*Critical Essays on*
*World Literature*

*Robert Lecker, General Editor*
*McGill University*

# Critical Essays on
## Albert Camus

# Critical Essays on Albert Camus

## Bettina L. Knapp

G. K. Hall & Co. • Boston, Massachusetts

**Library of Congress Cataloging in Publication Data**

Critical essays on Albert Camus/Bettina L. Knapp [editor].
     p. cm. — (Critical essays on world literature)
     Bibliography: p.
     Includes index.
     ISBN 0-8161-8838-6 (alk. paper)
     1. Camus, Albert, 1913–1960 — Criticism and interpretation.
I. Knapp, Bettina Liebowitz, 1926–    . II. Series.
PQ2605.A3734Z6288 1988
848'.91409 — dc19                                                    88-6091
                                                                        CIP

*This publication is printed on permanent/durable acid-free paper*
*MANUFACTURED IN THE UNITED STATES OF AMERICA*

# CONTENTS

INTRODUCTION     1
     Bettina L. Knapp

"L'Eternité à Lourmarin"     13
     René Char

*Articles and Essays*
     Presence of Camus     15
         Henri Peyre
     Camus's Libertarian Socialism     36
         Roger Quilliot
     Silence and the Desert: The Flickering Vision     42
         Micheline Tisson-Braun
     Sun, Sea, and Geraniums: Camus *en voyage*     56
         Alba Amoia
     Albert Camus and North Africa: A Discourse     73
       of Exteriority
         John Erickson
     Climates of the Mind: Albert Camus 1936–1940     88
         Germaine Brée
     *Supplementarity* in Camus     99
         Hanna Charney
     Existential Exile and a Glimpse of the Kingdom     107
         Diana Festa-McCormick
     Intertextuality in Albert Camus     116
         Jeanine Parisier Plottel
     Two Faces of Terrorism: *Caligula* and *The Just Assassins*     128
         Rosette C. Lamont
     The Fall: The Flight     140
         Maurice Blanchot
     The Compulsion of the Minimal: The Aesthetics of
       *La Chute*     145
         Michael Bishop

The Ethics of Albert Camus                          151
    Serge Doubrovsky
Tribute to Albert Camus                              164
    Jean-Paul Sartre

SELECTED BIBLIOGRAPHY                                167
INDEX                                               170

# INTRODUCTION

The critical sense is so far from frequent that it is absolutely rare, and the possession of the cluster of qualities that minister to it is one of the highest distinctions. . . . In this light one sees the critic as the real helper of the artist, a torch-bearing outrider, the interpreter, the brother. . . . Just in proportion as he is sentient and restless, just in proportion as he reacts and reciprocates and penetrates, is the critic a valuable instrument.

— Henry James, *Criticism*

Albert Camus's works have elicited conflicting responses — negative as well as laudatory, at times even mystifying — from the very start of his writing career. To react to Camus's writings overtly and aggressively as critics had done and still do suggests the import of the innovative, albeit radical, message of this twentieth-century writer. The manner in which Camus conveyed his existential experience — with all of its absurdity, its alienation, and, paradoxically, its excitement — was catalytic. And critics responded. Powerful issues were at stake that critics did not take lightly: the existence or nonexistence of God, colonialism, war, the death penalty, the notion of good and evil, and what constitutes the one and the other. Camus's polemical novels, essays, plays, travel journals, and short stories were not accepted passively. Perhaps Jean-Paul Sartre, when summing up his own point of view in his statement concerning *The Fall*, best expressed the reactions of commentators to Camusian thought: "We lived with or against his thought as it was revealed to us in his books. . . ."[1]

Leftists, rightists, and nonpartisan critics coming from all walks of life ventured reactions concerning Camus's works — *The Stranger, The Plague, The Myth of Sisyphus* — which were in the limelight almost immediately upon publication. Newspaper reporters as well as philosophers (Sartre, Merleau-Ponty), creative writers (Martin du Gard, de Beauvoir), polemicists and Marxists (Georges Lukacs), scholars, students — and anyone who wanted to voice his or her opinions concerning Camus's outlook on life — spoke up.

Most readers had — and still have — strong opinions concerning the breadth and impact of Camus's catalytic writings. To speak out on

1

intellectual and aesthetic matters during the forties, in the early days of Camus's career, was not, however, merely an example of one's intellectual faculties, but was part of a trend: to become engagé in the events of the day and to play an active part in shaping literary, economic, philosophical, and political policies. Camus's works became "conversation pieces," encouraging discussions in cafés, drawing rooms, libraries, and elsewhere.

Scholars as well as the intelligentsia who spoke out for or against Camus's writings reflected the problematic conditions existing in the western hemisphere. Their views, for the most part, followed in the tradition of normative criticism: a critic adheres to a specific moral, aesthetic, philosophical, and historical credo or standard and evaluates the work of art in terms of how closely or not it conforms to what he or she has in mind. A broad frame of reference, then, is used to judge the novel, play, or essay in question. Thematic criticism is also in evidence with regard to Camus's writings. Such an approach attempts to discuss the body of an author's works within the context of his writings, thus revealing their artistic complexities and ideational values within a tradition or the creation and application of a new and equally significant one.

Using thematic criticism as his point of departure, the politically oriented Roger Quilliot, who prepared the Pléiade edition of Camus's *Complete Works*, praised the writings of his compatriot for having evolved philosophically and politically. Indeed, Camus had succeeded in outgrowing his earlier negative stance. He realized he could no longer afford to indulge in the luxury of negativism or vindictiveness, as such views led to an impasse. When Camus attempted to come to terms with the difficulties facing him and humankind in general and started searching for ways of bringing to the fore new values that would replace *désuet* traditional theological and humanistic ones, critics like Quilliot, Pierre-Henri Simon, and Sartre began to realize the energetic pattern implicit in his writings.

*The Plague*, understandably, met with unequivocal approval from masses of critics. Thematic critics underscored Camus's value as an artist, the utter simplicity of his style, the mounting momentum and tension elicited in the course of the events. It was both classical and innovative, subjective and detached. Because *The Plague* dealt with people's reactions to such basic problems as survival with integrity, survival with humanity, and survival with dignity, it triggered the interest of those practicing normative criticism as well. They responded powerfully to Camus's concern for those forces that importuned individuals and society: the question of solitude and uncertainty, violence and the possibility of destruction, the notion of death and of evil. What seemed crucial to them insofar as *The Plague* was concerned, and perhaps made it unique among the novels of its time, was Camus's authenticity: his ability and *need* to dig deep into the hearts and minds of his protagonists in order to find some answers.

Each critic has his or her own way of functioning, of perceiving right or wrong, the human and inhuman, the positive and negative. The normative critic Gaëtan Picon, however, despite the larger issues of import, detected a strong macabre note in *The Plague* that disturbed him. He said it focused on a negative view of life and of happiness: "If happiness consists merely in escaping from the plague, this cannot be enough. . . . That one must fight against the plagues that enslave man: this is the sole conclusion which, according to Albert Camus, is not open to doubt." Picon searched for a more positive view, Camus's propensity for pessimism being too overwhelming for him. Nevertheless, let us recall that *The Plague* was published in 1947, two years after the end of World War II, when Camus was still smarting from the wounds endured during the holocaust. Had Picon banished the bloody years from his mind? Had he refused to face reality?

Camus's writings in the 1940s — and existentialism in general — were not only popular among most critics, eliciting both normative and thematic critical approaches, but they virtually dictated the intellectual taste of the period. When Camus's new humanism came into being, the nihilism so stunningly enunciated in his play *The Misunderstanding* (1944) fell by the wayside in time and was replaced by a more positive approach to life. With this in mind, Camus began directing a collection entitled *Hope* and published the works of René Char, among others.

Camus's understanding of hope was neither flighty nor unrealistic — it was born of his suffering, his harrowing confrontation with death. In keeping with traditional normative criticism, Emmanuel Mounier, describing Camus's notion of hope, underscored its oxymoronic nature — it echoed "the hope of the despairing." Camus's attitude toward hope, we might add, was also based on an acceptance of humankind's fundamental sense of solitude. As W. H. Auden wrote: "Aloneness is man's real condition." Yet Camus's fundamental and unflinching despair, both rationally depicted and subliminally felt, and his all-encompassing sense of anxiety, was enhanced by an intellectual and emotional need of solidarity, which served to inject new meaning into life. Critics, in keeping with normative and thematic credos, sensed Camus's new route: to endow human beings with a feeling of responsibility and worth, even though civilization may be declining rather than progressing, and to encourage them to forge ahead is to endow an individual's destiny with meaning and value.

Such is, in part, Camus's legacy to critics and readers today — not despair, not nihilism, but a concerted direction — to forge ahead, as Sisyphus had done daily, without illusion, but as part of life's work ethic. Hope, yes; blindness, no. Is it any wonder that Camus's fame and popularity soared in the fifties, sixties, and seventies? His popularity in the United States was unprecedented. Never before had the works of a French writer been so adulated, so discussed, so sought after. "Camus has had the luck, up to a certain point at least," wrote the critic and novelist Serge

Doubrovsky, "of being a prophet in his own country. Yet it would scarcely be a paradox to say that he is a great American writer even more than a French one, inasmuch as the public makes the writer."[2]

Not all critics looked upon Camus's works favorably. Patrick McCarthy, for example, stated that Camus was "a bad philosopher" who had "little to tell about politics. . . . His honesty could be devious and he was insufferably self-righteous." This is certainly a correct assessment of Camus the philosopher. Camus was not a philosopher. He was not a theorist. He was, rather, a humanist who dealt with reality — his reality. This is not to say, like McCarthy, that Camus was "devious" and "self-righteous"; although it was his own private view that he depicted, his ways were authentic and honest.

In sharp contrast was Germaine Brée's thematic assessment of Camus the man and his writings. Although it underscored the richness and complexities of Camus's writing, Brée's essay was objective — a remarkable feat in itself, for at the time Parisian intellectuals were at loggerheads over political and philosophical questions.

The novelist and critic Roger Martin du Gard assessed Camus from neither a political nor a philosophical view, but rather a humanistic one. His forte resided in the fact that he not only understood Camus the creative artist, but Camus the man, with all of his psychological problems. He is, Martin du Gard wrote, a person living in a "permanent state of rebellious bitterness . . . in keeping with a moral hygiene of his own creation. . . ." His struggle, insofar as Martin du Gard was concerned, was "without respite." Grave, restrained, despite his fundamental emotionality, Camus was a man who lived inwardly, delicately, in a world where melancholia was ever present.[3] Such an introverted condition, as Martin du Gard noted, is understandable when considering the poverty he experienced during his early years. The sole responsibility for his upbringing in Mondovi, Algeria, where he was born, rested upon his mother — his father was killed a year after his birth, in 1914, at the Battle of the Marne. Illiterate and partially deaf, Camus's mother worked long hours as a charwoman to see to the family's needs. Martin du Gard's comment on Camus's withdrawn and silent nature explains to a great extent the fundamental solitude of this writer. Studying hard, intent upon making something of himself, his world seemed suddenly shattered when, in 1930, he was told he had tuberculosis. Complete bed rest and the removal of all books was ordered. Such a fate could have led the lad to despair, but there was also a fighting spirit — that "invincible summer" — that helped him through his difficult period. He completed his studies and even joined — participating in an acting capacity — the left-wing *Théâtre du Travail*. Camus could easily have become a nihilist, a hedonist, or a solipsist. He chose, however, to be different — to be his own man, not subject to bitterness and hatred, and to exert a powerful will. He focused on serving himself and others in *fraternity*, authenticity, and forthrightness. His direction in life required him to reject escape mechanisms that would take him into a world of illusions, historical messianism, and Christianity, with its emphasis on sin and the afterlife.

The critic M. Saint-Clair, in his incisive appraisal of Camus's writings appearing in *Galerie privée*, is also impressive for the innovative nature of his approach and intent. He referred to Camus as "concentrated" and "spontaneous" — "original" in his ideations, "proud" in his comportment — and also applied Vauvenargues's statement to him: "There are simple exteriors which fit superior minds so well."[4] Discriminating on Saint-Clair's part, he sensed Camus's need to approach life in a concerted manner — not intellectually, but viscerally. Let us recall that Camus had to face the reality of death early in life so he understood more poignantly than others the meaning of life. Was it not for this reason, for the most part, that Camus developed a zest not only for earthly existence, but also for mysticism and philosophy? Having renounced, like Heidegger, Jaspers, and Sartre, the notion of a creator God and of a transcendent being who looked with beneficence upon humankind, Camus felt strengthened by accepting the fact that life was devoid of meaning, that hope was an illusion, and that, although people did not know why or how they had been placed in the world, they were part of it and related to it. Such an attitude freed him and others, he felt, from fear and subservience; it encouraged objectivity, which in turn endowed him with the ability to choose his course freely in life — in a world that is perpetually *becoming*, even though death is the inevitable culmination of existence.

"Camus' real merit," stated Gaëtan Picon, in a fine thematically oriented essay assessing Camus's style and the philosophical import of his works, "is to have elevated a truly modern sensibility, to the state of classical perfection. To him is accorded the honor of being the only one to have given *mythical expression* to contemporary man." Camus describes "this absurd sensibility" in the *Myth of Sisyphus* and incarnates it for us in *The Stranger*. In keeping with Picon's view, it might be said that Camus opted neither for stoicism nor for asceticism, but rather for the realization and acceptance of the notion of "nothingness as the essence of life." Such an approach to existence enabled him to experience and understand the discord and the harmony inherent within the human personality and the world at large. To look upon the mysteries of life in the world and in the galaxies, as Camus did so frequently, did not fill him with a sense of utter despair. What is remarkable in terms of Camus's writings is that hopelessness became a positive factor in his world, inviting him to get used to his own loneliness, thereby strengthening him, encouraging him to proceed courageously through the harrowing events making up the life experience. Camus remarked, and critics reacted most favorably to this view, that the very moment a person is struck down by despair, amazingly enough, "thirst is reborn," filling the individual with a livingness — a need for growth and fulfillment.[5]

The scholar Lev Braun, a practitioner of normative criticism, re-marked perceptively that Camus "has been unduly imprisoned in the concept of absurdity as expressed in *The Myth of Sisyphus*." Braun does not see Camus as the simple and facile writer whose beliefs concerning the "experience of absurdity" are explicitly detailed. On the contrary, he suggests, although the theme of absurdity may be the most perceptible, it is far from being the only one in Camus's works, nor perhaps, the most significant. The deceptive simplicity of Camus's language, so frequently alluded to as classical, is in part to blame for these erroneous conclusions. Camus's view of the *absurd*, as depicted in *The Myth of Sisyphus*, Braun continues, explores the conflict between humankind's desire to live eter-nally and the inevitability of death. It focuses also on the dichotomy between a person's intellectual need to understand what surpasses him — that is, a desire to rationalize the irrational and the inability to do so. Chaos, instead of a well-ordered world, greets the rational being. Pascal, Kierkegaard, and Bergson, as had the Symbolists and Impressionists, did away with the incredible claims of reason. Not so Hegel, who sought to reduce the world to rational categories. "The absurd," wrote Camus, "is the confrontation of this nonrational world with that desperate desire for clarity which is one of man's deepest needs. The absurd depends as much on man as on the world for its existence."[6]

When reviewing *The Stranger* in *Situations 1*, Jean-Paul Sartre was certain he understood Camus's message. His judgment was certainly interesting and intellectually stimulating. And he did understand him, but only in keeping with his own limited way of assessing anyone's personality. Could Sartre really understand Camus the artist? Although we would answer in the negative, credit must be given its due, and Sartre's rigorous analysis of *The Stranger* was impressive. He was wary of classifying this work under the rubric of novel: it was "so composed under its apparent disorder, so 'human,' so revealing once one possesses the key." Nor was it identifiable with the novel, he continued, since this literary technique implies the notion of continuous duration, that is, a sense of becoming, and "the manifest presence of the irreversibility of time." Nor did Sartre call *The Stranger* a narrative, in the strict sense of the word, since a narrative explains and coordinates events while retracing them, substitut-ing a causal order for chronological sequences of circumstances. Sartre, rather, compares it, to a certain extent at least, to Voltaire's philosophical and moralistic tales, *Zadig* and *Candide*.[7] The protagonist in *The Stranger* is alienated from society as well as from himself; he has rejected tradi-tional religious attitudes and social patterns of behavior and feeling, and has nothing to fill the void in his life. Only at the end, when he is about to lose his own life, does he finally learn to face himself. Life with its finality, its hazards and unpleasant entanglements *is* his only chance for happiness. Like Sisyphus, the protagonist understands that it is the very struggle and pain of experience that endows an individual with a sense of fulfillment and well-being.

Rachel Bespaloff's sensitive, thematic criticism views Camus's writings, surprisingly enough, as the work of a romantic. Emerging from Mediterranean climes, Camus remains, in her opinion, forever nostalgic for the finite world of the senses. Interestingly and impressively, she associates his essays and novels with the elegiac and lyrical writings of the Latins, as well as with the Greek tragedies. *Nuptials* (1938) is a case in point. The four essays included in this volume, set in the Mediterranean world, disclose Camus's sense of forlornness and human tragedy, and, concomitantly, his fervor for earthly existence. The images of visceral intensity that mark his text are transformed into energetic powers — protagonists of sorts. The sun burns and sears; the sea cleanses and purifies; the desert conveys its arid vacancy that, like a giant maw, stands ready to devour the naive and unsuspecting. Bespaloff — and here we are in complete agreement — maintains that Camus is also a classicist: his sentences are precise, intelligible, objective, restrained, and translucent. His plays, *The Misunderstanding* and *Caligula*, though thesis dramas, reveal a built-in understanding of tension — *agonia* — inherent in classical drama. Bespaloff admires Camus for his skepticism, comparing him to Montaigne and Saint-Evremond; for his passion, virile in all ways. In this regard, he is clearly a descendant of Corneille and Pascal. His metaphysical anguish is, for her, reminiscent of such creative spirits as Kierkegaard, Dostoyevski, and Shestov.[8]

In Germaine Brée's expert thematic view, the central idea of Camus's tales, *The Exile and the Kingdom*, concerns the "more or less fleeting reintegration of man into the kingdom of man."[9] Brée maintains that the same may be said of Camus's other works, such as *The Plague* (1947), in which suffering is looked upon as part of the life process. Evil, implicit in the novel's dramatic situation, is dealt with openly and powerfully. Camus depicts his character. Father Paneloux, delivering his sermon upon the death of a child from the deadly disease and blaming the demise of this innocent person on his sinful nature. To explain his stance with clarity, Camus stated in a lecture to the Dominicans of Latour-Maubourg in 1948: "I share your horror of evil. But I do not share your optimism, and I continue to struggle against this universe in which children suffer and die."[10]

The remarkably clear and incisive normative approach Henri Peyre has taken to Camusian criticism throughout the last four decades is deeply impressive. His profound understanding of Camus's need to be *aware* of the ramifications of one's attitude, to keep an open mind on such subjects as religion, politics, and aesthetics — a fluid point of view — helps in the evolution of thought and the heightening of aesthetic values. To be conscious of and involved in actual situations, as was Camus's way, and to side with justice and humanistic values require persistent vigilance, a willingness to act, and indicates a recognition of the absurdity of life, but also of its value, its uniqueness—views dramatized in *State of Siege*. Camus's desire to see to the "reintegration of man into the kingdom of man," is revealed in *The Rebel*. Rather than follow the Cartesian dictum, "I think, therefore I am," Camus suggested "I rebel, therefore we are." Revolt is beneficial in that it helps build one's individuality; it structures one's life—dignifying it in the process. The notion of reintegration is felt even more strongly in *The Fall*, where Camus's protagonist sounds out his depths, and, in the process, begins to understand, even relish, the magnitude of his guilt. *The Fall*, the most enigmatic and complex of all of Camus's works, like the biblical metaphor, intimates a descent onto earth, into a world of conflict and tension. In that such a trajectory marks the end of complacency, it ushers in the birth of awareness and consciousness and, with them, the personal anguish that might eventually lead to a harmonious amalgamation of being—on both an individual and a collective level.

We find Emmanuel Mounier's thematic critical discussion of Camus's writings highly insightful. His literary technique, which Mounier maintains is puritanical, was as ordered as his behavior patterns, to the point of being divested of everything that was not essential. Yet beneath this seemingly controlled and measured exterior existed Camus's secret inner world, bathed in its own inner light. Within these regions lived a torn and virtually dismembered being, drawn to both rational and irrational spheres. Summing up his reactions to the writings of this twentieth-century artist in an oxymoron, Mounier stated that Camus's was "a somber philosophy of lights."[11]

For the critic Pierre-Henri Simon, in his in-depth normative critical approach, which focused on traditional and organized religious beliefs, with their insights and their limitations, Camus was a humanist who sought to "save man through love and reason," to "protect him against natural evil and social oppression; to believe in his nature, which is good, while struggling against his destiny which is evil; and calling only upon human powers. . . ." Camus, he remarked, was honest when he stated that Christian beliefs were, and had always been, foreign to him. What preoccupied Camus, Simon pursued, was to discover a way people could structure their lives via their own set of values, without having recourse to Divinity. Simon did not view Camus as a nihilist, but rather as a spiritually oriented moralist involved in spreading the notion of justice and charity.[12]

The novelist Jules Roy may be a bit overindulgent in his thematic overview when considering Camus's fictional and empirical writings of exceptional merit. He was, in his opinion, one of "the most important writers" of this century and one "of the most sensitive and the most generous of our time."[13]

To the many laudatory essays and statements made by critics such as André Rousseaux, Jean Grenier, Dominique Rolin, and Jacques Lemarchand, may be added contrasting ones. Castigators, such as the critic for *L'Humanité*, the organ of the French Communist Party, found Camus guilty of spreading a climate of fancy, irreality, and idealism and of not dealing with contemporary problems adequately. He "is 'the philosopher' of the myth of abstract liberty; of illusion," one may read in *L'Humanité*. The critic's remarks were certainly not unbiased; rather, they reflected most assiduously the line promulgated by his paper and as such, may be understood as reflecting a limited view.[14]

In light of this history of Camus criticism, the time has come for a reevaluation of his work. For this reason new essays, rather than reprints, were solicited for *Critical Essays on Albert Camus*. Because a writer such as Camus lives with and beyond his times, his ideals and values — like those of Hamlet — evolve in impact and dimension. What are the political and social issues at stake *today*? What are the aesthetic and philosophical approaches? How do Camus's works affect contemporary critics? Can sustenance still be drawn from the novels, plays, and essays written by a man whose meteoric success culminated in the reception of the Nobel Prize for Literature in 1957?

The poem by René Char, "L'Eternité à Lourmarin," translated by Mary Ann Caws and Christopher Prendergast, which begins our volume, is not a commentary on the writings of *The Stranger*. Rather, it commemorates the feelings of a great poet for a longtime friend. It is in this spirit, as well as in a scholarly vein, that our volume proceeds.

Henri Peyre's "Presence of Camus" examines in a most meticulous and cogent manner the vast normative criticism surrounding Camus's body of work. With immense knowledge, coupled with an extraordinary ability to synthesize and to evaluate — virtually unique in today's world of critics — Peyre assesses the validity of statements made throughout the years concerning Camus's writings.

No one is better qualified than Robert Quilliot to deal with Camus's complex political ideas. In his normative critical essay, "Camus's Libertarian Socialism," he explores the most difficult question of Camus's political evolution throughout the years. He warns, and rightly so, against the pitfalls engendered by simplistic conclusions, particularly focusing on the years 1935–37, when Camus was drawn to the Communist Party; on the years 1943–47, when the Algerian-born author yearned for the creation of a socialist democracy; and on his last phase, when he identified with the intellectual Left.

Micheline Tison-Braun, who has written extensively on Camus, traces the lyrical current in his works in her brilliant thematical critical essay, "Silence and the Desert: The Flickering Vision." The expressive, direct, ardent, and pantheistic vein implicit in Camus's early writings, she maintains (and rightly so, I feel), runs through *all* of his later works in a variety of ways: *Nuptials*, *The Stranger*, *The Myth of Sisyphus*: in essays, such as *The Desert*; in his *Notebooks*; and short stories, *The Exile and the Kingdom*.

Camus's movingly elegiac pantheism is also expertly treated in a thematically critical manner by Alba Amoia in her innovative essay, "Sun, Sea, and Geraniums: Camus *en voyage*." She takes her readers through Camus's *Notebooks* and his *Travel Journals*; his essays, included in *The Wrong Side and the Right Side*, *Nuptials*, and *Summer*. As Amoia explores Camus's reactions to such places as "French Algeria," Venice, Florence, the islands of Palma and Ibiza, the Balearic Islands, the French Alps, she probes his mystical approach to life, pointing out the significance of the vitalism involved in his obsession with such images as sun and light, the blue sky, and the sound of water in a garden.

In John Erickson's monumental normative study and really the first of its kind, "Albert Camus and North Africa: A Discourse of Exteriority," we are invited to explore Camus's "North African" writings with all of their appealing descriptions and varieties of landscapes. "But," as Professor Erickson explains, "of its indigenous peoples, Berbers and Arabs, astonishingly little." The reasons for such a lacuna are probed in explications of such works as *The Stranger*, *The Plague*, *The Exile and the Kingdom*, *The Notebooks*.

Germaine Brée, whose important critical works on Camus have been studied throughout the world, has the advantage of having known Camus and of having lived in Algeria. Her normative approach in her essay "Climates of the Mind: Albert Camus 1936–1940" brings not only first-hand information to readers, but also the fruit of her vast learning. Brée focuses on the articles the novice reporter Albert Camus wrote for the short-lived local daily newspapers, *Alger Républicain* and *Alger Soir* disclosing new insights and perspectives on his later writings.

Hanna Charney invites readers to ponder the approach of New Criticism — thereby adding a different dimension to Camusian thought. Her fascinating study and the first of its kind, "*Supplementarity* in Camus," takes us into the Derridean world — to his work *Of Grammatology* — to explain some crucial notions concerning the affinities existing between Rousseau and Camus. Professor Charney elucidates most brilliantly Derrida's "complex argument" concerning Rousseau, which she then uses to "call forth Camus' double presentation of nature mute and hard, or striking with the burning heat of fate" in such works as *The Stranger* and *The Plague*.

Deft and sensitive is Diana Festa-McCormick's normative appreciation of some of Camus's short stories in her essay, "Existential Exile and a Glimpse of the Kingdom." Festa-McCormick shows with dexterity and cogency how Camus reached "perfection of craftsmanship" in *Exile and the Kingdom*, and she explores the psychological, aesthetic, and political impact of three of the stories included in the volume: "The Renegade," "The Host," and "The Adulterous Woman."

Jeanine Parisier Plottel's remarkable essay, "Intertextuality in Albert Camus," opts for New Criticism to broach this twentieth-century author's writings. Her Herculean vision, using structuralist, classical rhetoric in her intertextual exploration, universalizes Camus's thoughts — philosophical, political, and aesthetic — for her readers. Because of her extensive learning her study of the relationships between one or more parts of a Camusian text with segments from the works of other writers, reminiscent of traditional source criticism, nevertheless transcends it because of her use of *paratexts*. Such paratexts take into consideration second-hand material stemming from popular culture — duly influencing Camus's writing, albeit unconsciously. An early Camusian text may not be the sole reason for the writing of a later one, but the ideas implanted in rich and fertile soil may nourish later writings, accounting for expanded versions. Plottel leads her readers into a surprising and exciting world while also pointing out the many errors made by Camus and his critics. She is inspired to "construct a model of the textual self out of the author's genealogy" and "to imagine a paradigm for the textual production of this textual self."

Rosette C. Lamont, a renowned theater specialist, uses a normative approach to sound out a most important problem facing today's world: that of terrorism. Using the theater as her point of departure in her significant contribution "Two Faces of Terrorism: *Caligula* and *The Just Assassins*," Lamont traces the philosophical and political meanings and motifs surrounding notions such as revolt and revolution, individual acts of terrorism, and the "all-powerful terrorism of the state."

Maurice Blanchot, who kindly allowed us to reprint his essay "The Fall: The Flight" from his volume *Friendship*, translated with such skill and clarity by Amoia, draws us with his normative critical essay into the world of other great heroes of past and present. Clamence, the protagonist of Camus's *The Fall*, is compared with Oedipus, about whom Hölderlin had stated that, in his madness, he had "one eye too many perhaps." Evaluating the dichotomies between Clamence and Oedipus, readers of Blanchot's soul-searching essay are invited to examine such eternal notions as "flight" and "fall" not only in the light of Camus's work, but also in terms of their own lives.

Michael Bishop's poetic contribution, "The Compulsion of the Minimal: The Aesthetics of *La Chute*," is a paradigm of thematic criticism. For Bishop, Camus's imaginary universe as depicted in *The Fall* is considered to be "a self-synthetical *mise en abyme*." Suggesting that something is "out of kilter" in this patriarchal yet ambiguous and ambivalent sphere, Bishop invites the reader to follow him into Clamence's murky depths — and we do, fascinated by the play of the critic's imagination and his profound understanding of one of Camus's most sensitive works.

Serge Doubrovsky, in his important normative approach, "The Ethics of Albert Camus," alters the stereotypic picture that so many readers have of Camus: the existentialist, austere, just, and righteous moralist living and functioning in an immoral twentieth century. But what is Camus's morality? Is there a morality explored in his work? Doubrovsky's clear, concise, and profound rereading of Camus invites readers to focus on the "unreasoned" and unsystematic ethics of this writer who *lived* his ideas. As Camus wrote in *Actuelles II*, "I am not a philosopher and I know how to speak only of what I have experienced."

Perhaps the most deeply moving contribution to our volume is Jean-Paul Sartre's "Tribute to Albert Camus." Despite the fact that they had quarreled, Camus's presence had never been obliterated from Sartre's mind. On the contrary, he thought of him deeply and frequently; he also kept reading and rereading his works. Camus's *absurd* death in an automobile accident encouraged Sartre to convey his thoughts concerning his former friend's humanism:

> Insofar as Camus's humanism contains a *human* attitude toward the death that was to take him by surprise, insofar as his proud and pure quest for happiness implied and called for the *inhuman* necessity of dying, we shall recognize in that work and in the life that is inseparable from it the pure and victorious attempt of one man to snatch every instant of his existence from his future death.

## Notes

1. Jean-Paul Sartre, *"The Fall," A Collection of Critical Essays* (Englewood Cliffs, N.J.: Prentice-Hall, 1962), 173.

2. Serge Doubrovsky, "Camus in America," in *A Collection of Critical Essays* (Englewood Cliffs, N.J.: Prentice-Hall, 1962), 76.

3. Roger Martin du Gard, *Le Figaro littéraire*, 26 October 1957.

4. M. Saint-Clair, *Galerie privée* (Paris: Gallimard, 1947).

5. Gaëtan Picon, *Panorama de la nouvelle littérature française* (Paris: Gallimard, 1949).

6. Lev Braun, *Witness of Decline* (Rutherford, N.J.: Fairleigh Dickinson University Press, 1974), 13–14, 24–30.

7. Jean-Paul Sartre, "Explication de l'*Etranger*" (1943), in *Situations I* (Paris: Gallimard, 1947).

8. Rachel Bespaloff, "Le Monde du condamné," *Esprit* (January 1950).

9. Germaine Brée, *Albert Camus. L'Exil et le royaume*, ed. Benjamin F. Bart (New York: Charles Scribner's Sons, 1965), xviii.

10. John Cruickshank, *Albert Camus* (London: Oxford University Press, 1970), 178.

11. Emmanuel Mounier, *Esprit* (January 1950).

12. Pierre-Henri Simon, *L'Homme en procès* (Neuchâtel, Switzerland: Editions de la Baconnière, 1950), 93–123.

13. Jules Roy, *Les Nouvelles littéraires*, 24 October 1957.

14. *L'Humanité*, 18 October 1957.

# "L'Eternité à Lourmarin"

René Char*

### to Jean Paul Samson

No longer is there a straight line or lighted path with someone who has left us. Where, dazed and lost, does our affection go? Ring upon ring, if he approaches, it is to hide profoundly. Sometimes his face presses against ours, yielding only a frozen flash. That day which lengthened the happiness between him and ourselves is nowhere to be found. All the parts, almost excessive, of a presence, are suddenly dislocated. The round of our watchfulness . . . And yet this being, suppressed, remains in something rigid, empty, essential within us, where our millennia assembled make just the thickness of a drawn eyelid.

With the one we love, we have stopped speaking, and it is not silence. What then? We know, or think we know. But only when a meaningful past opens to give him passage. Here, he is now at our height, then far ahead.

At the time, newly contained, when we question all the weight of enigma, there suddenly begins the pain, from companion to companion, whom the archer, this time, will not pierce.

*From René Char, *Les Matinaux, suivi de la Parole en archipel* (Paris: Gallimard, 1962). Translated for this volume by Mary Ann Caws and Christopher Prendergast.

# Articles and Essays

## Presence of Camus

Henri Peyre*

More than a quarter of a century after his tragic death, Albert Camus remains vividly present among us. In France and elsewhere in the world his three novels, his short stories, and his lyrical essays reach sales unmatched by any other French author born since 1910. He was exalted early in his career to the perilous status of a classic; he is read, discussed, and dissected by college teachers, arousing the curiosity and often the enthusiasm of the young. Outside France—in the Far East, in South America, and particularly in the United States—he has remained close to many. A few and on the whole feeble attempts were made to belittle him as an author fitting "for terminal classes" in lycées, as providing a convenient storehouse of maxims to be proposed as moral and aesthetic comments by teenagers sitting for their exams. But the forcefulness of *The Stranger* and of *The Fall*; the pithy vigor of Camus's remarks on the themes that obsessed him (absurdity, revolt, history, death); and even his fragmentary reflections on the ancient Greeks, on Dostoyevski, on Kafka, and on Faulkner have hardly been affected by those reservations and occasional slurs. He victoriously survived the official glorification of the Nobel prize and the relatively early inclusion of his works in the two bulky volumes of the Pléiade in 1962 and 1965.

His accidental death in 1960 had grieved not only the millions who had read his books, but the men and women who had seen him mentioned in daily papers, heard some of his views discussed by politicians, priests, and pastors. To many he had assumed the stature of "a secular saint," of an intercessor between unbelief and traditional Christian faith. It is even reported that not a few addressed their prayers to him; a larger number endeavored to convert him posthumously and lavished much sophisticated subtlety in hinting that this "Pascal without Christ" (as he had been designated early in his career in an austere Jesuit review) would have seen the light if only he had lived longer and would have been redeemed from "the Fall."

*This essay was written especially for this volume and is published here for the first time by permission of the author.

15

The paradox is that such an accession of Camus to officialdom and to near sanctification has not as yet estranged him from independent minds and rebellious readers. The scathing, in part deserved, mockeries flung at him by Sartre during their bitter controversy of 1951–52 do not appear to have hurt Camus's standing lastingly. He has been spared the coolness or the outright hostility that appear to have followed the Hugo-like funeral of Sartre in 1980 and the sighs of relief heard after the demise of the tireless existentialist polemicist. Camus had repeatedly asserted that he was no philosopher and not even an effective dialectician. Much of the heat that had envenomed the partisan debates around the Algerian problem has cooled off after two decades. The fiction of Simone de Beauvoir, that of Sartre himself in his more ambitious technical experiments, that of Robbe-Grillet and Mme Sarraute, even that of Butor, have lost much of their glamour. Probably no one would contend that Camus is assured to be ranked with the very great masters of fiction. But he has not lingered long in the symbolical purgatory in which writers, having basked in fame and been laden with honors in the last decades of their lives, are made to atone for the praise lavished on them by their contemporaries. Thus far, Camus's novels and stories have not been meted out the fate that once chastised Alphonse Daudet, Maupassant, Anatole France, who had enjoyed too long a popularity with teachers and pupils. Since the middle of this century we have witnessed the eclipse of Jules Romains and of Georges Duhamel. Roger Martin du Gard, another recipient of the Nobel prize, has hardly grown in stature since his death; nor have Bernanos and Giono. Saint-Exupéry, for a time the only moralist and storyteller to have enjoyed a fame and wielded an influence comparable to Camus's, has become a pallid star in our firmament. A similar fate may perhaps await Camus. In the late 1980s signs of disaffection or of declining interest are not glaringly evident — at least if we judge by the critical and academic colloquia and the flood of publications on him in France and the United States.

The many critical studies on the philosophical or ideological works by Camus inevitably fail to reach a consensus on the validity or the originality of *The Myth of Sisyphus* or *The Rebel*. All, however, agree that the survival of the author as a significant figure in the thought of this age will not rest on those controversial and often contradictory works — nor would it on Camus's achievement as a playwright. The most searching critical analyses and appraisals have dealt with *The Stranger* and *The Fall* and two or three stories in *Exile and the Kingdom*. Varied and sharply conflicting meanings are read by scholars who have lavished a great deal of ingenious subtlety on their interpretations. Since those works of fiction were being probed, analyzed line by line in college classes and seminars, treasures of scholarly erudition and of ingenious exegesis were spent on clarifying meanings and allusions that might have escaped other commentators. Camus's technique of storytelling, his creation of characters, and even the stylistic devices he used have generally received less attention. Yet

Camus is primarily an artist. He provided relatively scant information, however, on the secrets of his creation. He kept no diary of his work such as the journal Gide kept while he was reflecting on his *Counterfeiters* or Martin du Gard's correspondence with Gide while he was laboriously composing *The World of the Thibault* and weighing the respective merits of Tolstoy and Dostoyevski. Purposely perhaps, Camus allowed a great deal of mystery to wrap his characters. He expressed himself more willingly on other aspects of his personality and of his tales, his North African origins and environment, poverty, the sea, Hellenism, Christianity, the debates in his conscience, his political and ethical attitudes and beliefs. Much of the journalism concerning him in the years 1950–65 dealt with the Algerian question and with the debates that then raged in Parisian circles: the Communist or para-Communist Left and the capitalist (often called pro-American) Right, how to end or transform colonialism, and the justification or the condemnation of violence both in history and in history in the making, which present politics is.

Documents throwing some light on Camus's life, travels, and journalistic, editorial, and theatrical activities were available to researchers in the years 1960–75. A number of friends who had known Camus well were willing to provide biographers with information and reminiscences: Max-Pol Fouchet, Pascal Pia, and Emmanuel Roblès. His first wife, Simone Hié, died in 1970; his second, Francine, née Faure, was to attend a conference on her late husband's works in Florida in 1980 but died on Christmas Eve of 1979. The first thoroughly documented biography and to date the richest in precise information was published in English in 1978 with a simultaneous French translation. *Albert Camus: A Biography*, by Herbert R. Lottman (an American journalist living in Paris), lays no claim to being a psychological interpretation of Camus the man or an appraisal of Camus the thinker and the artist. Lottman has a passionate curiosity for the details of French literary life and an inexhaustible patience in the pursuit of minor incidents, some revealing, others inconsequential. On the ancestry, family background of the young Algerian, on his travels in Czechoslovakia (Prague, where he stayed only briefly, impressed him lastingly), on Camus's friends in their youthful theatrical enterprises, and in journalistic attempts in North Africa before and during World War II, Lottman rectifies errors, establishes facts and dates, and maintains an impartial balance between Camus and friends from whom he became estranged. His recurrent bouts with tuberculosis, his long struggle against poverty in his youth, and some native impetuosity and brutality in his makeup often rendered him irritable and self-righteous, intolerant of contradiction. Lottman's book is far too bulky; it lacks stylistic brilliance as well as psychological insight. It is an exterior biography from which the pangs of the creator in Camus, his struggles with the Don Juan in him, the sentimentalist, the would-be philosopher unsure of himself, are left out. Modestly and wisely, it refrains from asking questions and from offering personal interpretations. It is a storehouse of precise details and incidents from which more venturesome critics have since drawn — not always with gratitude.

The next comprehensive volume on Camus, to a large extent biographical, was published in 1982. Patrick McCarthy's *Camus* is more discriminating and severely critical than Lottman's book. It was written in English, as were the most significant works on an author who, untouched and certainly unmoved by Britain and America, found his most fervent audience in English-speaking lands. McCarthy, of Irish extraction, was educated at Oxford and Harvard. He is fully informed on Camus's life and reticent in acknowledging his debt to Lottman or to others of his predecessors, such as Germaine Brée and John Cruickshank. His judgment on Camus, peremptorily stated at the beginning of his volume, is severe, dogmatic, and youthfully insolent. Camus was "a bad philosopher and he has little to tell about politics. . . . His honesty could be devious and he was insufferably self-righteous. . . . His vision of Algeria is uncomplicated and barbaric." One senses at once that the young author (he was forty-one when the book appeared) firmly intended to separate himself from the crowd of early enthusiasts who had acclaimed Camus as their inspired prophet or, as the French like to put it in their ludicrous and touching phrase, their "maître à penser." Diffidence, and even sheer dislike, can turn out to be more perceptive than uncritical admiration. Shrewd insights appear in many a chapter of McCarthy's intellectual biography. They evince a sharp literary judgment and a familiarity with history of thought for which one would look in vain in Lottman's heaping up of factual details. But the judgments proffered on the novels, their parareligious quest, and their craft are often hastily subjective, unsupported by any reasoned argument or by a close analysis of texts. They are thrown at the reader in a disconnected fashion and are more irritating than challenging or enlightening. McCarthy drops a few hints here and there on aspects of Camus that had been touched upon in too gingerly a manner by earlier critics: the part played by poverty in his early development, which he proudly belittled; his role as a Don Juan, or as a rather vulgar womanizer. "Love making was . . . a participation in natural beauty" for Camus, hints McCarthy.[1] "Contact with women involved a dehumanization which suited the pantheist." The subject of Camus and love is more vexing and troublesome than it appears from rash assertions scattered here and there. So is that of Camus in relation to Algeria. McCarthy lends special attention to North Africa, with which he appears to be familiar, and to Camus as a *pied-noir*, who was unable "to face the fact that the French must leave. His attitude was not very heroic nor very moral." Would it have been more "heroic" of him to turn against his native land and, as he said, his mother, at a time when the lad from Belcourt had been one of the first to denounce misery in Kabylia? The summary indictment of Camus on the Algerian issue harshly and haughtily formulated by another

Irishman, Conor Cruise O'Brien, seems to have been too hastily endorsed by McCarthy. The latent or implied hostility of this biographer toward his subject deprives his ambitious volume of warmth and even of plain fairness.

Donald Lazere's long study, rather infelicitously entitled *The Unique Creation of Albert Camus*, was published in 1973. Lazere had the advantage of approaching Camus with a youthful sympathy that he had developed in part from discovering the French writer through his American translator, the late Justin O'Brien, who taught for many years at Columbia University. Lazere specialized in English, not French, literature, and he draws parallels with English-speaking authors or makes allusions to them. His approach to Camus is circular rather than chronological and is intended as eclectic; it lacks, and refuses to have, a focus and does not delve in depth into any one aspect of Camus's writings. Rather disconcertingly, Lazere places himself at several points of view (metaphysical, psychoanalytic, artistic) and touches upon, rather fleetingly, contradictory aspects of Camus's personality. Respected critics such as E. R. Curtius and Leo Spitzer had often proceeded in that way, but their aperçus had more depth and revealed an underlying mastery of the whole of the author approached from a variety of angles, which one misses in this effusive and at times naïve work. It is often true that several books by one author fail to reveal any evolution, and Camus's do not. They may be works provoked by some circumstance — a passing incident in his life, a casual remark by a friend or by a critic — that leads an author to dip into a deeper layer of his own personality. Some themes recur under varied symbols that point to obsessive concerns of the author: in the case of Camus, death, an omnipresent menace in his writings, exile, estrangement or alienation, revolt, and the theme of *claustration*, which permeates the novels of Malraux, the plays of Sartre, *The Stranger* and *The Plague*, and predated the *concentrationary* literature depicting Europe at mid-century. In his zeal not to omit any facet of Camus's works, Lazere cursorily offers too many ways of access to his author, but he explores none of them in depth or with conviction. He is redeemed by his fervor and his attempt to share the political attitudes of the French Left, which in the 1970s had treated Camus's position on Algeria with a severity that, fifteen years later, already appeared excessive. In his final chapter, Lazere attempts to integrate Camus into the current of American literature, on the grounds that, as Serge Doubrovsky had hinted after the Frenchman's death, "Camus is the great writer American literature had waited for and who never came," to fill the gap left by the disappearance of Faulkner, Dos Passos, and Hemingway. There is scant validity in portraying the author of *The Stranger* as a follower or a relative of American novelists and even less in contending that the American success of Camus might have owed to his alleged affinity to the American novelists of 1920–35, when Sartre had praised and imitated them more than had Camus. American readers thought they found in Camus ethical and aesthetic values that they failed to encounter in Hemingway and Mailer.[2]

The best overall evaluations of Camus as a man, but chiefly as a writer and man of thought, are by Germaine Brée, the French critic who writes in English, and John Cruickshank, one of the most acute English critics of our time. Their volumes have helped most to mold that view of Camus which is still ours in the late 1980s. Germaine Brée enjoyed the advantage of having lived in Algeria and of personal contact with Camus and his widow. Living and teaching in America, Brée remained impartial to the polemics that tore through the Parisian intellectual circles, brandishing ambitious political theories and philosophies of history. She sought to inform her readers by means of intelligent summaries of Camus's books and ideas and with warm but always lucid and never pretentious or pedantic criticism. She sympathized with Camus in his political feuds with Sartre, as she did with the French Algerian author on the question of Algerian independence. In her subsequent writings she evinced some occasional impatience with Sartre's dogmatism and verbal intoxication, as she did when taking issue with the stubbornly "impenitent" judge Conor Cruise O'Brien. Few if any subsequent studies of Camus are likely to survive the test of time as victoriously as her general and smooth presentation.

Cruickshank's book, *Albert Camus and the Literature of Revolt*, does not treat Camus with hostility. It grants his novels their due and interprets them incisively, maintaining a detached British attitude toward the peculiar ways in which the French politicize literary debates. Much of the quarreling between former friends who grossly overstate their differences and forget all they have in common appears, to a more pragmatic Anglo-Saxon, as child's play or petty family quarreling. Wisely, in this reviewer's opinion, Cruickshank underlines the basic if unavowed agreement between Camus and Sartre in their much publicized controversy. Despite the vehement denial by each of them and differences of emphasis, Camus had been and to a large extent remained, very near existentialism. They came out of the war, argues Cruickshank, "with a common concern for political questions. They denounced the same things: bourgeois hypocrisy, economic exploitation, colonialism, the color bar, Franco's Spain."[3] Both had pinned their hopes on the possible emergence and eventual survival of a non-Marxist Left. Sartre persuaded himself that it might remain a possibility, though he could not convince himself, after the Hungarian repression of 1956, that he could still entertain such a belief without some bad faith. He never actually joined the Communist party, and after the reluctance of the French Communists to act as revolutionaries during the 1968 riots in Paris, he swerved away from communism to another and bolder extreme Left which, as he was well aware, stood not a chance of winning in France. Camus hoped against hope for a French non-Marxist Left. Events during the second half of the Mitterrand presidency, after the

Socialists parted ways from their Communist allies and indirectly brought about their defeat in the 1968 elections, have to some extent fulfilled Camus's hope. He turned out to have been shrewder than the ideologists of the journal *Les Temps modernes*.

Cruickshank coolly lays bare the intellectual confusion of Camus, who failed to define one of his favorite terms, "revolt," and to separate it from "revolution"; who proves "a better moralist than he is a logician"[4] and blends historical generalizations and argumentative ideology with rapturous hymns to the sun and "la clarté de midi," Mediterranean wisdom, and "la mesure" hyperbolically lauded. He offers dispassionate reservations on the contradictory assertions with which both the book on Sisyphus and the one on man in revolt are replete. But his detached and pragmatic appraisal of the turbulent Parisian literary stage enables him serenely or skeptically to dismiss clichés to which the intellectual Left uncritically subscribed in France and which Camus had the courage to question: the cult of Sade as a deep thinker and as a talented writer; the near unanimous acceptance of Marxism as still valid one hundred years after Marx; the conviction that Algeria, once free from the French colonists, would turn into a genuine and tolerant democracy; and the contention endlessly debated amid the "mandarins" of 1960–65 that it was justified and intellectually defensible not to reveal that concentration camps existed in Soviet Russia and that the accused were forced through hypnosis or torture to confess crimes that they had not committed. Camus was certainly not infallible in his political judgments; he was confused and evasive, and torn inwardly, when faced by the question of Algeria. Still he did not have to reverse his positions as his contemporary and for a time opponent Merleau-Ponty did or, later, flocks of former leftists who, like Jean-François Revel, hailed America (which Camus never came to appreciate when he visited it in 1946) as the savior of civilization.

No attempt is made in this essay to compile an exhaustive bibliography of the numerous volumes, pamphlets, and articles devoted to Camus. An arbitrary selection of books deemed to be of some novelty or importance is made—chiefly of those which appeared after the death of the writer in 1960. The present state of the questions most hotly debated and most relevant for today's readers is sketched, again with some arbitrariness and with no claim to eschew value judgments. Literary commentaries, like history itself, *pace* Tacitus (a partial and wrathful historian if ever there was one) can only be worthwhile if written "cum ira et studio."

Camus's early writings published since his death have added substantially to our knowledge of his development as a creative artist and as a moralist relentlessly probing into his own self. The two volumes of *Notebooks* (*Carnets*), published in 1964 in Paris and in America soon after, are often revealing. Even more than Benjamin Constant, Balzac, Malraux, and Proust, Camus was endowed (some would say afflicted) with the French passion for scattering maxims in his works. One should not expect to find in those jottings of his early years the pointed and biting definitiveness of the ironic thoughts Valéry sharpened and polished throughout his career. But they reveal an apprentice thinker arduously striving to understand himself and to struggle in the midst of his inner conflicts. Unlike Gide's daily remarks in his lifelong journal and even Valéry's occasional moments of impatience recorded in his early morning hours of solitude, Camus's "thoughts" are never sneers at his contemporaries. They may be at times tinged with harshness against himself and his dependency upon women. To the future student of his words they will serve as a rich storehouse of insights, more revealing than his early and very tentative attempts at fiction, the publication of which has perhaps not served our understanding of Camus. *La Mort heureuse*, which first appeared in volume one of the *Cahiers Albert Camus* (1971) was composed in 1936–38. The young apprentice shows himself as an able stylist. His obsession to discover "how to die happy" is not rendered very convincingly; Patrice Mersault contrives to die in the last chapter, sick, hardly charitable to the women who nurse him, untouched by remorse for his gratuitous murder of Roland Zagreus. He had killed him in cold blood in order to appropriate the treasure of that invalid who trusted him. The immaturity and the clumsiness of the récit caused some embarrassment to the editors. The scattered pieces put together in the second number of the *Cahiers Albert Camus* in 1973, under the title *Le premier Camus, suivi des Ecrits de Jeunesse* (translated and published in New York by Alfred Knopf in 1973), are also tentative sundry pieces of scant merit in and of themselves. They date from the years preceding 1934, Camus's twenty-first year. They are ably edited and introduced by Paul Viallaneix. Already then Camus was preoccupied by the religious impulse in man, leaning not toward a revelation but rather to a pantheistic union with nature. Even then the young Algerian student was torn between the temptation of tragedy (fostered by his reading of Nietzsche's early work) and pagan or allegedly Mediterranean sense of *mesure*. He went on meditating assiduously on tragedy, delivered an important lecture on it in Athens in 1955[5] and tried to write some.

It is hardly worthwhile to dwell on the attempts made thus far to psychoanalyze Camus posthumously. He grew up without a father — not an unusual occurrence among writers like Racine, Baudelaire, Rimbaud, Nietzsche, Zola, Gide, and Malraux. Jean Grenier and half a dozen famous novelists have been generously granted a surrogate paternity over the future Nobel prize winner. Such at least is the contention of Alain Costes's very elementary psychoanalytical attempt at "explaining" Camus, *Camus et la Parole manquante*. More has been made of his early relationship with his mother, illiterate and afflicted with a speech defect that condemned her to silence, and with an imperious and harsh grandmother, even less conclusively. The first syllable of his first hero, Meursault, and the approximate similarity between "mère" and "mer" (the sea into which Camus and his characters like to dive for purification) and other even more preposterous rapprochements have been suggested by Costes. Jean Gassin has showed more tact as well as more prudence in his 1980 volume, *L'Univers symbolique d'Albert Camus*. He aims not at the man and author Camus but at his writings. His approach is lexicological as well as psychological; through the frequency of certain words and phrases, he reaches conclusions of modest import on what he pompously calls the "symbolic universe" of Camus. The same professor from Australia has submitted an ingenious interpretation of the Van Eyck triptych at Ghent, "le panneau des juges intègres," which plays a prominent part in *La Chute*. The empty spaces in the center might stand for the barrenness of both the mother of Saint John the Baptist and the mother of Christ; they were no longer young when they gave birth. Infant Camus, perhaps in his subconscious, imagined that he could identify with infant Jesus. The knights in their steel armors riding in front of the judges supposedly "recall the castrating symbolism often linked by Camus to the figure of the father."[6] Many a reader may be put off by such subtleties, ingeniously calculated to bewilder and impress academic audiences.

It is fortunate that hunters of influences have not rushed in large numbers to Camus. Yet he himself had not been chary of pointing to what he might have owed to some of his predecessors, with the same overgenerous "misplaced intellectual loyalty" that characterized W. B. Yeats. Camus embarrassed his former teacher, Jean Grenier, by repeatedly overstating his debt to him. Grenier himself protested against being thus magnified, and perhaps devoured, by his student of the Algeria days. In fact, his self-professed disciple failed to share his teacher's interest in the Oriental religions, Hinduism and Taoism. Camus had grown up in Algeria close to Moslems and Jews but he nowhere evinced any curiosity for the mystics of Islam or for the writings of a fervent interpreter of Moslem theology who was also one of the great Catholics of twentieth-century France — Louis Massignon. Readers of Grenier's volumes, *Les Isles* (1932) and an essay on "the spirit of orthodoxy," are not likely to experience the same thrills of rapturous illumination that had shaken the untrained and lonely student in Algeria. An English scholar, J. S. T. Garfitt wrote, for his Oxford degree, a modest and restrained monograph on *The Work and Thought of Jean Grenier 1898-1971* in 1983.

The similarities between Camus's early lyrical essays and Gide's *Fruits of the Earth* are superficial and have been rashly magnified by critics. The temperaments of the two men and their hedonistic proclamations of sensuous intoxication are at opposite poles, as are the textures and the tones of their lyrical prose. Camus was assisted by Gide, who put him up in his Paris apartment on rue Vaneau, encouraged him, but never claimed him as a disciple.

Camus expressed in 1955 his esteem for Martin du Gard. It was a personal esteem for the integrity of the artist in the elder writer and for his attitude toward political and ethical problems in *Jean Barois* more than for the sage of the *Thibault*. Both were, in Martin du Gard's words, "atheists, but not without faith." At best, a parallel stressing the deep differences between the two Nobel laureates may be warily sketched. It was attempted in an article by Lionel Cohen. Among the French predecessors of Camus, the one whom he respected most and whose novels, *Man's Fate* and *Days of Wrath* (or, rather, of *Contempt*), struck him most powerfully was Malraux; a study of their works in this connection would repay a searching inquiry. Although he commented upon Kierkegaard, in reference to Don Juan, and on Kafka in *The Rebel*, Camus owed each of them very little, if anything, and a comparative study linking them would merely overstate a very frail philosophical relationship. "Camus and Dostoevsky," resting on the French writer's adaptation of *The Possessed*, or his obsession with Ivan Karamazov's passionate speeches on the most revolting of crimes, the death of children, and especially on the monologue-dialogue in *The Fall*, recalling the Russian's *Underground Man*, would prove a more challenging and more daunting subject. On the American novel, whose impact had early and probably rashly been denounced on *The Stranger*, Camus expressed himself candidly in a conversation with Jeanine Delpech in 1945 (*La Table ronde*, February 1960). He had borrowed some devices from Hemingway when they seemed to suit him, as he was intending to present a character without a past. But he soon repudiated that technique, which if generalized, would impoverish the novel and reduce its characters to automatons. A more lasting influence was that of Melville, in whom Camus recognized what Edouard Morot-Sir has called "a fraternal model." *Billy Budd*, *Moby-Dick*, and probably *Benito Cerreno* counted in Camus's development more than any of his American contemporaries, excluding Faulkner. The thinker to whom he owed most in his early training, and even unto the last, was Nietzsche. Camus read him eagerly in the translations of Henry Albert, and later of Geneviève Bianquis. Only partial attempts have to this day been made to embrace the huge impact of the German thinker on French imagination. On Camus's affinities with Spain, on his readings in Spanish drama and fiction of the Siglo de Oro, or even of nineteenth-century plays on Don Juan (by Zorilla), it is surprising that so little was said by the half Spanish author himself. His 1958 address, "What I owe to Spain," is only a few pages long; the other texts in the Pléiade volume of *Essais* are of a political character. How well he knew the language, how skillfully he adapted Spanish plays, what he may have received from Maria Casarès, the daughter of a Spanish politician of note, are questions which, like many others concerning Camus, have never been adequately answered.

More attention has been lavished on Camus and Algeria. Fierce partisanship envenomed the polemics that raged in the Paris political circles when the country was torn asunder by controversies on the Algerian question. There prevails more tolerant understanding of Camus's hesitations and always tentative positions on that subject in the late 1980s than was possible thirty years earlier, when they clamored for an immediate solution; many non-French then jumped into the fray to indict French colonialism. One of the harshest critics of Camus then and since in the English-speaking world is Conor Cruise O'Brien. He submitted that Camus was "a stranger on the African shore" and, through his education, "more French than Algerian." He pointed out the basic lie of which Meursault is guilty — he lies to the police and lies to himself in never regretting that he shot the Arab four times when the victim could not fight back. To O'Brien, Meursault not only refused to dramatize his own feelings in the conventional way, but also did not experience one ounce of remorse about murdering an Arab since the latter is "not quite a man." The novel is "colonial in a certain sleight of hand." *The Plague* proves even more indifferent to the plight of the Moslems, who should in all likelihood have perished from the epidemic in far larger numbers than the French. But "the strategy of the fable required the disappearance of the Arabs." All in all, according to that Irish prosecutor, Camus was guilty of failing to attack colonialism, while proving hostile to communism. "He flinched from the realities of his position as a Frenchman in Algeria," is the verdict.[7]

O'Brien's hostility to Camus's lack of sympathy (in his fiction) for the plight of the Arabs in North Africa reflected the mood of many of those in the French Left around 1960–70 who rose against the tergiversations of French policy toward Algeria. It took issue with what the polemicist considered as excessive leniency toward Camus's ambiguous position in the writings of Germaine Brée and others who sympathized with Camus. The bitter polemics of the 1950s around the Algerian question have died down today. In the United States, Germaine Brée refuted several misinterpretations put forward by O'Brien: Camus's innocent statement that if he had to choose, he would side with his Algerian mother, had been grossly caricatured by O'Brien as implying that he chose to be with the "special forces" advocating torture by the French army.[8] Brée protested against the arguments ad hominem put forward by Sartre in the polemics around *The Rebel.* "An anti-Communist is a dog. I shall never change my mind on that," shouted irate Sartre in his articles against Ridgeway, in which he proffered accusations against the American general that turned out to be based on patent forgeries. Sartre never took the trouble to withdraw them. He sharpened polemical sentences against Camus "the bourgeois" and mocked him as carrying with him a portable pedestal on which to be hailed as "the prosecutor general for the republic of beautiful souls." In fact, there was more nobleness and even more humility in Camus's attitude than there was in Sartre's. Not very long after the acrimonious debate of 1952 in *Les Temps modernes,* Bernard Murchland submitted that Sartre may have proved a clever polemicist, but that "he does not seem to have understood Camus": "he was poorly disposed and poorly equipped to answer him."[9] Poirot-Delpech, in *Le Monde* of 5 August 1977, justified Camus against the sarcasms of his accuser. Indeed, it had taken fewer than twenty years after the debate for Sartre to repudiate all collaboration with the Communists who had, in his view, become "the biggest French conservative party" (in 1970).[10] They had turned their backs on the revolution during and after the student riots and sided with the hated bourgeoisie.

So had philosopher Merleau-Ponty who had, soon after World War II, advocated revolutionary terror and discarded humanism contemptuously.[11] A close friend of Sartre in those days (they parted ways later), elated as were many by the Russian victory at Stalingrad, feeling remorseful at the immense sacrifices made by the Russians in 1941–45, Merleau-Ponty adduced sophisticated reasonings to justify the trial of Bukharin in 1938 and the Russo-German pact of 1939. If there was violence in the Soviet regime (and millions jailed in labor camps, besides the other millions put to death), the philosopher argued that such violence was "progressive," unlike humanistic bourgeois justice that was obsessed by the past. If Stalin had in 1939 sided with Hitler and thus unleashed war in Europe, it was in order to preserve the gains of the Bolshevik revolution. The tribunal of history would ultimately justify him. Schiller's line at the end of his early poem, "Resignation," might have been the motto of those post-Hegelians—"Die Weltgeschichte ist das Weltgericht"—world history constitutes the ultimate judgment. Camus's outcry against that historicism substituted for "the tribunal of beautiful souls" was to resound in his later writings. The argument to which the French fellow travelers with communism then resorted bore a perilous similarity to what the Nazis and those among the French who collaborated with them in 1940 had contended: history and a realistic submission to facts justified them. They were realists.[12]

In a subsequent book, *The Adventures of the Dialectic* (1973), Merleau-Ponty reversed himself. He ceased to proclaim that "Marxism is THE philosophy of history and that to renounce it is to dig the grave of reason in history."[13] He took refuge in silence; he died in 1961 before he could have made amends to Camus. Dialectics, with a "yes" turning into a "no" and a "no" into a "yes," seemed to open up a way out of his contradictions, as Sartre, reconciled with his once estranged philosopher friend after the latter's demise, admitted in a touching article in *Les Temps modernes* in 1961, as he had "forgiven" dead Camus the year before. The most judicious appraiser of the shifting positions of the three Frenchmen is a Swiss teacher of philosophy born in 1940, Eric Werner. His sympathy is with Camus more than with his critics, as seems to be that of the generation now reaching the middle of their lives. In *De la Violence au totalitarisme* (1972) he stated Merleau-Ponty's arguments in his early work in favor of the wished-for violence of the slaves (the proletarians) which deserved to succeed the violence, too long unchallenged, of the masters (the capitalists). Werner pointed to the flaws in such a thesis, resorting to

Camus's arguments that the former slaves, turning into tyrants, would victimize their former masters. He preferred Camus's slogan: "Neither victims nor executioners." Both communism and fascism, resting on ideologies and contending that they alone embody the course of history, end up in a totalitarianism that tramples ethical values underfoot. Prometheus is soon metamorphosed into Caesar. Jacobins of 1973, Marxists, and fellow travelers of the twentieth century immolate the present to a future and remote justice; the end eventually to be reached would justify the means. Such transcendence spurns the present. Camus's choice is for Nietzsche's everlasting "yes" — a "yes" that refuses to subscribe to violence and to surrender to the irrational. There are many non sequiturs and many a preposterous assertion in Camus's *Rebel*, a confused and imperfect volume that fails to come up to its philosophical claims. Yet it is, said Camus, of all his books the one dearest to him. Its basic contention may well outlive many of its flaws.[14]

Throughout his life Camus repeated that he was not a philosopher and not anxious to pass for one. He repudiated all systems. He contended that he spoke for no one but himself and found it arduous enough to formulate his views in his own language — the last time in an interview given to *Venture*, in December 1959. He added: "I ask myself the same questions as do men of my own generation; that's all . . . A mirror informs; it does not teach."[15] He was aware of the risk he ran when he attempted to present his ideas with some systematic coherence, or the appearance of it, in *The Rebel* and *The Myth of Sisyphus*. Those volumes should be read only as loose collections of fragments and storehouses of maxims. They reflect the doubts and often the anxieties of a man interested in ideas and fond of meditating on history, but one who would be repelled by the reading of Sartre's heavy philosophical works, or Hegel's, or Aristotle's, even of Plato's *Dialogues* (if he ever attempted it).

He was, however, fascinated, even obsessed, by vexing questions of the history of thought, particularly on the conflict, at times artificially magnified by him, between Hellenic paganism and Christianity. That conflict underlies much of his fiction and almost all of his meditations on moral and spiritual values. Like many of us, he groped toward a formulation of his own ideological and religious positions while studying philosophy in his last year at the lycée, and then while writing a minor thesis, corresponding to a long master of arts essay, called "Diplôme d'Etudes Supérieures," which came after the Licence ès Lettres and was a prerequisite for the competitive exam of the "agrégation."[16] Camus was not allowed to sit for the latter after his health had deteriorated. The essay's ambitious title was *Métaphysique chrétienne et Néo-Platonisme*. The date was 1938. It seems, on the surface, to be an impressive piece of work by a young man of twenty-three, familiar with Saint Augustine and perhaps with other Latin Church fathers or early theologians, but much less so with the Greek and Gnostic writers. Camus's knowledge of Greek was nonexistent or very elementary. Nowhere does he give evidence of direct familiarity with Homer and the Tragic poets, or indeed with the philosophers. Repeatedly he asserted that "the world wherein he felt most at home was that of Greek myths" and that he had a Greek heart. He liked to declare that he was a pagan, respectful of the Christian faith but obstinately outside it. Ancient Greece was for him, as it had been for many a modern, the land of his heart's desire. He visited the country twice, but left no written impressions of the people and their art. He romanticized Heraclitus and particularly Empedocles, lavished allusions to Plotinus, which he appears to have borrowed from the Russian Lev Shestov who impressed him strongly, and from historians of Hellenic and of early Christian thought: Emile Bréhier and Pierre de Labriolle. He shut himself determinedly to the concept of incarnation as he did to the notions of sin and resurrection, inconceivable, he maintained, for a Greek mind. Peremptorily, he argued that the Greeks had no sense of history and he opposed Christianity (blaming it as moral, dramatic, obsessed with history) to Hellenism, which he praised as aesthetic, tragic, and close to nature.

That youthful essay, "more literary than philosophical," as was the verdict of his thesis director, Poirier, was clearly put together in feverish haste and with scant urge to resort to primary texts and to read them in depth or even with accuracy. Camus discovered and formulated a number of views on Greek antiquity, on his own inner conflicts, which he found already adumbrated in Alexandrian Gnostics and in two North Africans writing in Latin, Tertullian and Augustine. The essay is well organized and pleasantly readable for the none-too-scrutinizing reader who looks into it for an early expression of Camus's yearnings. It does not, however, bear the searching examination of a scholar intent on checking Camus's sources and on appraising his originality. One at least of Camus's readers, Paul Archambault, a distinguished scholar at Syracuse University, had the scholarly competence and the patience to explore the sources and the smooth and eloquent developments of the thesis. The result is devastating. In *Camus' Hellenic Sources* (1972) and in two essays[17] Archambault proved, tactfully but unflinchingly, that many of Camus's ideas and, literally, his facile developments had been borrowed (or "lifted") from scholars to whom the young student failed to acknowledge his debt. The information thus obtained by Camus is, to say the least, "badly digested." Much of the essay is a patchwork of phrases summarily stolen from others. "Camus is either delinquent or erratic in indicating his references." The confrontation of Camus's text and that of his sources, presented in two columns on the same page, is indeed disturbing. Camus's Hellenism was sentimental and passionate, and like most passions, partial. It overlooked slavery, the slighting of women, the political cruelty, and the tyranny of the Greek city states. But it inspired Camus with some of his most fervid and glittering prose — in "L'Exil d'Hélene," for example, first published in a bulky and remarkable number of *Les Cahiers du Sud* entitled *Permanence de la Grèce*.

Camus's praise of Greece was proclaimed by him too often and too loud to be questioned, even if the combative tone on which he celebrated it may elicit doubts as to whether he was not seeking to persuade himself of it. His attitude toward Christianity has aroused more discussion. Not a few Christians he knew would have liked him to undergo a conversion. They contended, on very frail grounds indeed, that he might have converted if he had lived longer. It grieved them to think that an author deserving to be a saint would have the gates of paradise closed to him. Articles and books have been devoted to Camus's alleged, or unorthodox, Christianity. One of them—descriptive and perspicacious but in no way argumentative—is even entitled by author Bruce Pratt *L'Evangile selon Albert Camus* (1980). Its content and its manner are more prudent than the title might lead one to surmise. The commentators on *The Fall* have been impressed by the Christology suggested by the title, the name of the prophetic Jean Baptiste discoursing tirelessly in his spiritual desert, the pretense of self-flagellation, and much of the imagery. At least two of the stories in *Exile and the Kingdom* recalled the solitude and the chastisement of Christ. The novelist could not but be aware of that obsessive role of para-Christian symbols. Perhaps half-consciously, he made use of them in order to broaden his appeal. They certainly enlarged his audience among the Protestants in English-speaking countries and in the religious institutions in his own. Camus himself, never baptized, would not have accepted to be ranked among the nominal Catholics. It is nevertheless certain that his essays and his fiction are tinged with Christian hues far more than are those of Giraudoux, Malraux, and Sartre. He liked to declare (as he did to Brisville) that he had "a sense of the sacred," without making it clear what he put under that catchall phrase liberally abused in our time. Sartre pronounced God "a useless passion," seems not to have been pursued in his creative years by reminiscences of the Gospels, by the "nemo bonus" that outraged Camus rather childishly, or by Augustine's summary condemnation of the children dead without baptism. Sartre welcomed violence, which outraged Camus. He ignored Christ's invocation (through the twenty-second Psalm) in the Garden of Gethsemane to his father who had forsaken him. He would not, he who disdained external nature, have taken the trouble to deny Christ's assertion and to contradict him by repeating that his own kingdom was "of this world."

The most concise, most penetrating, and most impartial exposition of Camus's attitude toward religion is that formulated by the well-known (and self-confessedly Roman Catholic) French professor Jean Onimus in the 1965 collection "Les Ecrivains devant Dieu."[18] Onimus does not transfigure Camus into a Christian. He repeats that he was an atheist, perhaps even an antitheist, marked early by Nietzsche. "It is up to us to create God," Camus had jotted down in his *Notebooks* of 1942–51. "It is not he who is the creator. . . . We have but one way of creating God which is to become God."[19] Camus spurned all sense of sin; he rejected the urge for salvation or the mere possibility of it. He accused Christianity of slighting the beauty of the world. Onimus remarks that not a few convinced Christians, Bossuet, for example, Claudel and Teilhard de Chardin in our century, had in no way ignored the world's material splendor. Camus would rather have echoed Maeterlinck's remark: "If I were God, I would be ashamed of having created this world." Still, there lurked in him a deep-seated disquietude. His firm denials (in oft-quoted texts such as "L'incroyant et les chrétiens"[20]) point to a constant preoccupation in him with the religious problem. The wisest words on the subject are probably those of two eminent religious leaders, P. Festugière and Rev. Samuel Miller. A Dominican, Festugière wrote in the same issue *Permanence de la Grèce* (*Cahiers du Sud*, 1948) in which Camus's "Exil d'Hélène" appeared. Festugière, a well-known Greek scholar, had long been concerned with Platonism, Neoplatonic Renaissance literature, and with the relations between Hellenism and Christianity. In religious matters, he submitted, "there are two kinds of people: those for whom religious problems count and those for whom they do not exist." Among the latter are many orthodox, practicing Christians who fulfill their "religious duties" in order to be no longer bothered by what they might owe to "the divine." But it is quite possible to subscribe to no creed, never to practice, yet to be tortured throughout one's life by the problem of God and the relations between God and man. Rev. Samuel Miller, then Dean of the Harvard Theological School, delivered an address at the Princeton Theological Seminary on 6 June 1961 and mentioned Camus along with Malraux and other French unbelievers. "These atheists are asking for greater honesty about the human condition, demanding severer dimensional responsibility and opening both freedom and compassion to new depths. . . . Such atheism is the movement of the spirit by which religion itself may be saved from itself."[21]

If some mystery hovers over Camus's parareligious yearnings and his dual attraction-repulsion to the symbolic representation of Christ, another side of his personality has remained wrapped in even darker mystery. We know from his biographers how sensitive he was to the appeal of women — that he was easily and frequently distracted by them. But he remained extraordinarily restrained in his writings both on his first wife, on his long liaison with Maria Casarès, and on other women who may have meant much to him. Twenty-five years after his death, no letters have appeared comparable to those which Sartre sent to some of his lady friends. The role assigned to women in his imaginative work is insignificant, nonexistent to a degree unequalled in today's fiction. They are banished from *The Plague* and from all but one of his stories. Mothers are dismissed. His early notebooks, jotted down while he was in his twenties and early thirties, are mysteriously reticent on the subject. The pagan that Camus proudly proclaimed himself to be appears as an ascetic, advocating chastity — "asceticism, when voluntary, is a reserve of real energy."[22] "Sex is pointless. . . . Chastity alone can lead to personal progress. . . . it endows the world with meaning."[23] Again, "sex life was given man to turn him away from his true path. It is his opium. In it, all goes to sleep. Outside it, things resume their life."[24] And in 1942, "Those who love truth must seek it in marriage; that is to say, entertain no illusion."[25] Are those warnings to himself by the fulfilled and weary lover, returning to his writings after sexual "conquests" by which he felt chained and with his creative energy depleted? The pages on Don Juan in *The Myth of Sisyphus*[26] are strangely lacking in ardor. The theme haunted Camus who was perhaps contemplating variations on Don Juan when he died. He praised nudity and the embrace of bodies in his lyrical essays. But few great writers have proved as reserved on the subject as he was. Only one such case may be recalled — Victor Hugo, whose ancillary loves and indiscriminate yieldings to faunlike urges are recorded in his notebooks and meticulous financial accounts. Through a puzzling process of compensatory remorse, shame perhaps, or the will to play the part of a moralist in all that was not his erotic poetry, he banished physical love from his novels or, as in *L'Homme qui rit*, he made it perfunctory, unbelievable and strangely chaste. The enigma (it is the title of one of Camus's essays in *L'été*) is more impenetrable with Camus than with any of his contemporaries. Stubbornly, the author refuses to be interpreted as present in his imaginative creations. His wish was to be an objective writer and to preserve his freedom from any identification with his characters. In a similar vein and with a singular courage, while other men of letters in Paris were collecting disciples in "cénacles" or demanding obedience in their "seminars," Camus declared in a Swiss journal in March 1954: "The artist, the writer were not put in this world to please the youth. They are here to tell the truth. If the young reject them, they will do without the young. If their ideas coincide with those of the young, they will rejoice."[26]

A vast amount of critical commentary has accumulated on Camus's novels — more so quantitatively than on those of any French writer of this century, excluding Proust and Gide. That may owe in part to the enigmatic character that their author imparted to them and that opened them up to a variety of ingenious interpretations, which the fiction of Romains, Duhamel, Montherlant, and Martin du Gard does not encourage to an equal degree. Camus's plays failed to provoke or to stimulate a similar wealth of critical appraisals. The consensus, in the late 1980s (and despite the New York Civic Repertory Company's attempt to rejuvenate the best of Camus's plays, *Caligula*, in February 1986 by staging it in modern dress), appears to be that those plays are too intellectual, too geometric in their architecture, too haughty in their diction, to move audiences. The verdict of critics amounts to a reluctant recognition of an ultimate failure, even for *The Misunderstanding*, for which its author confessed a special fondness. Camus's lifelong interest in the stage, his zeal for working on a team with stage managers and actors, his oft-proclaimed esteem for theatrical works as "the highest form of literature and the most universal,"[27] his address on tragedy delivered in Athens in 1962, lay bare a profound concern of his. Ultimately, however, it seems doubtful that Camus's plays, even the ones he adapted from other dramatists, will ever enjoy a successful revival. The fiction and the lyrical essays, the passionate moral and aesthetic declarations of Camus constitute the firmest basis for his being included among the four or five important mid-twentieth-century French authors.

One of the most acute commentators on *The Stranger*, Jules Brody, has termed it "the most abundantly discussed novel of the century and, what is more, the most widely read."[28] It had sold, according to André Abbou, nearly four and a half million copies by 1980 (and *The Plague* close to four million), translations into other languages not included. Obviously, success proves little if anything and is not even a sure proof of the mediocrity of a book that enriches its author. The ambiguity of the title, its studied, overclassical simplicity, the ease with which the prose can be enjoyed by the least sophisticated of readers, and particularly the youngest among them, are some of the reasons for such a success in the case of Camus. Surprising is the small number of hostile or dissenting critics: Leo Bersani is one of them, and not a very harsh one. The subtle and searching minds of several well-known scholars teaching in America have deciphered and appraised the short novel, without becoming impatient with its effective skill: Brody, Champigny, Girard, Viggiani. One of those critics, Girard, has reinterpreted *The Stranger* in the light of its successor, *The Fall*, and read into it an indictment of the judges singularly lacking in "integrity." Camus himself helped throw some of his commentators on strange byways through the choice of his enigmatic title, *The Stranger* or *The Outsider*, and by his unwary (perhaps sly) remark in the American school edition of the novel that Meursault was a Christ-like figure and perhaps the only Christ that our age, steeped in pettiness and desiccated by abstraction, deserves. Fellow novelists such as Nathalie Sarraute and Robbe-Grillet were shrewd in pointing to Camus's novel as a virtuoso tour de force technically impressive in its mastery of varieties of prose, now hyperclassical in appearance, now lavish in its use of metaphors and in its poetic suggestiveness.

In contrast to the avalanche of appraisals of his first novel, *The Plague* has been restrainedly and scantily dealt with by critics, while meeting with a wide favor with the general reader. Camus repeatedly revealed in his posthumously published *Notebooks* how painfully he struggled while in the throes of composing that long allegory. He could not but realize that the symbol of the plague in the city of Oran was inadequate to render the inhuman cruelty and the cowardice that had been granted free rein during the German occupation of France. He himself had suffered from the anguishing separation from his family and from his tuberculosis during those years 1942–45. He felt unsure as yet of his own ability to compose another novel that would not prove a brutal letdown after *The Stranger*. He had to wrestle with a plot almost totally uneventful and with the absence of all feminine element in the story of the besieged city. He had a message to deliver but the characters with whom he entrusted that message could hardly be presented dramatically and colorfully. It was almost impossible to avoid a monotony of diction and not to lapse into the pitfall of didacticism. The novel reached an excessive length, and its author gave the impression of becoming too weary or sterile to make it shorter. Despite obvious shortcomings and a general lack of humor as relief from the oppressive tragedy, the novel has moments of tragic intensity that grip today's reader. Still it does not leave the reader puzzled and personally concerned as *The Fall* was to do a few years later. If *The Plague* has not brought out conflicting exegeses by critics displaying their own subtlety, *The Fall* is proving to this day one of the favorite battlegrounds for professors and students, who are eager to read enigmas and allusions into it. Its formal mastery and its complexity have won for it the rank of a masterpiece, not unequal to Dostoyevski's *Notes from the Underground* man or to Malraux's fiction.

Several of the essays devoted to Camus in volumes presenting the learned debates on Camus's legacy twenty years after his death deal with sundry aspects of *The Fall*: among them are Brian Fitch's *Le Sentiment d'étrangeté chex Malraux, Sartre, Camus* (1964), *Bibliographie d'A. Camus* (1972), and *Camus Nouvelliste* (1973); Jacqueline Lévi-Valensi's essay "Le Temps et l'espace dans l'oeuvre romanesque de Camus; une mythologie du réel," in Raymond Gay-Crozier's *A. Camus* (1980); Lionel Cohen's essay "Signification du sacré dans *La Chute*," also in the Gay-Crosier volume, and his article "Une lignée humaniste au vingtième siècle: Martin du Gard et Camus" in the autumn 1973 issue of *Hebrew University Studies in Literature*; and Jean Gassin's essay "*La Chute* et le retable de l'agneau mystique; étude de structure," also in the Gay-Crosier volume. Entire monographs have been devoted to the elucidation of the *récit*: that of Pierre-Louis Rey among others, in a series for students published by Hatier in Paris. Camus's own statements on the meaning and the technique of his *récit* made shortly before his death in *Venture* are enlightening on his choice of the novelistic form, though they are in no way self-assertive or pompous: "I have utilized a theatrical technique (the dramatic monologue and the implicit dialogue) in order to picture a tragic comedian. I adapted the form to the substance, that's all."[29] But Camus often declared that techniques to him are mere tools; they do not condition a work. It may be regretted that too much of the elucidation that was attempted on *The Fall* centered on the circumstances preceding it — notably the acrimonious debate in *Les Tempes modernes*. The short novel was interpreted variously as a direct attack on the existentialists, prone to declaiming freedom and universal responsibility; as a remorseful self-indictment of Camus himself, conceding that he had more than once been self-righteous and solemn; also that his private life as a husband and a lay preacher of virtue and honesty had hardly remained unsullied by his bouts of Don Juanism and his explosive fits of anger at his companions. In truth, the novel has a far more general, even a universal import. It is a rich and complex masterpiece of irony, with allusions to Christ or some form of Christology much more prominent than in Camus's previous works. The moral concern pervading it is the same that Camus was to express more solemnly in his Stockholm address of 1957. It extends the longstanding meditation of Camus on the function of literature in our time. In November 1948, Camus had delivered at the Salle Pleyel in Paris a vibrant address on the artist as a witness of freedom. It appeared the following year, in December 1949, in the American review *Commentary* as "the Artist as witness of freedom" and was soon set beside the finest pages in Sartre's *What is Literature?* It has lost little of its fervor forty years later. With *The Fall* (his best work, Sartre pronounced after the death of his former friend,[30]) Camus displayed a mastery of technique, a skill in the art of distancing himself from his own self, which ranked him, in world literature, close to Dostoyevski himself.

The same detachment from his personality and a similar control over his material are noticeable in several of the stories collected under the felicitous and hardly enigmatic title of *Exile and the Kingdom*. "The Renegade," that "parable of nightmarish perfection" as its most perceptive commentator, Victor Brombert, has called it, may well remain as the most powerful short story and dramatic monologue of this century in French. Symbols have, inevitably, been read into it, anti-Christian ones in particular, since it is true that the person of Christ (and the gloom that haunted him, according to Camus, for having been the occasion for the slaughter of the innocents by Herod) remain insistently in the background of atheist Camus. Like many who watched the near-unanimous acclaim of Hitler by the German and Austrian masses until 1944, Camus had been impressed by the ease with which once civilized people could yield to hatred. His eloquent, if too haughty, 1943–44 *Letters to a German Friend* had showed how easy it had been to slide from fanatical love of one's country to universal hatred and masochist self-destruction. The story, laid in a barbaric African setting, conjuring up an atmosphere of bestial torture and ritualistic savagery, is unmarred by any didacticism. Seldom has sheer cruelty been rendered so powerfully. It affords the evidence that, despite his recurring bouts with the fear of becoming dried up by the intellectual climate of Paris and his impatience at having become idolized, Camus's imaginative power had remained undiminished.

Ultimately it is on his achievement as an author of novels, récits and short stories that Camus's place rests. His plays and his ideological works are less assured of survival. Lyrical and moral essays, once disengaged from the circumstances by which they were inspired, and a number of maxims culled from the *Notebooks*, would make up another volume worthy of being placed alongside the French classical moralists whom Camus praised as not very far from Nietzsche. By 1988 the political controversies that had raged in the 1950s have lost much of their bitterness. The intellectual circles of Paris and those that duplicate them in American academia have shed their dogmatic conviction that one brand of political, social, and aesthetic doctrine alone is valid, or that Marxism, impervious to aging, is assured to remain the creed of the working class and of the antibourgeois intelligentsia. Camus, after all, may not have fought in vain the worship of history. He is present among us and may be so among our successors for more time to come.

## Notes

1. Patrick McCarthy, *Camus* (London: Hamish Hamilton; New York: Random House, 1982), 99.

2. Donald Lazère, *The Unique Creation of Albert Camus* (New Haven, Conn.: Yale University Press, 1973), 245–46. Lazère quotes Jack Newfield's biography of Senator Robert Kennedy, who, at thirty-eight, discovered Camus while grieving his brother's death. By 1968, "he had read, and reread, all of Camus' essays, dramas, and novels. . . . He memorized him, meditated about him, and was changed by him" (in Robert Kennedy, *A Memoir* [New York: Dutton, 1963]). In New York a critic familiar with French literature, Lionel Abel, ranked Camus among the "Seven Heroes of the New Left."

3. John Cruickshank, *Albert Camus and the Literature of Revolt* (London, New York: Oxford Press, 1959), 121.

4. Ibid., 64.

5. Albert Camus, *Théâtre, Récits, Nouvelles*, vol. 1 (Paris: Bibliothèque de la Pléiade, Editions Gallimard, 1962), 1701–11.

6. Jean Gassin, "*La Chute* et le retable de l'agneau mystique; étude de structure," in *A. Camus*, ed. Raymond Gay-Crosier (Gainesville: University of Florida Press, 1980), 134.

7. Conor Cruise O'Brien, *Albert Camus of Europe and Africa.* (New York: Viking Press, 1980).

8. Germaine Brée, *Camus and Sartre: Crisis and Commitment* (New York: Dell, 1972).

9. Bernard Murchland, appendix to Michel Antoine Burnier, *Choice of Action: Existentialists and the Political Frontline* (New York: Random House, 1968), 188, 193.

10. Thirty years after the debate and Sartre's assertion that Marxism and the French Communist party embodied "the march of history," the Italian Communist organ *L'Unità*, approved by French observers, predicted the disappearance of the French Communist party (*Economist*, 29 March–4 April 1986).

11. Maurice Merleau-Ponty, *Humanism and Terror* (Boston: Beacon Press, 1969).

12. See Jacques and Claudie Broyelle, "Il y a vingt ans mourait Camus," *Le Monde*, 5 January 1980; "Camus," Poirot-Delpech, Bertrand, *Le Monde*, 24 December 1982; Emmett Parker, *The Artist in the Arena* (Madison: University of Wisconsin Press, 1965); Henri Peyre, "A. Camus Vindicated," *Laurels* 50, no. 2 (Fall 1979):83–92; Jean-François Revel, "Le Silence de Camus," *L'Express*, 3 November 1979.

13. Maurice Merleau-Ponty, *The Adventures of the Dialectic* (Evanston, Ill.: Northwestern University Press, 1973).

14. In America, a balanced presentation of Camus's attitudes — often contradictory — on Marxism, nihilism, and history was offered by Lev Braun, *Witness of Decline: Camus, Moralist of the Absurd* (Rutherford, N.J.: Fairleigh Dickinson University Press, 1974). Without concealing the flaws in Camus's logic, Braun lays bare the grounds on which the French moralist stands when he denounces the pitfalls of Marxist idealism (used as bait to strengthen the Soviet power machine). Braun stresses the deeper significance of Camus's indictment of historicism as willful intoxication with abstraction, ending in the demise of man's freedom.

15. Albert Camus, *Essais*, vol. 2 (Paris: Bibliothèque de la Pléiade, Editions Gallimard et Calmann-Lévy, 1965), 1925–28.

16. The text of Camus's essay is reprinted in *Essais*, 2:1224–1313.

17. Paul Archambault, "Albert Camus et la métaphysique chrétienne," in Gay-Crosier, *A. Camus*, 210–20; "Augustine et Camus," in *Recherches augustiniennes*, vol. 6 (Paris: Etudes augustiniennes, 1969), 195–221.

18. Published originally as "Les Ecrivains devant Dieu" (Paris: Desclée de Brouwer, 1965); *Camus and Christianity*, trans. Emmett Parker (Tuscaloosa: University of Alabama Press, 1970).

19. Albert Camus, *Notebooks*, 2 vols. (New York: Knopf, 1963), 64; *Carnets* (Paris: Gallimard, 1962).

20. This was delivered by Camus in December 1946 at the Dominican convent of La Tour Maubourg (*Essais*, 371–78).

21. Samuel Miller, Oral address delivered at the Princeton Theological Seminary on 6 June 1961; text was communicated to author in a private letter.

22. Camus, *Cahiers*, 2:59.

23. Ibid., 2:49, 55.

24. Ibid., 2:55.

25. Ibid., 2:101.

26. Camus, *Essais*, 154–656.

27. Camus, *Théâtre, Récits, Nouvelles*, 1726.

28. Jules Brody, "Camus et la pensée tragique: *L'Etranger. Saggi e Ricerche di Letteratura francese.* (Rome: Bulzoni, no date), 515.

29. Camus, *Essais*, 2:1927.

30. Jean-Paul Sartre, "Albert Camus," in *Situations* 4 (Paris: Gallimard, 1964), 127. Article dated 7 January 1960, a few days after Camus's accidental death.

# Camus's Libertarian Socialism     Roger Quilliot*

It may seem surprising in this day and age that we concern ourselves with the political thought of a writer who has been dead for twenty-five years. We forget, however, that since 1944, many students, among them

*This essay was derived from a speech commemorating the twenty-fifth anniversary of Albert Camus's death, delivered in Rome in January 1986. It was translated for this volume by Myriam Boucharenk and Enda McCaffrey.

myself, were introduced to the literary output of Albert Camus through articles in the newspaper *Combat*, inspired by Roger Grenier. We also overlook the fact that in the following decade, Germany and Japan, the two major defeated powers, sought through the work of Camus reasons to enable them to survive the nihilism in which they had been sunk. Finally, we fail to realize that Camus himself has tried on many occasions to define the position of the artist — he liked to picture himself alone and firmly rooted in an angst-ridden world. The artist cannot ignore the age in which he lives nor can he detach himself from the political and social context.

This being so, it is possible to distinguish three stages in the political thought of Camus: first, the period from 1935 to 1937 when he was tempted to join the ranks of the Communist party; second, that time from 1943 to 1947 when he aspired to a socialist democracy; third, the years of his connection with the free-thinking Left. But one can see clearly that this type of classification leaves areas untouched and deals with what is essentially arbitrary.

This classification does not take into account Camus's sensitivity, his reactions to events, and the enduring nature of this feeling of revolt which colors all his viewpoints. For Camus, negation, the individual's right to say no as a protest against everything that oppresses him, and the risk of nihilism that he admits readily, is paramount. Every time the world reaches a point of crisis, a revolt is the first thing to break out. Only after this, when man has saved his face, must he get down to living, to accepting life modestly but begrudgingly. Modest with regard to the ends, begrudgingly with regard to the means.

Let us go back to 1935 and that day when Camus, at the behest of Jean Grenier, wrote of his intention to join the Communist party. It was a strange letter addressed to a strange mentor. Strange inded one might say. Here we had a professor cum writer who, at the same time, was drafting a fiercely anti-Communist article entitled *Essai sur l'Esprit d'Orthodoxie* and was encouraging his former pupil to have dangerous thoughts. Here we had a neophyte communist who was ridiculing the illusion of progress, historical materialism, and the potential triumph of the working class. How great was the amount of dogma put to bad effect in one period of time.

A free-thinker was Camus and he intended remaining so even within the confines of absolute commitment: "I will always resist placing a volume of *Das Kapital* between life and man." A case of *lèse*-Marxism which was to be found again in 1947 when he made the following remark to Emmanuel d'Astier de la Vigérie: "I have not learned about freedom in Marx, I have learned about it in poverty." However sacred a text may be, it is based on experience in the same way that man's sensitivity is the basis of all doctrine. "This is all I need to willingly subscribe to ideas which bring me back to my origins, to my childhood friends, to all that which forms my sensitivity." One must always return to the beginning; a beginning characterized by inner experience, place of abode, the poor classes and one's earliest writings.

However much a Communist he may have been, Camus's approach to such an ideology was no less personal. While engaged in writing a collective play entitled *Révolte dans les Asturies*, he accentuated the play's reactionary side as opposed to the revolutionary side: at the Algiers' Cultural Residence, he organized an open debate on the very anticommunist work *Retour de l'U.R.S.S.* In treating Mediterranean culture, he recommended a Mediterranean collectivism which in his opinion was more favorable than the glacial Soviet collectivism. We will not discuss here the relevance of such a stance, this being the domain of the historian.

But as soon as the tensions increased between the Algerian Communists and the members of Messa Li Hadj's North African Star; as soon as the international crisis reached Czechoslovakia after Spain, Albert Camus realized the full potential of his freedom. Having taken up his pen as a journalist for the *Alger Républicain*, he launched a vitriolic attack against the actions of the Mayor of Algiers, M. Rozès, and against the bigoted law enforcement imposed by the police and the Gouvernement Général. These were followed by bitter articles concerning the Hodent Affair, a man suspected of anti-colonial sympathies, the Sheik el Okhy accused of harboring feelings towards independence, and the alleged "Auribeau arsonists." Soon, there were to come eleven articles in which Camus denounced blatantly the misery of the Kabylie. There were so many cries of revolt, expressed in the most majestic language, against an intolerable state of affairs.

The more imminent the prospect of war, the more insistent became Camus's protests: he criticized the harmful effect of the Treaty of Versailles; he denounced Hitler as the brown plague; he condemned outright the war mentality; he satirized the ludicrous censorship of the *Alger Républicain*; he lead *Soir Républicain* to ruination by his refusal to toe the line. At the same time, from 1936 onwards, contrary to what had been previously believed, he wrote the first and second versions of *Caligula*, a kind of theatrical reflection on the nature of revolt against death and human misery, as incarnated by the demented emperor Caligula, who dreamed of the triumph over both but was led to terror. As our colleague Vertone has underlined, Caligula turned against himself not only senators, whether upright, fickle, or ridiculous, but also Chéréa, a man of sobre reflection, who later delivers the fatal blows. Revolt, therefore, is met with revolt. And already there emerges a picture of those who resisted Nazism in the same way as they did the Goulag.

In some respects, *Caligula* is a prophetic play: Chéréa is by nature peace-loving, even a pacifist. And yet he will go as far as committing murder in order to preserve his freedom. For similar reasons, many peace-loving men were to emerge in France and in all of Europe harboring no feelings of hatred towards the Resistance, just like the author of the *Lettres à un ami allemand*.

As Roger Grenier recalls in his correspondence, Albert Camus joined the Resistance, I was about to say the revolt, following the death of Gabriel Péri. He became actively involved during his stay in Chambon-sur-Lignon when he met frequently the Christian René Leynaud or the then Communist Francis Ponge. He took up a position with the team of reporters working for the newspaper *Combat*, replacing the deported Claude Bourdet, before meeting Pascal Pia, his journalistic mentor.

It was the latter, according to Roger Grenier, who chose the subtitle for *Combat, de la Résistance à la Révolution*. This marked once again the shift from negation to affirmation, from revolt and its implied nihilist temptation to revolution and its organic and constructive supposition. He defined this revolution in a number of important articles as a collective enterprise of the resistance, closely linked to the socialist tradition, which in turn was injected with new blood: "all of us must reconcile justice with Freedom. Our objective is to make life free for each person and just for all." This was an unhappy reconciliation, he did not hide the fact, which still had not been fully understood even in what he called a "principle of contradiction." In addition, he did not forget the absurd backdrop against which he played out his professional life, that Pascalian condition in which man struggles with himself: "the demanding and wondrous task of this century is to invent justice in a most unjust world and to maintain the freedom of those people who, from their birth, have been born into subservience." This implied the introduction, little by little, of politics into metaphysics and of morality into politics.

Time and time again, Camus came back to these analyses. "The only social order is that one in which there is fear, a sparing attitude, caution and a harsh-heartedness which authorize all injustices. There is no order without justice and the ideal order of peoples is to be found in their happiness. . . . It is not order which reinforces justice, it is justice which gives its certainty to order." And he concluded, as a free-thinking socialist, that he was one of those who would "forever prefer disorder to injustice." To be more exact, "our idea is that one must make justice prevail on the economic level and guarantee freedom on the political level. . . . Our desire is to see in France a collectivist economy and a liberal politics. Without a collectivist economy which takes away from money its privileged position and gives it back to work, a politics of freedom is an illusion. But without the constitutional guarantee of political freedom, the collectivist economy runs the risk of absorbing all initiative and all individual expression." This is a difficult arrangement, a precarious equilibrium, a Sisyphean task!

One can understand why the young Camus of 1935 took no interest in progress, "a futile question," since the war of the revolutionary fighter was also being waged outside the limits of all "infallible and absolute ideology" through a sort of obstinate, chaotic but relentless improvement of the human condition. A keen foresight for predicting the future was required, "one which would restrain us from thinking of the individual every time a social problem had been solved and one which would prevent us from considering the well-being of everyone each time the individual sought our attention." There is a constant coming and going which leads us to believe that revolution is not a simple, spontaneous, radical upheaval of values and structures, but rather a perpetual adjustment the reference for which at least, if not the exact model, he sought in the Scandinavian democracies. In short, there is no such thing as a definitive revolution, because "all human effort is relative . . . we believe in relative revolutions."

However, the word itself was soon to be effaced by events. It was not only problems relating to food supplies or man's abuse of justice; it was, in particular, global changes which made a revolution inappropriate and in other words obsolete. Since Hiroshima and Nagasaki, our universe has assimilated the logic of terror. The cold war, the first signs of which few observers discerned, was revealed in Churchill's speech to Fulton at the end of 1946. At that time, Camus was drafting a famous series of articles for *Combat*, *Ni Victimes ni Bourreaux*, republished in 1947 by Jean Daniel in a special issue of *Caliban*. In this article, he analyzed the new balance of power in the world and the impossibility of both Soviet and Atlantic camps agreeing to important changes without the risk of a World War. This was the balance of dissuasion.

The very notion of revolution has no longer any meaning "in current historical circumstances . . . I trust I am forgiven in mentioning so openly, since everyone knows it already, but the fact is that, as French people we are not free to be revolutionaries." He had an acute perception of Soviet advancement through Europe under the shadow of the "bayonets." But supposing that the U.S.S.R. was still revolutionary, which Camus doubted, did there exist a revolutionary politics or a politics based on power? "The idea of revolution," he wrote with great shrewdness, "is being replaced today by the notion of an ideological warfare. Or to be more exact, there can be no international revolution without an extreme risk of war."

From this point on, "we must deny the importance given to internal politics." First, peace must be saved. In place of the notion of revolution, Camus was to substitute that of "relative utopia." Realizing that the German problem, which still obsessed the French generation of 1946, was nothing when seen in the context of the "clash of empires" which in itself was secondary in comparison with the "clash of civilizations" that he prophesied in the next fifty years, it would be the predominance of western civilization that would once more be questioned. It was Camus who proposed a world parliament, the first element in the organization of the world, an institutional demonstration of a "New Social contract." But how could such a change come about if it did not express itself, first, within nations, through communities based on a work ethic (and he referred here in his manuscript to the Barba cooperative in Valence, which had been inspired by Proudhon's thought), and second, beyond national boundaries, through communities where ideas are formed. The first group, according to the voluntary contracts on the cooperative level, would help relieve the greatest possible number of individuals. The second would seek to define the values according to which this international order would live, while at the same time, defending its case at every occasion. On this particular occasion, Camus defied so-called strict government policies and put his trust, as in all moments of crisis, in his independence of mind and the cell-structured organization in order to combat those fears which beset social bodies and would lead us to confrontation. The revolutionary spirit died and revolt, that force of indignation and love, was reborn.

Thereafter, Albert Camus was to juxtapose two approaches — the first, modest and working-class to a degree, was to increase partial reforms; it was also to lead him to support the Labour leader Atlee against Churchill in 1951, or of Pierre Mendès-France against the conservative coalition in 1955; the other, more intransigent and all-inclusive, was to bring him nearer to the extremely small R. D. R. Party, the occasional weekly *La Gauche* or the daily *Franc-Tireur*. This approach was to lead him to unite with the exiled Spanish Republicans, to the point where he accepted from them the order of the Liberation of Spain and celebrated the Nobel Prize with them. It was the same spirit that he wrote for *Témoins*, a discreet monthly founded by J. P. Samson, as well known an anarchist as the anarcho-trade-unionist Monatte, or for *La Révolution prolétarienne* of Roger Hagnaret, which disappeared at the very beginning of 1986.

This double temptation has nothing contradictory about it. It is coherently presented in the final pages of *L'Homme révolté*; Midé's thought is indeed balanced, moderately reformist in a working-class way, with a mutualist, cooperative and a trade-unionist substratum, charged with as many adjectives as one finds in liberal thought and practice which claim to reconcile the individual and society by means of a conscious and organized solidarity. It was not for nothing to have to plead for freedom. He did so in 1953 at St. Etienne during a meeting organized by the Inter-Trade-Union Liaison Committee (C. F. T. C., Working Class Force, the anarchic C. N. T. and F. E. N.) at the Bourse du Travail; no, Camus affirmed, freedom was not "a bourgeois see-saw. . . . The important thing today is this: without giving an inch on the judicial level and without abandoning anything on the level of freedom . . . the revolutionary struggle, the push for liberation is defined first as a double and constant rejection of humiliation. Freedom is not a gift that one receives from the State or from a leader, but rather a benefit that one conquers every day through the effort of each person and the union of all."

We have come full circle and the artist has never left the center. With a passsion for happiness, Camus confronted a tyranny that admitted neither silence nor neutrality. "One must come clean, either for or against. In this case, therefore, I am against." And he went on to add "that the opportunities to act were not lacking. Trade Unionism is the leading and most productive organisation of them all. . . . From my first articles to my last book, I have written so much, maybe too much, only because I cannot prevent myself from being pulled away from the everyday things of life, whatever they may be, that we humiliate or debase." This is a question of sensitivity, instinct and solidarity. "Even if, militant in real life, we speak in our works of deserts or egoistic love, it is enough that our lives be militant for a more secret energy to fill this desert and this love with people." In this respect, *La Peste* produces Rieux and Rambert who temporarily fulfilled their lives.

# Silence and the Desert:
# The Flickering Vision        Micheline Tisson-Braun*

There is an inveterate tendency to pigeonhole Camus as a novelist, playwright, and mostly philosopher of the absurd and revolt — which he undoubtedly is; but is he only that? The purpose of this essay is to follow, beneath the mainstream of his work, the lyrical current that springs forth in his youth, persists underground during his theoricizing period (the so-called cycles of Sisyphus and Prometheus) and timidly reappears later on in an inconclusive new trend, abruptly interrupted by Camus's death.

"In the spring, Tipasa is inhabited by the gods, and the gods speak in the sun and the scent of the absinth leaves. At certain hours in the day, the countryside is black with sunlight."[1] On the very threshold of Camus's poetic universe, the gods are present. They dwell in "the desert." Not the actual Sahara, several hundred miles south of Algiers, but the arid, luminous Mediterranean shores of Camus's childhood: Tipasa, Djemila swept by dry winds, their ruins merging into the stony ground surrounding them, and the metallic glimmer of the sea. In such vehement landscapes, with shapes and colors vibrating in the sunlight, nothing is commensurate with man, neither with his mind, nor his heart, nor even

*This essay was written especially for this volume and is published here for the first time by permission of the author.

his senses. Nothing is even visible, because of the excessive glare. Sight, the most intellectual of all the senses, is submerged in more primitive sensations, blinding sun, inebriating scents. This absolute violence heralds the presence of the gods, whose very essence is their self-sufficient simplicity. In referring to such landscapes, Camus rejects the banal adjective "dionysiac:" "I describe and say: this is red, this blue, this green, this is the sea, the mountain, the flowers." (*LCE*, 68). In short, here are the Homeric gods, in the simplicity of their absolute presence.

The language of pure presence is silence. It is unintelligible to man as defined by his reason and feelings, but akin—so it seems—to erotic desire at its most imperious and enigmatic. "To clasp a woman's body is also to hold in one's arms this strange joy that descends from sky to sea." (*LCE*, 68). Nevertheless, even erotic joy is deceptive since it does not address itself to one particular object, but tends to the unlimited and inevitably leads to the apprehension of death. "Under the morning sun, a great happiness hovers in space" (*LCE*, 68)—a happiness from which man is somehow excluded, since he knows he must die.

A pantheistic experience underlies the best pages of *Nuptials*, but joy at the glory of life is mixed in it with the dread of passing time, each feeling enhancing the other. "That is what youth must be like: this harsh confrontation with death" (*LCE*, 77). This, not pure revolt, is Camus's initial experience—a longing for a bittersweet communion. The pantheism of *Nuptials* is born of this ambivalent perception of nature's beauty both enthralling and alien. The "benign indifference of the universe"[2] or "the tender and inhuman something that dwells in me today" (*LEC*, 30) make up Camus's deepest experience. Much more complex than frustration, alien to romantic love—even to unrequited love—it is love for a sleeping beauty or rather for a silent mermaid whose message cannot be understood. To this dumbness, the mind says both yes and no. The discrepancy is not to be found between the feeling and its intellectual interpretation. Camus's rule of absolute lucidity precludes any such confusion ("Ne pas tricher"—do not cheat). He prefers silence to half-truth. Where, then, is the discrepancy? The answer is outlined for the first time in the essay on "The Wind at Djemila."

Djemila is the site of an ancient Roman town whose arches and columns rise skeletonlike on an arid windswept plateau—another "desert." The scorching wind seems to imprint on the visitor's skin the unknown cypher in which the gods' message is couched. We know already that this language is neither that of reason—for it is absurd—nor of the "heart"—for it frustrates—nor even the unconscious, since Camus demands lucidity. What is it, then?

Without renouncing the Tipasa experience, the essay on Djemila carries a broader meaning, born of a deeper insight into the cosmic experience. Here we find Camus joining the long line of seekers after the lost sense or faculty that would enable man to feel cosmic unity and grapple with what the post-Hegelians call "the Other." Can such a faculty exist? Can we capture Heidegger's "Being," to which other thinkers refer as "higher truth" and Camus simply as "beauty"? The secret sought by poets from Mallarmé and Breton to Camus is not the idealist's "Other World." In the case of Camus, it is not any kind of mysticism, either of God or of the divine emptiness that would entail detachment from the flesh; it is, least of all, a surrender to the unconscious and the plunge into instinctual life. He is most articulate in his refusal of comfort. He wants to experience — indeed to savor — the tragic confrontation. He wants to die disconsolate. Djemila, "inhuman" as a "great shout of stones" (*LCE*, 79) is, for him, a perfect symbol of "the Other." There he becomes sure of the true nature of the rift between human and cosmic consciousness.

"There are places where the mind dies so that a truth which is its very denial may be born" (*LCE*, 73). (The mind stands here as the respected principle of individuation.) Many texts in Camus's early lyrical works express a feeling on pantheistic communion. This is the clearest message of the gods in Djemila.

> I am the wind and within it the columns and the archway, the flagstone warm to the touch, the pale mountains round the deserted city. I never have felt so deeply and at the same time so detached from myself and so present in the world. . . . The wind was fashioning me in the image of the benign nakedness around me. . . . I was a portion of the great force on which I drifted . . . confusing the throbbing of my own heart with the great sonorous beating of this omnipresent natural heart." (*LCE*, 75)

Such communion can be reached only at the price of personal emotions. This is the detachment Camus was trying to achieve at Djemila — although he became fully conscious of his aim only in Florence. It has been seen that his pantheistic relation to nature satisfies both the senses and a secret feeling of harmony before and beyond personal consciousness, while leaving a gaping void in the region of man's nostalgia for understanding and brotherhood. Could it be, then, that the lost paradise — or the promised one — is to be found in an impersonal consciousness? That would be man's awareness of nature's great rhythm of desire and of death. Thus, not consciousness but personal consciousness would bring about the rift and the discrepancy that are felt as absurdity. "It is to the extent that I cut myself from the world that I fear death most, to the degree I attach myself to the fate of living men instead of contemplating the unchanging sky" (*LCE*, 78).

The experience of detachment is analyzed in all its bitterness in the essay on Florence (*The Desert*). Here, the Tuscan hills and Florentine painting lead to the same meditation. The beauty, the serenity of the landscape and the stately indifference of the figures painted by Giotto or Piero point to the same truth: they all proclaim that "the mind is nothing, nor even the heart" (*LCE*, 103) and that "plunged deep in beauty, the mind feeds off nothingness" (*LCE*, 101). Hence we see the harmony that Camus felt long before but realized only in Florence, between "the earth and man delivered from the human." (*LCE*, 100). In the serene equivalence of "beauty," poverty and luxury, detachment and passion, nothingness and plenitude are one and the same thing. In Fiesole's cloister, the roses in the garden match the skulls on the monks' tables. Detachment from self is the precondition for the sensuous possession of the world. "This world annihilates me" and the annihilation must be accepted. Since nothing will mitigate the dread of death, neither God nor any transcendent principle, the only certainty is lust for life and the despair of it: "a bitterness under a flame" (*LCE*, 78).

The beauty of the world is felt thanks to a certain form of attention that holds consciousness at a precarious — almost unbearable — degree of acuity. This insight reaches Camus in Fiesole in a cloister garden with a well at the center, while pigeons fly about. This "unique game of appearances" keeps him enthralled, in a constant fear that the spell might break. And yet it lasts, colored, as it were, by the premonition of its own end. "There lay all my love of life, Camus comments: a silent passion for what would perhaps about to escape me, a bitterness beneath a flame." (*LCE*, 56).

This is not pure revolt. The lesson of Florence is that "at the heart of my revolt, consent is dormant" (*LCE*, 105).

It did not take long before the poetic vision of *Nuptials* began to fade. Circumstances were unfavorable to poetic inspiration: the looming war, Camus's illness that interrupted his studies, and finally the necessity to work. (He described the filing shelves in his office as a columbarium in which dead hours were rotting away.[3]) At the same time, the vision also suffered from certain shortcomings in human relations. In spite of the compassionate and sensitive friendliness expressed in *L'Envers et l'endroit* (*The Wrong Side and the Right Side*), human relations are poor — no love, no friendship, and Camus even reproaches himself with a "natural indifference" (*LCE*, 6–7) in which he takes refuge. At the center of the psyche — his own and the psyches of others — he senses a void, an inner emptiness that erodes it as soon as the passions of youth have subsided.

More surprising still, considering the voracious reading to which the *Notebooks* of that period bear witness, no intellectual enthusiasm is apparent in Camus's lyrical account of his inner life, and very little interest for literature or for the arts. The adventure of civilization — which fascinated the young Malraux — awakes in the young Camus neither admiration nor curiosity.

This absence of cultural interest Camus sees as a characteristic, indeed, a merit, of what he calls "the Mediterranean Man."

> Intelligence does not occupy the place here that it does in Italy. This race is indifferent to the mind. It worships and admires the body. From

this comes its strength, its naïve cynicism. . . . Here are a people with no past, with no traditions, though not without poetry. Their poetry has a hard, sensual quality I know very well; it is far from tender, even from the tenderness of the Algerian sky. . . . These barbarians lounging on the beaches give me the foolish hope that, perhaps without knowing it, they are modeling the face of a culture where man's greatness will finally discover its true visage. These people, wholly engaged in the present, live with neither myths nor consolation. . . . Everything people do in Algiers reveals a distaste for stability and a lack of regard for the future. People are in a hurry to live. (*LCE*, 89)

Camus may be right in so describing the man of the future. The success of *The Stranger* among intellectuals seems to confirm his prediction. As for the eulogy for this healthy philistine, it reads sometimes like the *pro domo* of a victim of *inquiétude* determined to bury his inner life.

A period of relative emotional dryness intervenes between *A Happy Death* and *Cross Purpose*,[4] during which Camus's initial vision undergoes profound changes. In the works written under the spell of Sisyphus — including *The Myth* itself — the negative aspect of the initial ambivalence prevails. Instead of asserting both love and despair of life as an unbreakable unit to be lived through lyrically, *The Myth* proclaims life as absurd. Evil fate replaces the enigma. The discrepancy felt in human existence is no longer in the mind, between ego consciousness and cosmic consciousness, but rests squarely "between the mind that desires and the world that disappoints"[5] or "between the human appeal and the unreasonable silence of the world" (*Myth*, 28).

Camus's earlier attitude could lead either to detachment as practiced in the Orient, or to tragic love of life, as is known to the Greek and to some Renaissance poets. The new attitude leads straight to nihilism, possibly to violence (as happened in Nazi Germany). In France, *The Myth* became a sort of bible of despair. Yet Camus was advocating precisely the opposite — neither suicide (including that kind of, to his mind, spiritual suicide he calls "the jump into God"), nor aggressive nihilism. Both aspects of the absurd had to be lived consciously — the appeal and the absence of an answer.

*The Myth* reflects other changes. Man is now a stranger in the world, deprived of those enigmatic, lost motherlands that were Tipasa, Djemila, Florence, which "negated" only his personal consciousness.

Time is now perceived as an unmitigated evil, although in *Nuptials* the horror of passing time could be balanced by the sense of a timeless present (as in the cloister in Fiesole). Most important of all, in Tipasa and Djemila the gods "spoke" in their silent language, delivering a message that was real — indeed the only thing in life; now the gods have retired in dumb silence. Instead of a concealed truth, there is only nonsense and chaos. The unity sensed in *Nuptials* is replaced by the absurd play of chance. In short, what remains of the initial vision is the refusal of nihilism. The spontaneous joy of life persists only as a will to happiness. "We must imagine Sisyphus happy" (*LCE*, 123). Be this as it may. Such is the theoretical account of Camus's transformation as recorded in *The Myth*. How far it coincides with the imaginative account as expressed in *Caligula* and *The Stranger* remains to be seen.

In *The Myth of Sisyphus*, Camus offers three models of behavior for the absurd man: Don Juan, the Comedian, and the Conqueror. It is noteworthy that none of them is portrayed in his major works. Instead, the two figures of Caligula and the Stranger stand out as examples of absurd heroes.

*Caligula*, the first version of which was written as early as 1938, shows a more complete departure from Camus's youthful works than *The Myth*. It probably originated in an ethical meditation on the Karamazovs' paradox — if God is dead, everything is permitted. Then why not Caligula? It was not until *The Rebel* that Camus found an answer. Here, he seems to be bedazzled by Caligula's "logic," which other characters (and presumably Camus himself) can neither accept nor refute.

Taking the absurd as a starting point, Camus shows the transformation of an idealistic young man into a life-destructive and self-destructive maniac. The origin of Caligula's madness is not so much a personal loss as the discovery that "men die and are not happy." Accordingly, Camus insists throughout the play that Caligula has to be "understood," as he is by Caesonia, Helicon, and even the young Scipio, whose father Caligula murdered abominably. He should be understood, that is, not out of compassion for a disturbed mind, or of love for a lost friend one would like to save, but as a perfectly logical human being, whose pattern of life all men would follow if they dared. In the 1938 version, the murdered Caligula reappeared to announce the survival of "this monster or angel who lives in each of us."[6] In the postwar version, this couplet is replaced by one line, "I'm still alive!"

Camus seems to take for granted that Caligula's revolt derives exclusively from his frustrated wish for happiness. Since this wish is innocent and legitimate, it follows that Caligula's conduct must be innocent too. Therefore, Camus tries hard to legitimize his monster, against his better judgment. This may be why Caligula has to explain his position too often and lacks the simplicity of a living character, while the whole play bears the stamp of a demonstration and sometimes sounds like a court debate with a surfeit of devil's advocates.

On the other hand, Camus is somehow aware that the frustrated desire for happiness is not the *only* element in Caligula's madness. For if it were, then Caesonia's argument would impress him: "At my age one knows that life is a sad business. But why deliberately set out to make it worse?" "No," answers Caligula, "It's no good, You can't understand."[7] What is there to understand, except that Caligula's logic is not that of a frustrated desire and that some other element has been smuggled in, namely insane pride, and the wish to compete with the gods?

Another major departure from *Nuptials* is Caligula's concept of the gods. They no more speak to man in the enthralling, mysterious language of nature. They have become hostile and contemptible, "cruel," with a "stupid, unintelligible face" (*LCE*, 59). They have assumed the role and attributes of fate. Not that there is no friendly or charming power left in nature. The "tender indifference of the Universe" has not vanished, but it has become deceptive. It still haunts the demented emperor, but he has seen through it; this "caress of the gods" Caligula now perceives as a poisonous gift, or one that is sadistically withdrawn from his hands. The underlying myth here is not that of Sisyphus but that of Tantalus. Nature and life have become allies of Fate—a betrayal that calls for revenge. Hence we have Caligula's obsession with destroying all that is beauty and love. As for his own former love of beauty and poetry, we can watch it massacred in a decisive scene. In a lyrical dialogue, in which each partner completes the other one's thoughts as a tribute to former friendship, Caligula and Scipio evoke a world of unity and innocence—Roman hills in the twilight, the sound of crickets, the smell of grass and all the magic of *Nuptials* (II, xiv). At this particular moment, everything can be restored—friendship, happiness, sanity. Caligula's "soul," as Scipio would say, is still in the balance. Everything depends on him. This is a moment of promise. Caligula crushes it with one butcher's blow—all this lacks blood.[8] He has learned the technique of tantalizing and rejecting. The lyrical temptation will return to him twice. He evokes the Moon goddess's visit to his couch "like a milky pool in a dark wood." (*C*, 62) But the poetic memory is destroyed even as it is recalled, both by the prosaic setting (Caligula is tending his feet) and by its vulgar conclusion: "I can say without boasting that I have had her." The last blow dealt the youthful vision comes in the third act, when Caligula grotesquely masquerades as Venus, while an invocation to the goddess is read (and repeated in a choir) as if to rub in Caligula's lesson to the world. In the style of Homeric hymns, the goddess of love and beauty is stripped of her idealistic attributes; she is but a tempting demon instructed by fate to hide the meaninglessness of the world.

While pursuing this suicidal revenge on his youthful illusions, Caligula uses his imperial power to emulate fate ("To emulate the Gods is to make oneself as cruel as they are") (*C*, 57). Here, Camus seems to remember an idea expressed in Malraux's *Man's Fate*, namely, that man reacts to fate as a slave to a cruel and insane master. He can either try to institute an order in which there would be neither masters nor slaves, or, simply, emulate his master by enslaving other men. This second choice—born of vindictive pride—is that of Caligula. Powerless against "the gods," he emulates them and behaves as they do toward his subjects: "I wear the stupid and incomprehensible face of the gods" (*C*, 59).

When the dying Caligula admits that his solution was not the right one, the stage is set for his opposite: The Stranger.

*Caligula* sometimes reads like an exorcism. *The Stranger*, on the other hand, seems like a *pro domo*, since the hero is so dear to Camus's heart that he still describes him (in the preface to the American edition) as "the only Christ we deserve" (*LCE*, 337).

Everybody remembers Meursault's comments on his mother's burial, the vigil disturbed by the old people's sniffling but enlivened by the café au lait ("I am very partial to café au lait"), the heat on the way to the cemetery, and how wonderful it would have been on the beach "if it had not been for Mother." And so it goes on. The reader does not feel so much shocked as mystified. What is it that makes the Stranger so strange? Camus himself admitted that his character was built deliberately (*"très concerté"*). He does not reveal the gimmick, but there is a gimmick. The reader soon discovers that Meursault's strangeness is the result of a lack. What Husserl calls the "meaning endowing faculty" was skillfully removed from him. He registers facts, but not their meanings; his consciousness is purely instantaneous; he lacks the principle of unity and continuity that characterizes man. Accordingly, Meursault has desires and affects but no sentiments. He has neither memory nor projects, and his synthetic faculties do not operate above the immediate physical level.

There is no doubt that this amputation fits into Camus's theory of the absurd: if, indeed, the world has no meaning, then, the absurd man should adjust to the fact, and refuse to pretend. Although less overtly proclaimed than that of Caligula, Meursault's logic is, in Camus's eyes, more compelling.

Yet Meursault's personality cannot be reduced to this conjuring trick. One could argue that, rather than being the absurd man, a special, as yet unrecognized species, Meursault is a very common type indeed.[9] His mother's death did not upset him too much. Yet he liked her, always refers to her affectionately as *Maman* and often quotes her. But they had quietly drifted apart: "They had nothing to say to each other anymore." A very common fact indeed, however distressing. As for his girlfriend, although he would marry her if she wished to, he refuses to call his feeling "love." Then, she asked:

> Suppose another girl had asked you to marry her—I mean a girl you liked in the same way as you like me—would you have said Yes to her, too?—Naturally. (*S*, 53)

Most unromantic, to be sure. Yet if marriages were investigated, the majority would turn out to have started that way. All of Meursault's relations follow the same pattern. He becomes a "pal" of his immediate neighbor—a pimp, by the way, but who cares—just because he has no reason to refuse. Nothing exceptional here either. How many friendships rest on genuine and idealistic affinities?

The readiness with which simple people accept him shows how perfectly ordinary Meursault is, "just like anyone else." He is, in fact, a well-meaning, indifferent, shallow, and perfectly boorish young man — probably another specimen of what Camus describes approvingly as "the Mediterranean man."

Yes, but Meursault is perhaps not the commonplace person he professes to be.[10] Not only because he is more intelligent, more educated than his surroundings, *"un Monsieur,"* not only because of a word he drops here and there ("when I was a student. . . . when I was travelling. . . .") but, first of all, because he keeps a diary. One does not record in the first person what any third person would notice at first sight. Here lies the gimmick. Meursault is not shallow, he is multileveled; not simple, but simplified deliberately.

This leads to the suspicion that his aloofness was not natural but induced and that Camus intended to portray a man, perhaps himself, who tried to escape the painful awareness of absurdity by blocking the complexities of his inner life, just as he limited his social connections to uncomplicated, undemanding people. Similarly, his near namesake in *La mort heureuse* (*A Happy Death*) admits that he was using all his strength to quench the flame in himself.

There are other means to commit spiritual suicide than the "jump in God." There is Caligula's jump into hell and Meursault's flight into insignificance. Yet it failed, for Meursault got involved in spite of himself, a victim of his own passivity, an unwilling murderer, "because of the sun." We have reached the lower ebb of Camus's ethical message, far away from the sensitive — if deeply indifferent — young man of *The Wrong Side* and far away from *Nuptials* and the vision of tragic happiness.

At this moment, when Camus seems most determined to vindicate his hero's right to think and feel nothing, when he seems to have moved further away from the tender melancholy of *The Wrong Side* and from the tragic fullness of *Nuptials*, unexpectedly the pantheistic vision comes back.

The vision comes back gradually and, as it were, cautiously. Although Meursault had stifled it with the rest of his inner life when he became normalized, simplified to the level of the "Mediterranean man," in fact it had always been there, in beach scenes for instance, but not reaching lyrical consciousness. It had haunted him insidiously in his prison, where he could hear the sounds of life — the trumpet of the ice cream merchant who reminded him of "the poorest, the most penetrating of his joys"; it had come to tempt him at twilight, that "nameless hour," of which he refused to think — "There are some things of which I have never cared to talk" (*S*, 89).

At the same time, the Sun God is present all the while but as an avenging deity whose power had not been properly honored. A raging sun was streaming like a rain of fire during the mother's funeral — a premonition of divine vengeance. It came back with blinding fury on the beach where the murder of the Arab took place. "Everything began to reel before my eyes" (S, 76).

No explanation is offered for the act, and one can think of none, except the demented reaction of a man who had vainly tried to escape the gods of Tipasa. As for the additional four shots fired on the dead enemy, they were "like four loud fateful raps at the door of my undoing" (S, 76). What else could they be but fate's revenge at the mortal who had sought to escape it in spiritual slumber? From a certain angle, *The Stranger* might be read as an example of *Nemesis*, as ruthless to slumbering angels as to the fallen ones, like Caligula.

If Meursault's crime was a punishment meted out to a Chosen One who shunned his mission, then, as in Greek tragedy, balance has to be restored in the end, and to Meursault on his last day (as to Oedipus in the sacred grove where his tomb was prepared) the lyrical vision comes back. He wakes up "with stars over his face" and suddenly understands that he had been happy and still could be — that the meaning of life can be revealed near the end, in a timeless moment. Just like the mother has acquired a "fiancé" in her last days, the son renews his nuptials with the nocturnal skies and the "tender indifference of the universe." Then the cycle is closed and once more the language of images has prevailed over the dubious ideology of simplifying wisdom.

In spite of the success of *The Myth* and *The Stranger*, Camus seems conscious of having strayed into a blind alley. Meursault and Martha of *Cross Purpose*, as well as Caligula, could say that their solution was not the right one. Of course there was no solution, but it was possible to create meaning when it was not given. Accordingly, the stress in Camus's new works is no longer on the absurd, but on the fight against it. Beginning with his war-time articles in the underground paper, *Combat*, Camus enters a period of *littérature engagée*, culminating in *The Rebel*. His theoretical positions are well-known; but, here again, the analysis of his imaginative works might, perhaps, cast a new light on them.

It requires no great insight to read *The Plague* as an allegory of the German occupation, or of Nazism, or of history as the enemy of happiness and civilized life. All these interpretations are correct but insufficient. Why choose a bacillus as a symbol of these evils? Many critics — Sartre among them — pointed this out acidly, but they did not ask themselves why Camus was avoiding the facilities of such an obvious scapegoat as Nazism. In fact, Camus was aiming at something else as well, which left some readers puzzled and slightly suspicious. What of his insistence that we are all germ carriers? How could the maintenance of the death penalty compare with Hitler's crimes? Was Tarrou one of these "pharisees in reverse," to quote P. H. Simon, whom the straw in their own eyes prevents from seeing the beam in the enemy's eyes? Was he trying to drown the responsibility of precise evildoers in the general abstract guilt of mankind?

No doubt there was some confusion in Camus's mind. Nevertheless, those critics who demanded sternly that the bacillus symbol be explained were guilty of a worse confusion—they read a myth as if it were an allegory. Let us call allegory the concrete representation of an idea and a myth a spontaneous product of the unconscious, all twisted with entangled meanings and loose ends. Camus might have been referring to a distinction of this kind when he answered Barthes that *The Plague* should be read on several levels.[11] And indeed, there is no lack of texts of the same period from which one can obtain, if not an explanation, at least useful pointers.

One of these is a clear intimation of hell—or rather Hades, the kingdom of shadows where Sisyphus and Tantalus suffer. The undistinguished town of Oran is such a place, as described both in the initial chapter of *The Plague* and the essay in *Summer* called "The Minotaur." Oran is described as an entirely modern town. Now what better symbol of modern aberration could there be, in Camus's eyes, than a city that turns its back to the sea, ignoring its magnificent bay, as if it feared the appeal of natural splendor; than a city entirely absorbed in commerce (*"le négoce"*) and in shallow pleasures, foreign to contemplation; a city without trees, disfigured by pretentious public monuments; and dismissing the sea, that symbol of freedom and beauty, as something unwanted, disquieting (*"inquiétant"*)? In short this entirely modern city—as Camus sees it—was forfeiting the gifts of the gods, thus laying itself open to divine punishment. It was visited by an anachronistic curse, a "scourge of God," as a reminder of the awesome mysteries it was trying hard to forget. Once again the sun god, raging in every street during the summer of pestilence, darted his rays as the Homeric Apollo his arrows, at those who had offended beauty and mystery.

At the same time Camus was so impressed by the circular structure of the city that he compared it to the Labyrinth, and of course, found a Minotaur in it—boredom. The physical pain and the moral suffering of separation and loss were the tribute paid to him.

A similar labyrinth of circular streets (and canals) leading nowhere is Amsterdam in *The Fall*. It does open on the sea but a sea of mist, without horizon or contours or colors, a stifling void on which one can sail without feeling motion. This pale labyrinth in the middle of nowhere also has its Minotaur, a squirming little devil called Clamence/*clamans (in deserto)*, the Jean-Baptiste of nothingness whose only occupation is to watch himself watching himself in the endless game of parallel mirrors. Boredom, guilt, anxiety, destructive pride—such is the tribute exacted by the devil from those who willfully deprived themselves of beauty and friendliness.

Clearly the remedy for the plague is material prophylaxy and the associated virtues of courage and patience. But even that would be useless without the presence of men and women of good will in the plague-stricken city. Love, friendship, dedication — be it Tarrou's quest for total harmlessness or Grant's absurd search for literary perfection — contribute to the healing process, no less than the luminous glance of the doctor's mother who helped the dying Tarrou.

Roger Quilliot tells how Camus complained to him that the more he delved into politics, the less he was able to perceive and describe nature. Now nature is present in *The Plague*, in the background, and nocturnal. The starry sky appears several times. Then one day, when the plague is raging, Rieux and Tarrou escape to the beach at night for a kind of ritual swim, a baptism that seals their friendship.

"Boy scout's ethics, Red Cross outlook," railed the Caligulists who deplored what they regarded as Camus's conversion to bourgeois virtues. Camus's answer can be surmised from an essay in *Summer* called "Helen Exiled" that starts with a majestic musical chord:

> The Mediterranean has a solar tragedy that has nothing to do with mists. There are evenings, at the foot of mountains by the sea, when night falls on the perfect curve of a little bay and an anguished fullness rises from the silent waters. Such moments make one realize that, if the Greeks knew despair, they experienced it always through beauty and its oppressive quality. (*LCE*, 148)

Then starts a parallel between Greek thought and modern European attitudes, a slightly unfair parallel since the best in Greece is compared to the worst in our world. Nevertheless, Camus's point is clear and carries far.

With the reminder of the Greek tragic poets, the "oppressive fullness" of *Nuptials* has returned and starts a long chain of associations. Helen, of course, is beauty but she is also measure according to the classic canon of nature, rectified and idealized by the law of number and rhythm. Helen stands here for what is called in *The Rebel* "thought at the meridian." The concept of beauty is also akin to contemplation of what is eternal and serene in the world. It comes close to Heidegger's notion of being and his concept of beauty as equilibrium of opposite forces. In this context, man finds his freedom and dignity in a just appreciation of his limits.

Our modern world, on the other hand, is ruled by *hubris* — will to power, as illustrated by its addiction to history and its wars of domination; absolute trust in science as a means to power; a quest for moral absolutes expressing itself in the devilish "all or nothing" (analyzed in *The Rebel*) and its fierce intolerance. The cult of history excludes all forms of permanence. The modern world first substituted preoccupation with the ego for contemplation of the world and then having lost its anchor, perceived everything in a flux. By this unreasonable conduct, it called upon itself the swarm of the Erynnies.

We were all told that the plague had disappeared from the modern world. So had, in our opinion, such archaic evils as tribal chauvinism, torture, the inquisition (political), slavery, wholesale extermination — yet they are all back among us. Then why not the plague? Men are smitten by anachronistic disease for having ignored the eternal law of measure.

Camus's last years offer no major work after *The Fall. Summer*[12] is a collection of essays, most of them written earlier. This leaves us with the short stories in *Exile and the Kingdom*. No one can tell whether this silence showed that Camus's inspiration had dried up, like that of the artist in *Jonas*, or that he was collecting himself in view of a renewal. The mythical Jonas, after all, emerged from the belly of a whale. A few months before his fatal accident, Camus told a friend that his work was hardly begun and he was thinking of a novel called "The First Man" (possibly in connection with Nietzsche's "last man").

Camus's premature death makes it impossible to ascertain what kind of renewal, if any, would have taken place. Yet he himself sought it in the recapturing of his early sense of nature. He mentions it in the blurb of *Summer*. And in the preface of "The Sea Close By,"[13] he celebrates the return of his "familiar gods": the earth, the sea, the night. As if to confirm this prediction and reassert his "faithfulness to the earth," *Summer* contains a victorious — if melancholy — "Return to Tipasa" that can read not only as a real episode in a journey to Algiers, but as a double symbol — of Camus's own life darkened by broken friendships but ready to recover its earlier inspiration; and also as a symbol of human life alternatively smitten and visited by peace and wisdom, like that of Sophocles' *Oedipus*.

In spite of obstinate winter rains and his mistrust of efforts to recapture the past, Camus returned to Tipasa. The sight of the rain-soaked landscape distressed him. But a second attempt gratified him beyond all hopes:

> . . . in the glorious December light, as happens only once or twice in lives that may later be described as heaped with every blessing, I found exactly what I had come in search of, something which in spite of time and in spite of the world was offered to me and truly to me alone, in this deserted nature . . . It was as if the morning stood still, as if the sun had stopped for an immeasurable moment. In this light and silence, years of night and fury melted slowly away. I listened to an almost forgotten sound within myself, as if my heart had long been stopped and was now gently beginning to beat again. (*LCE,* 167).

Thus the exile realizes that "in the worst of our madness, the memory of this sky had never left [him]" (*LCE,* 168) and that "in the depth of winter . . . within [him] there lay an invincible summer" (*LCE,* 169). Later on, while musing over an ancient coin he brought from there, with one side eaten up, a graceful phantom speaks to him — perhaps that of his youth, perhaps a Greek wandering soul, or even the lost spirit of Europe. "I long to go and lie down in the valley, under the unchanging light, and learn for one last time what I know" (*LCE*, 171). Then the circle will be closed and the curse of time abolished.

Camus's last suggestions of his favorite landscape are in two texts of *Exile and the Kingdom* — very briefly in "The Host" and prominently in "The Adulterous Woman." The first text just hints at the line of Saharian hills as a French schoolmaster gazes at them from the window of his poverty-stricken village school; the second tells of a wife, on a journey to the South with her mediocre husband, whom she neither loves nor esteems. She escapes their hotel room at night to contemplate the starry night above the desert and dreams of limitless expanses of freedom.

These are the last reminders of the youthful vision. Both will come to nothing — the adulterous woman will stay with her mediocre husband and the schoolmaster will be murdered for a betrayal he did not commit. The initial vision is there inded, but blurred by tears and soiled with blood.

## Notes

1. Albert Camus, *Lyrical and Critical Essays*, ed. and trans. Philip Thody (New York: Knopf, 1968), 65; hereafter cited as *LCE* followed by page number. This volume includes, among various articles, *The Wrong Side and the Right Side (L'Envers et l'endroit)*, *Nuptials (Noces)*, and *Summer (L'Été)*.

2. Albert Camus, *The Stranger*, trans. Stuart Gilbert (New York: Random House, 1971); hereafter cited as *S* followed by page number.

3. Albert Camus, *A Happy Death (La Mort heureuse)*, trans. Richard Howard (New York: Random House, 1971).

4. Between 1938 and 1944; although Camus was in fact thinking of and preparing works of very different inspiration at the same time.

5. Albert Camus, *The Myth of Sisyphus and Other Essays*, trans. and ed. Justin O'Brien (New York: Knopf, 1969), 50.

6. See Albert Camus, *Théâtre, Récits, Nouvelles*, vol. 1, introduction by Roger Quilliot (Paris: Bibliothèque de la Pléiade, Editions Gallimard, 1962), 1735.

7. Albert Camus, *Caligula and Cross Purpose (Le Malentendu)*, trans. Stuart Gilbert (London: Hamish Hamilton, 1947), 22.

8. The English translation is "All that is a bit . . . anemic" (49) does not render the unexpected brutality of the French text, "Cela manque de sang" ("This lacks blood").

9. See Robert Champigny, *Sur un héros païen* (Paris: Gallimard, 1959).

10. See Nathalie Sarraute, *L'Ere du soupçon* (Paris: Gallimard, 1973).

11. See Albert Camus, *Essais*, introduction by Roger Quilliot (Paris: Bibliotheque de la Pléiade, Editions Gallimard, 1965).

12. Camus, *Théâtre*, 2997.

13. Camus, *Essais*, 1829. In this text, Camus mentions "sa longue fidélité" (prolonged faithfulness) to his early inspirations.

## Sun, Sea, and Geraniums:
## Camus *en voyage*                                    Alba Amoia*

> Et jamais peut-être un pays, sinon la Méditerranée, ne m'a porté à la
> fois si loin et si près de moi-même.[1]

The names of many great writers are linked with the places where
they were born or lived, or which they recreated for us in their works.
Sappho of Lesbos, Dante the Florentine, Dr. Johnson the Londoner, Emily
Dickinson, "The Belle of Amherst" — such hybrid designations are part of
the common coin of literary discourse. In using them, it is true, we run the
risk of inadvertently limiting our appreciation of a writer's range and
significance. Great writers become so because what they have to tell us is
of universal, not merely local, significance. Yet even a universal message
must owe a part of its impact to a sense of the time and place in which it
was nurtured, the physical, palpable details of soil, climate, and human
ambiance out of which it grew.

Of no literary figure is this more true than of Albert Camus, who is
closely identified with what was still known during his lifetime as "French
Algeria." The blinding North African sun, the tang of the Mediterranean,
permeate much of his work, and the pictures of his native land and its
people that he has left us will survive as unique witness to their time and
place.

Yet Camus was infinitely more than a merely "local" or "colonial"
writer. He was, in the widest sense, a citizen of the world, and his message
was and is addressed to all people everywhere. Nor were his life and
activity by any means confined to the Algerian scene. In addition to his
years in metropolitan France and his leading role in the French Resistance
during World War II, he was familiar with other parts of Europe and
twice crossed the Atlantic on professional missions, to North and South
America.

It is true that Camus did not enjoy traveling. "Travel is no fun, nor is
it easy,"[2] he wrote on one occasion. The airplane, for him, was "one of the
elements of modern negation and abstraction which effaces nature's
landscapes"[3] — a metallic coffin, he frequently called it. "What gives travel
its importance is fear. Traveling smashes our interior decoration,"[4] he
alleged, reminding us of the "slight anxiety that accompanies each
departure."[5] The very notion of "pleasure travel" was alien to him. Travel,
if anything, was a duty. "It is for education that we travel, if by education
we mean the exercise of our most intimate sense, which is the sense of
eternity. Pleasure takes us away from ourselves, as Pascal's *divertissement*

*This essay was written especially for this volume and is published here for the first time
by permission of the author.

takes us away from God. Travel, as a deep and serious science, brings us back."[6]

Such views could hardly fail to limit the scope of Camus's own voyagings. Although his two transatlantic journeys belong to the immediate postwar years (1946 and 1949), it was not until the 1950s that he was able to visit Greece, the country that for him was synonymous with Beauty in the most complete sense—and which he did not, unfortunately, describe in his travel notes.[7] He altogether refused to visit Japan, and his 1957 journey to Stockholm to receive the Nobel Prize for Literature was undertaken only on the insistence of Roger Martin du Gard and of his publishers.

The deeper source of this reluctance undoubtedly lay in Camus's intensely "Mediterranean" consciousness and his habit of carrying with him, on all his travels, the memories and predilections of his original milieu. Other lands and peoples, to him, were acceptable to the degree that they resembled those of his Algerian homeland. Italy, Spain, the Mediterranean lands, held familiar elements that qualified them almost to be regarded as parts of a "greater Algeria." At times he spoke of the entire Mediterranean as constituting a single, dodecagonic country, of which he felt himself to be a citizen. Beyond the Mediterranean, in metropolitan France, Central Europe, or the Americas, he was seldom truly at ease. Yet at such times his very nostalgia, his longing for the southern sun, gave rise to some of the unforgettable images that stud his writings, from the more or less autobiographical *Carnets* and *Journaux de voyage* to the essays gathered in *L'Envers et l'endroit*, *Noces*, and *L'Été*.

The reader seeking to trace Camus's footsteps would be hard put to develop an exact itinerary or a specific catalog of places to be visited. Eschewing guidebook details, Camus prefers to offer us poetic images and artistic impressions. The minutiae of time and place are submerged in a flood of personal sensations and associations.

In describing a locality or a landscape, Camus would not attempt a map, content instead to record those soaring emotions, fantastic analogies, or mythological references the scene awakens in his mind. The Mediterranean, for him, is not so much a geographical feature as " a living country full of games and smiles."[8] Gibraltar is the spot where Antaeus died.[9] Brazil is a "land without men," and Sâo Paulo an "outsized Oran."[10] New York City is a "dried-up iron- and cement-scented cistern,"[11] while London emerges as "the opposite" of his recollections of gardens and birds, Oxford is "silence," and Edinburgh, "the Athens of the North . . . has no north" and is built around a "false Acropolis."[12]

Camus defined his almost mystical obsession with the life of the Mediterranean in the formula:

God — Mediterranean: structures — absence of nature.
Nature = equivalence.[13]

These mathematical propositions offer a key to what Camus was looking for in all his travels. God is in the beauty of nature; the beauty of the Mediterranean is in its sun and light (the words *soleil* and *lumière* appear innumerable times in his descriptions); and these in turn are the source of truth. "Happily, there exists a light which we Mediterraneans have never lost";[14] and, again, "[l]ight on the olive trees in Italy . . . gives witness to truth."[15]

Even outside of Algeria, Camus found homes and hills bathed in golden sunlight. But, he insists, "it's not the same sun. I know very well that it's not the same sun."[16] Convalescing from a lung ailment in a remote French village in 1950, he writes, full of yearning: "This afternoon, sun and light streaming into my room, the sky blue and veiled, the sound of water in the garden . . . and then the hours of Algiers come back to me"[17] — for his physical illness was compounded by nostalgia for his country, "proportionate in its lines, disproportionate in its light."[18] Though he could enjoy a brief "secret affair" with France, it was toward Algeria that he felt what amounted to an unbridled passion and voluptuous abandon.[19] The Algerian sun, the Mediterranean sea, and the sensuous North African landscapes were his source of light and truth, from which he felt far removed in foreign lands.

The city Camus loved most — Algiers — is "full of sun: warm streets, full of women. Flowers are sold on each corner. And these girls' faces that smile."[20] The only European city that could offer an alternative satisfaction was Florence: "Gentle, fine light over Florence. . . . [A]t each corner, vendors' stands with thick, bright flowers. . . . I drank at the fountains, and the water was a bit warm, but so fluid. . . . I stopped to look at faces, and I drank smiles."[21] In *L'Été*, he characterized the mild softness of Algiers' climate as "rather Italian, while the cruel refulgence of Oran is somewhat Spanish."[22]

Though North Africa's intense sunlight offered a panchromatic palette for Camus's descriptions of the "hours of Algiers," it could also impose a vision in stark black and white. "At certain hours, the countryside is black with sun."[23] "The revelation of this light, so bright that it becomes black and white, at first is somewhat suffocating";[24] or, "this white and black brightness which, for me, has always been the brightness of truth."[25] At other times, he described the Mediterranean's "greenish light" that filled him with a joy akin to Mircea Eliade's childhood experience, in which sunlight streaming through green curtains gave him the delicious sensation of finding himself inside a grape.

Sun and light (or sunlight), then, are symbols of truth and a source of strength for Camus. This is true even in philosophical terms, since his concept of the absurd takes him back full circle to the sun.[26] They are the very opposite of the cold northern grayness, devoid of panchromaticism, which fills him with a deep sense of despair. For Camus, the person who turns from the sun and the sea to the rain and concrete of northern cities is bound to feel solitude and anguish, and to realize the absurdity of having left truth and pleasure behind. Oran — for Camus, a desert place, without soul and without escape[27] — is the city that "turns its back to the sea."[28] This alone would seem to explain sufficiently the author's choice of Oran as the setting for his novel *La Peste*.

Referring to the "miserable tragedies" of his contemporaries, Camus accuses them of "turning their backs to nature" and of being "ashamed of beauty."[29] An environmentalist before the time, he inveighs against human constructs as opposed to natural ones (cf. God — Mediterranean: structures — absence of nature), calling man's reckless effacement of nature "the modern cancer." "Deliberately," he writes, "the earth has been amputated of what makes for its permanency: nature, the sea, the hills, evening meditation."[30] Even in his own *Carnets*, he notes ironically, landscapes gradually disappear as the entries accumulate. "The modern cancer is eating at me, too."[31]

In Paris, Camus is chilled by the colorless urban scene, where gray skies, pigeons among the black stones of the Palais Royal, and artificial lights cause the quality of love to be strained.[32] The color gray, for him, is associated with sadness, ennui, and absence of sensuality. Along the streets of Paris, he sees "black trees in the gray sky and pigeons the color of the sky."[33] On a rainy morning during his sea voyage to North America in 1946, he records: "The color of the Atlantic, pigeon wing."[34] His first glimpse of New York harbor is a melancholy mixture of skyscrapers, gray mist, cold wind and flat sky that leaves him "dry" and "untouched."[35] Yet even in France or in New York, the return of sunshine and blue skies permits him to recapture something of his Algerian happiness: "Because the sky is blue, the snow-covered trees, thrusting their white branches low over the icy river waters, look like almond trees in bloom."[36] When the spring sky in New York finally turns blue, he recalls that the city does, after all, lie on the same parallel as Lisbon, and "it's a good moment."[37]

If panchromatic sunlight is associated with joy and sensual pleasure, the sound of the sea is pansonorant — a balm for his hurt mind. On the long voyage back to France after his North American lecture tour in 1946, his anguish is calmed by the sea, an infallible tranquilizer.[38] Wherever he finds himself, if the sound of the sea reaches his ears, he is "repatriated." The sea contains the entire world; it is his eternity; its incantatory power telescopes time and space for the tormented adult obsessed by early recollections of sunning, swimming, and loving at the Algerian beaches.

From complete exposure of his body to sunlight at high noon, sea bathing, and struggles with the wind, Camus derived a feeling of unlimited strength. "Poverty was no obstacle to this strength: in Africa, the sea and the sun are free,"[39] he writes in *L'Envers et l'endroit*, and in his *Carnets*: "The sea: I didn't become lost in it, but rather found myself in it."[40] Often, plunging naked into the sea at Algiers, his body perfumed by the essence of the earth, he sought to feel that voluptuous embrace of lips against lips—the eternal kissing between land and sea.

A sun- and sea-bathed atmosphere of pagan sensuality is everywhere diffused in *Noces*, the collection of essays written in 1936–37. These essays are saturated with Camus's love for Algiers and its surroundings: the sea, visible from every street corner or framed by the ancient ruins outside the city; a certain weight of the sun; the prodigality of nature; and the beauty of the race.[41] Camus and his fellow Algerians enjoy complete freedom on the beaches, swimming and running with "the magnificent gestures of the athletes of Delos."[42] He achieves complete gratification of the senses as his naked body enters the dialogue between stone and flesh, between the sun and the seasons.[43] The blood in his veins beats the same pulsations as the sun at high noon.[44] To these sensations his heart and mind unceasingly return: "When I am away from this country for some time, in my imagination its twilights become promises of happiness."[45]

The opening lines of Camus's very first essay, "Noces à Tipasa" (a Mediterranean village about seventy kilometers east of Algiers), convey the tone of the entire collection: "In the springtime, Tipasa is inhabited by the gods and the gods speak through the sun and the perfume of absinthe, the silver-clad sea, the raw blue sky, the flower-covered ruins, and the billowing light in the heaps of stones."[46] He revels in the "libertinage of nature and the sea,"[47] which attracts and takes possession of him like the Eleusinian mysteries, which were essentially agricultural rites but often included the ritual of sea-bathing. Filled with force tempered by tenderness, he lies upon and caresses the flat stone slabs of Tipasa's ancient ruins, crushing the scented absinthe beneath him, and trying to synchronize the rhythm of his breathing with that of the earth. Accomplishing this, his heart grows calm with certitude: "I learned to breathe, I became whole, and I was fulfilled."[48]

Returning on a passionate pilgrimage to Tipasa some fifteen years later, after a flight from "the night of Europe,"[49] Camus finds the sun and sea of his idealizations unchanged. Reverently, he touches the ancient stone beauties of the Tipasa ruins, regaining sufficient strength to return to what, for him, is the dark continent of Europe.

At Djemila, another archaic North African site that lends its name to the enthralling essay "Le vent à Djémila," the author bathes in the violence of sun and wind, actually *becoming* the wind which sweeps through the ancient arches. In still another ceremonial mystery, the wind synchronizes the beating of his blood with nature's heavy, sonorous heartbeat, which echoes through Djemila's mountains while the living face of a horned god in the pediment of an altar looks on.[50]

Camus's first trip outside of North Africa (documented in the *Carnets* and in *L'Envers et l'endroit*) was to Central Europe in June of 1936. During a lonely and lugubrious stay in Prague, his mind dwelt desperately upon his native city and the gentle Mediterranean nights, "bathed in a green light, and full of young, beautiful women."[51] All that will remain of his visit to Prague is "that odor of cucumbers soaked in vinegar," which arouses deep feelings of anxiety in him.[52] In Vienna, he fared no better. "I arrived in Vienna, and left after a week"[53] is all he has to say of his stay in the Austrian capital. Eight months later he stated: "I spent two months in Central Europe, from Austria to Germany, wondering where this strange weight on my shoulders and this dull uneasiness came from." The answer, for him, was the absence of a certain indescribable perfume which "Mediterraneans smell with their skin."[54]

It was with relief that Camus turned south from these unfruitful scenes, traveling homeward via Italy (Venice and Vicenza) and the Balearic Islands (Palma and Ibiza) and delighted to find himself once again among his unrestrained and noisy fellow Mediterraneans. "Light was beginning to appear. . . . I was approaching Italy. Land made for my soul. . . ."[55] Italy's hubbub and disorder, Italian cypresses, fig trees and olive groves, aroused him to the point of tears. Here he found himself and again was part of the world, for over Vicenza the sun was at its zenith, the sky was deep blue and airy, and *light* inhabited the trees.

In the Balearic Islands, Camus saw landscapes "crushed under the sun."[56] In the café-chantant at Palma, he spent almost an entire night among the shouting men, in whose joy he noted a certain ease that he qualified as the mark of true civilization: ". . . the Spaniards are one of Europe's rare civilized peoples."[57] At Ibiza, sitting in one of the port cafés at sundown, "the evening turned green" — just as in Algiers — and the color green, representative of fertility, productivity and abundance, arouses his desire to make love. ". . . I was immobile and tense, powerless against this overwhelming ardor that sought to place the world in my hands."[58]

Camus was no effete spirit, frightened by noise and rude energy. The common denominator, perhaps, of the twelve nations that form his dodecagonic "country" is their boisterously shouting men — in Spain's cafés, along the colorful waterfront of Marseilles, on the docks of Genoa, or in Tunis or Algiers. During his later trip to the United States, he felt uncomfortable among white Americans and asserted that only the blacks lent life, passion, and nostalgia to the country. In the oppressive atmosphere of New York, it was in Chinatown that he breathed more freely, thanks to the crowded streets and the seething life and movement.

The summer of 1937 took Camus to Paris, to Embrun (a village in the French Alps), and to Florence and Fiesole, whose impressions inspired the fourth essay in *Noces*, "Le désert." Here there was much that recalled his native Algeria. The sun that shines on Tuscany is the same that shines on Djemila, the breeze in the Boboli Gardens is that same "deep breathing of the earth" that he had heard in Tipasa, and the warm flagstones in the Fiesole cloisters, the deep blue sky and the scent of Tuscan trees and plants arouse in him the same voluptuous feelings as in Algeria itself. His instinctive desires, summed up in the motto "paganism for oneself, Christianity for others,"[59] are stirred in Pisa at night, when his body becomes taut with the ardor that transformed him into a giant. "I hear the first strains, deep in the Italian night, of the innermost song that one seeks here. . . . [T]his evening, here I am, god among gods. . . ."[60]

All of Florence, viewed from Fiesole, is "the splendor of the earth." Struck by the magnificence of the countryside, the beauty of the afternoon sunlight on vineyards and olive groves, the sensuous grace of the Tuscan cities, decked at night in their black and gold Arno and bejewelled by day in yellow and green monuments, Camus entered into blissful harmony with the Italian sun. He finds a kindred soul in Saint Francis of Assisi, lover of poverty, nature and life.[61] "In the life of these Franciscans cloistered among their columns and flowers, and the life of young people . . . in Algiers, who bask in the sun the year 'round, I sensed a common resonance."[62]

Fired by what he calls the three virtues of the Tuscan masters— silence, flame and immobility—Camus plunges into an appreciation of Florentine art and undergoes a quasi-purification of his own soul. It is in Florence that he best crystallizes his conviction that asceticism and pleasure are equivalents, and that at the farthest point of poverty lie luxury and richness. He who has nothing material revels freely in nature, and is keenly sensitive to sun, sky, flowers, plants, trees, perfumes, the birds, and the sea. Camus and Saint Francis are of the same "noble race" that "envies nothing."[63] If Saint Francis's asceticism implies renunciation of material goods to embrace a life of poverty, Camus's concept of willful impoverishment (*dénuement* or *dépouillement*) is not different. Both find themselves midway between destitution and love;[64] both participate in the dialogue between nature and man; both are "naked" in the sense of being poor, but also of enjoying physical freedom and a loving entente with the earth. "Ah!" exclaims Camus, "I'd convert [to Franciscanism] if it weren't already my religion."[65]

Since childhood, Camus, who "grew up in the sea," had considered his poverty a luxury. When he was not in contact with nature, all luxuries appeared gray to him, and his poverty unbearable.[66] He recorded in one of his early diary entries that the beauty of the landscape of La Madeleine (on the outskirts of Algiers) had inspired in him a taste for poverty: "On the path at La Madeleine—again this tremendous desire for impoverishment (*dépouillement*) in the face of natural beauty such as this."[67] Similarly at the church of Saint Barbe du Tlélat, a barren plain southeast of Oran, he exhorts Saint Barbe, in a long prayer which harmoniously combines faith and atheism, skepticism and innocence, to grant him "this indivisible freedom called poverty (*dénuement*)."[68]

The closing passage of "Le désert" is Camus's apostrophe and salutation, addressed from the Boboli Gardens, to Florence, city of ascesis and pleasure, of austere self-denial and profuse voluptuousness. It is perhaps the greatest metaphysical tribute the city has ever received: "Florence! One of the only places in Europe where I understood that deep within my revolt slept an assent. In its sky where tears and sun mingle, I learned to accept life and burn in the dark flame of its feasts."[69]

Camus's encounter with Metropolitan France was inevitably conditioned by the experience of World War II, the German occupation, and his work in the Resistance. The period of France's military collapse in June 1940 was spent in Bordeaux, Lyons, and Clermont-Ferrand, far from his beloved Mediterranean. His notebook entries for that period offer little beside negative impressions. The years 1942–43, also spent in France's central regions, were even more dark and depressing. Politics and nature conspired to cast a pall over this entire period. If hell existed, Camus commented, it certainly would resemble those endless gray streets where everyone was dressed in black.[70]

By the end of the war, Camus had gained sufficient celebrity to be in demand as a lecturer and literary lion in both North and South America. Traveling ostensibly as a journalist, he set out for New York on 10 March 1946, crossing the Atlantic by cargo vessel as one of the five occupants of a four-berth cabin. Preferring for obvious reasons to spend most of his time on deck, he was fascinated by the mixture of water and moonlight in the ship's wake — "liquid marble" in one image, and, in the next, a fine lace which is repeatedly worked and then unravelled. Throughout the *Journaux de voyage*, Camus keeps seeking an image for the "blooming" of water and light, which he considers a "continuous symbol,"[71] combining and recombining in constantly changing configurations.

The first glimpse of New York — "hideous human city" — fills his heart with trembling at the thought of such admirable "inhumanity" (implying power, order, and economic strength). He realizes that he may change his opinion later on, but subsequently finds no reason to do so. After a visit to Washington, D. C., where he saw long-legged girls whose splendid faces were devoid of love, his diary entry of April 19th is a curt: "I have suddenly ceased to be curious about this country."[72]

In New York, he is continually struck by details: gloved garbage collectors, orderly traffic, long blocks of bridal shops in the Bowery, and the impression that everyone looks as though he had stepped out of a film. Broadway is a "luminous fair" whose violent lights stultify him; he realizes he has reached a "new continent" because *real* smoke comes out of the mouth of a soldier smoking a Camel cigarette in a fifteen-meter-high billboard in Times Square. He admires the magnificent food shops, the women and the color of their dresses, and the colors of taxis, which look like insects dressed up for Sunday in reds, greens, and yellows; but he finds the tie shops perfectly horrendous, with a concentration of bad taste that is scarcely imaginable.[73] He is puzzled about the function of the Funeral Home and the fact that cemeteries are private property, where space is reserved in advance. Thousands of operetta Generals and Admirals catch his eye: they are New York's doormen, bell captains, and elevator boys in the big hotels.

One of Camus's best-contrived images is his personification of New York's elevated railway train, speeding along out of the Bowery, surrounded by slowly dancing skyscrapers; the machine swallows up little red and blue lights, allows itself to be digested momentarily by the stations, and then speeds off again into the poorer neighborhoods beyond Manhattan.[74] One can easily image Camus, lonely nocturnal passenger in another "metallic coffin" — desperately peering out of the window and vainly searching for the panchromatic nature of his beloved Algeria.

East Orange and the surrounding New Jersey countryside are a "pretty postcard," with thousands of clean cottages, nestled like toys among poplars and magnolia trees. Traveling from New York to Canada, his eye catches little and big homes with white columns and lawns unseparated by any kind of fence, so that the impression is of one big lawn that belongs to everyone, and where children laugh and play.[75] As for Maine and New England, his only diary entry is "land of lakes and red houses"; while Canada is a big, calm, slow country, oblivious to the recent war, and Montreal, with its two hills, on a Sunday afternoon, fills him with "Ennui; Ennui."[76] Quebec, on the other hand, offers a thrilling impression of beauty and grandeur. The "prodigious landscape" of Cape Diamond and the Saint Lawrence River are characterized as "air, light and water, which merge in infinite proportions."[77]

Although Camus found Americans to be generous, hospitable, and cordial, he was oppressed from the moment of his arrival by an indefinable "tragique américain," which he was to feel again during his trip to South America to deliver a series of lectures in the summer of 1949. Exhausted by a drive to Marseilles in his automobile, named Desdemona, Camus embarked on 3 June of that year and, always the "loner," promptly recorded his satisfaction at having been assigned a single cabin, though he felt uncomfortable about the fourth-class passengers huddled in the immigrants' dormitories below. "I prefer this narrow, simple cabin, this hard bunk, and this impoverishment (dénuement),"[78] he wrote, in a renewed reminder of his affinity for Saint Francis's asceticism.

The South Atlantic crossing was marred by fever, loneliness, and social constraints. The other passengers were a strange assortment of people whose conversation was of very little interest. Admitting that his impulses were directed not toward human beings but towards the sea,[79] his diary entries often sum up his social encounters in one word — "triste." Sometimes he took refuge in the crowded fourth-class lounge, to watch the immigrants' drinking and singing; among them, he felt happy "for ten seconds."[80] His preference was to watch the ocean from the ship's deck, and to rise early in the morning to work in the sun on the lectures he was to deliver in South America.

A character wholly antithetical to Camus and his love for color, nakedness, and the sea was the passenger who, even under the tropical sun, was dressed in a dark gray suit, stiff-collared shirt, and black shoes. Trailing him four times around the deck, Camus noted that "he didn't once look at the sea."[81] What more scathing judgment could be pronounced?

The ship crossed the Tropic of Cancer "under a vertical sun that kills all shadows"[82] on 5 July, and the following day, during a stopover in Dakar, Camus was happy to find again the "smell of my Africa, smell of misery and abandon, virgin smell, and strong, whose seductiveness I know."[83] The Equator was crossed on 10 July but the usual ceremonies were omitted because most of the passengers had disembarked at Dakar. The twenty-odd who remained were treated instead to a Laurel and Hardy film. Camus took refuge in the bow of the ship, to contemplate the moon and the Southern Cross. How few and anemic were the stars in the southern skies, he observed, compared to Algeria's nights, "swarming with stars."[84]

The long days between Dakar and Rio, during which no land was visible, were filled with prolonged contemplations of the ocean, work on his lectures, and reading the *Journal* of Vigny, in whom Camus found "many enchanting things except that part of him which is like a constipated swan."[85]

The lights of Rio de Janeiro and Sugarloaf Mountain finally came into sight on 15 July together with "an immense and regrettable luminous Christ"[86] on the highest mountain top, Corcovado. In Rio, Camus was again happy to find himself completely alone in a "charming room" of the French ambassadorial residence. His first annotations, on the day of arrival, concern Brazilian motorists, who are "happy madmen or cold sadists."[87] He was impressed by the harsh contrast between the luxury of the fine hotels and modern buildings and the poverty of the *favelas*, where a miserable black and white population lived without water or electricity. All in all, the mountains, the bay, the warm air, and the stars over Rio made him "more melancholy than happy."[88]

As time went on, Camus became increasingly exasperated by formalities, the shortcomings of the diplomatic services responsible for his travel arrangements, the delegations that failed to meet his planes. The climate was oppressive, and he was frequently ill. He relates his peregrinations in the *Journaux de voyage*, sometimes with tongue in cheek but more often with ill humor and biting sarcasm. Flying over the Andes at night, he "saw nothing—which is the symbol of this trip."[89]

Perhaps the only city he really enjoyed was Recife, at Brazil's eastern tip. "I really like Recife. It's the Florence of the tropics, tucked among coconut groves, red mountains and white beaches."[90] The nearby historic town of Olinda, with its old churches and beautiful Franciscan monastery, also interested him, but he returned to his hotel shaking with fever after the visit.

One redeeming feature of the stay in Brazil was the opportunity to observe some of the exotic rites associated with what he called the "catholicism of the Blacks,"[91] a blend of Roman Catholicism and traditional African practices that no doubt reminded him of the Eleusinian mysteries. At Caxias, a village forty kilometers from Rio, he witnessed a *macumba*, a night-long ceremony whose participants, having become possessed by a god, sought to enter a trancelike condition through dances and songs conducted under the guidance of a priest and principal dancer, known as the "father of the saints," who was responsible for authorizing the ceremony and verifying the trances of his "children." Wedged into an overcrowded mud-and-straw hut, Camus watched the ceremony unfold to its climax, but left at two in the morning after being told that it would continue until dawn. Coming out into the cool night air, he remarked succinctly that he preferred "the night and the sky to the gods of men."[92]

A *bomba-menboi*, which Camus found "quite extraordinary," was witnessed in Recife itself. It too was of religious origin, but its dances were diabolical in character. Camus describes it as a kind of grotesque ballet, executed by masked and totemic figures, its unvarying theme the killing of a bull which is then reborn to carry off a young girl between its horns.

In the fishing village of Itapoa (Bahia), with its straw huts, beautiful untouched beaches, and foaming sea bordered by coconut groves, Camus was able to view a *candomblé*, this one danced by richly costumed women led by a matron, in contrast to the all-male character of the *macumba*. Executed in front of a table laden with food, the dancelike ceremony was accompanied by three drums and a flattened funnel struck by an iron bar. A group of young black girls entered the scene in a semihypnotized state; they danced rhythmically, and Camus became enraptured by the infinite grace of one of them whom he dubbed a "black Diana."[93]

Most remarkable of all was the pilgrims' procession to the "growing stone" (*la pierre qui pousse*) at Iguape, three hundred kilometers and ten hours from São Paulo over roads covered with red dust and dry mud. Iguape is the town of the Good Jesus, whose effigy had been found by fishermen. Bringing the effigy into a grotto, they washed it, whereupon there miraculously grew a stone which continues to grow even though slivers are constantly being cut off by the Iguape pilgrims, who consider the stone highly efficacious against infirmities, shipwreck, and other calamities.[94]

After visits to Fortaleza and Porto Alegre, Camus left Brazil on 10 August for Montevideo, a city he found attractive with its necklace of boardwalk and beaches and whose mimosas and palm trees reminded him of Menton. He boarded a ship the following evening, traveling overnight on the Rio de la Plata to his next destination, Buenos Aires—a metropolis "of rare ugliness."[95] Proceeding thence by plane to Chile, he admired Santiago, nestled between the Pacific and the Andes, offering violent colors and almond trees in bloom against a white backdrop of snow-capped mountains. Camus felt comfortable among the splendid mimosas and weeping willows of the Chilean countryside. "I wouldn't mind living a while [in Chile] under different circumstances."[96] A state of siege had been declared due to demonstrations and student riots, forcing Camus to deliver his lecture at the French Institute rather than at the University, as planned.

On the whole the South American trip was a serious disappointment, marred by poor health no less than by the stolidity of his audiences. The reader of the *Journaux de voyage* cannot but be struck by the weight, stress, and strain of these months abroad. The tone of the diary entries is somber and bathed in gray light, relieved by only a few spots of humor. ("I always wonder why I attract society women. So many hats!"[97]). Boarding his plane for Paris on 31 August, he was saturated with feverish perspiration and pencillin. "The trip ended in a metallic coffin, in between a mad doctor and a diplomat," the *Journal* glumly concludes.

The South American journey did, however, inspire one memorable composition: the last essay of *L'Été*, "La mer au plus près" (1953), which is subtitled "Journal de bord" and takes the form of a curious ship's log, supposedly written by an ocean traveler who "weds" the sea.[98] "What can I do about it," asks Camus on the first page of the essay, "if the only image I can ever remember [is that of the sea]?"[99] "The days at sea all resemble each other, like happiness," he writes in hindsight.[100] Often during his travels he would half awaken at night, thinking he heard the sound of the waves and the breathing of waters, but fully awake would realize that it was only the wind in the trees and the mournful, dismal sound of some "ville déserte"—that is, some city far from the sea.

In New York, where he had felt trapped in the concrete city, he had subconsciously sought the sea: "the uninterrupted line of cars moving smoothly [along Riverside Drive] sang dull and distant—exactly the sound of waves."[101] At night "a tugboat blast came into my sleep to remind me that this desert of iron and cement was also an island. So I could find the sea, and I was close to my native land."[102] The closing paragraph of his North American diary is a declaration of love for the sea: "Marvelous night on the Atlantic . . . Yes, I have loved the sea very much—this vast calmness, this churning wake, these liquid paths. . . . My model is the sea and everything on the face of this earth that resembles it. . . ."[103]

But it is in his essay, "La mer au plus près," that Camus's involvement with the sea finds its most moving expression. Here every aspect and movement of the sea is described poetically, voluptuously, and sensuously, as though a pagan wedding were taking place. The ocean's spray is strewn with camelias; off the coast of some vague southern continent, the sea is covered with "strange yellow flowers," and an "invisible song precedes [the ship] for many long hours."[104] The ocean's foam is the "saliva of the gods"; in the ship's wake, unfolding patterns create an image of a blue and white cow; under the burning heat of high noon, the sea is personified as an extenuated mistress, scarcely able to lift herself up, lying face down on the ocean's bed; then, pale, as the waves swell and darkness falls, she turns to offer her humid face to her lover.[105] Under the moonlight, a corridor of sea is a rich river of milk flowing into the dark ocean.[106]

So absorbed is Camus's narrator in the sea, his "bride," that he scarcely takes notice of the lands lying along the ship's route. Telescoping long distances into four short sentences, he passes the Azores, Cape Horn and the Cape of Good Hope, Vancouver, Easter Island, Desolacion, and the Hebrides in one fell swoop. The tone of his descriptions continues ceremonial and symbolic: latitudes wed longitudes and the Pacific drinks the Atlantic.[107]

From the ship the narrator finally discerns the coast of South America: forests of coconut trees whose feet bathe in green lagoons, the skyscrapers of Rio, interminable beaches, flocks of Uruguayan sheep, the Argentine seashore, Tierra del Fuego, and finally, the coast of Chile. But nothing seems to interest him except the experience of swimming for an entire day at a deserted beach and drying in the sun. This, indeed, would seem to be the highlight of the entire trip.[108] After this day in physical contact with the sea, he returns to his ship. The calm sea has grown even more peaceful, as though it were his own soul, and he senses that it will be the sea that will ultimately help him to die.

If the sea was the continuing source of Camus's "royal happiness,"[109] a contrasting leitmotiv that runs through his travel notes is that of the red geranium against the backdrop of a cemetery. Frequently these two elements appear in juxtaposition, evocative and premonitory of Camus's own illness and imminent death. The symbolic combination of the red, pink, or purple geranium (representing passion, blood, and suffering) and the cemetery (whose white tombstones represent oblivion, extinction, and the silent sadness "that accustoms us to the beautiful pure face of death"[110]) reflects the author's own susceptibility to alternating states of exaltation and depression. He speaks of the "gentleness" of Arab cemeteries in Algiers but then goes on to describe, in the midst of Oran's "bones of the earth," a "purple geranium" which "gives its life and its fresh blood to the landscape."[111] In the cemetery of El Kettar, he sees "hills full of white tombs . . . pigeons among the white stone slabs [and] a single pink and red geranium. . . .";[112] and, among the ruins of the forum of Tipasa, resting place of the past, the stone slabs are like white tombstones, and "red geraniums spill their blood on what used to be homes, temples and public squares."[113]

This same image reappears in Camus's European and American travels: ". . . the little Gothic cemetery of Bautzen [in eastern Germany], the bright red of its geraniums, and the blue morning."[114] In the Franciscan cloister at Fiesole, he reflects at length that the same friars who live among the "red flowers" in the courtyard have, in their austere cells, a skull to feed their meditations.[115] On the other hand, "nothing speaks of death" in Florence's sun-bathed Cloister of the Dead of Santissima

Annunziata or in the Cloister of San Marco, neatly tucked among rows of bright flowers.[116]

Everything speaks of death, however, in Camus's cold images of other cemeteries where black ravens fly (in the Isère département of France[117]), in New York's "whitish skyscrapers," which "stand like giant tombs of a city of the dead,"[118] and in Philadelphia's "little cemeteries full of flowers under huge gas tanks."[119]

Today, exactly fifty years after Camus's writing of *Noces* (1936–37), the Mediterranean Sea has ceased to be that temple to beauty and light in which Camus worshipped and to which he dedicated his hymn, "Poème sur la Méditerranée."[120] The twelve countries he loved so deeply, and which he linked in a special, congenial relationship, are now gripped in antagonisms, strife, and acts of terrorism. The Mediterranean has become a sea of turmoil and conflict, which escalates dangerously in daily politico-religious battles and military shows of force. Its waters have taken on the hue of a lake of blood, from which would-be tourists in search of Hellenic beauty and Roman grandeur are advised to shy away. Polluted and lying under an invisible pall of nuclear fallout, Camus's beloved Mediterranean has gradually come to resemble a blood-stained cemetery. Its basin glows red, not with the flames of sunset but with the fire of weaponry and the burning of bombed-out settlements. "We light, in an intoxicated sky, whatever suns we want," Camus had written in "l'Exil d'Hélène,"[121] in which he denounced man's criminal folly in destroying the beauties of nature and of civilizations. The symbolic and prophetic image of Camus's red geraniums, spilling their blood on what used to be homes, temples, and public squares, has become a reality.

Has Camus, then, become irrelevant? Is his message obsolete? On the contrary, we need him perhaps more than ever, though it is mainly to other aspects of his work and personality that we now must turn. Scenes of violence and desecration were as familiar to him as to us, and he had pondered deeply the contradictions and vagaries of the human condition. If he offered no conclusive answers to the human enigma, he offered understanding, comfort and courage both to his contemporaries and to all of us who come after.

## Notes

1. Albert Camus, *L'envers et l'endroit, Les Essais* 88 (Paris: Gallimard, 1958), 110.

2. Albert Camus, *Carnets*, I, mai 1935–février 1942 (Paris: Gallimard, 1962), 92.

3. Albert Camus, *Carnets*, II, janvier 1942–mars 1951. (Paris: Gallimard, 1964), 232.

4. Camus, *L'Envers et l'endroit*, 108–9.

5. Albert Camus, *Journaux de voyage*. Texte établi, présenté et annoté par Roger Quilliot. (Paris: Gallimard, 1978), 17.

6. Camus, *Carnets*, 1, 26.

7. Greece and its heritage permeate much of Camus's work and had inspired his

doctoral dissertation (1936) at the University of Algiers on the relationship between Hellenism and Christianity. In May 1955, in Athens, Camus delivered a lecture on the theatre entitled "The Future of Tragedy," and planned to stage an outdoor performance of his *L'Etat de siège* the following year, but the production did not materialize. Cf. *Théâtre, Récits, Nouvelles.* Préface par Jean Grenier. Textes établis et annotés par Roger Quilliot. (Paris: Gallimard, 1962), 1699.

8. Albert Camus, *Essais.* Introduction par Roger Quilliot, textes établis et annotés par Roger Quilliot et Louis Faucon. (Paris: Gallimard, 1965), 1321.

9. Albert Camus, *Noces, suivi de L'été* (Paris: Gallimard, 1959), 173.

10. Camus, *Journaux de voyage*, 91, 115.

11. Ibid., 31.

12. Camus, *Carnets*, II, 245–6.

13. Camus, *Carnets*, I, 36.

14. Camus, Interview prise par Gabriel d'Aubarède en 1951. *Les Nouvelles littéraires,* 10 May 1951. In Camus, *Essais,* 1341.

15. Camus, *L'Envers et l'endroit*, 26.

16. Camus, *Carnets*, I, 146.

17. Camus, *Carnets*, II, 303.

18. Camus, *Carnets*, I, 146.

19. Camus, *Carnets*, II, 73.

20. Camus, *Carnets*, I, 147.

21. Ibid., 69.

22. Camus, *Noces, suivi de L'été*, 125.

23. Ibid., 11.

24. Ibid., 126.

25. Ibid., 141–42.

26. "Avec tant de soleil dans la mémoire, comment ai-je pu parier sur le non-sens? . . . Je pourrais répondre, et me répondre, que le soleil justement m'y aidait et que sa lumière, à force d'épaisseur, coagule l'univers et ses formes dans un éblouissement obscur. Mais cela peut se dire autrement et je voudrais, devant cette clarté blanche et noire qui, pour moi, a toujours été celle de la vérité, m'expliquer sur cette absurdité que je connais trop pour supporter qu'on en disserte sans nuances. Parler d'elle, au demeurant, nous mènera de nouveau au soleil." Ibid.

27. Ibid., 77.

28. Ibid., 85.

29. Ibid., 136.

30. Ibid.

31. Camus, *Carnets*, II, 206.

32. Camus, *Carnets*, I, 195.

33. Ibid., 208

34. Camus, *Journaux de voyage*, 23.

35. Ibid., 28.

36. Camus, *Carnets*, II, 73.

37. Camus, *Journaux de voyage*, 34.

38. Ibid., 50

39. Camus, *L'Envers et l'endroit*, 14–15.

40. Camus, *Carnets*, II, 314.

41. Camus, *Noces, suivi de L'été*, 33.

42. Ibid., 36.

43. Ibid., 37.

44. Ibid., 48.

45. Ibid., 39.

46. Ibid., 11.

47. Ibid., 13.

48. Ibid., 14.

49. Ibid., 155.

50. Ibid., 32.

51. Camus, *L'Envers et l'endroit*, 93.

52. Ibid., 89.

53. Ibid., 95.

54. Camus, *Essais*, 1322–23.

55. Camus, *L'Envers et l'endroit*, 95.

56. Ibid., 113.

57. Ibid., 106 n.

58. Ibid., 115.

59. In an interview with Gabriel d'Aubarède in 1951, Camus stated: "C'est un destin bien lourd que de naître sur une terre païenne en des temps chrétiens. C'est mon cas. Je me sens plus près des valeurs du monde antique que des chrétiennes. Malheureusement je ne peux pas aller à Delphes me faire initier!" (Camus, *Essais*, 1343). See also Camus, *Noces*, 14: "La basilique Sainte-Salsa est chrétienne, mais chaque fois qu'on regarde par une ouverture, c'est la mélodie du monde qui parvient jusqu'à nous."

60. Camus, *Noces, suivi de L'été*, 58.

61. Camus, *Carnets*, I, 70.

62. Camus, *Noces, suivi de L'eté*, 62–63.

63. Camus, *Carnets*, II, 326.

64. Camus, *Noces, suivi de L'été*, 56.

65. Camus, *Carnets*, I, 74.

66. Camus, *Noces, suivi de L'été*, 169.

67. Camus, *Carnets*, I, 89.

68. Ibid., 186–87.

69. Camus, *Noces, suivi de L'été*, 70.

70. Préface aux Poésies de René Leynaud. Quoted in Camus, *Théâtre, Récits, Nouvelles*, xxxiii.

71. Camus, *Journaux de voyage*, 26.

72. Ibid., 42.

73. Ibid., 30.

74. Ibid., 40.

75. Ibid., 44.

76. Ibid., 45.

77. Ibid., 47.

78. Ibid., 60.

79. Ibid., 66.

80. Ibid., 56.

81. Ibid., 63–64.

82. Ibid., 62.

83. Ibid., 63.

84. Ibid., 68.

85. Ibid., 60.

86. Ibid., 72.

87. Ibid., 73.

88. Ibid., 111.

89. Ibid., 134.

90. Ibid., 99.

91. Ibid., 105.

92. Ibid., 91.

93. Ibid., 106.

94. Ibid., 125. The story forms the last of the five tales of *L'Exil et le royaume*, *Théâtre, Récits, Nouvelles*, 1653–84.

95. Camus, *Journaux de voyage*, 132.

96. Ibid., 136.

97. Ibid., 112.

98. Camus, *Noces, suivi de L'été*, 174.

99. Ibid., 169.

100. Ibid., 175.

101. Camus, *Journaux de voyage*, 41.

102. Camus, *Essais*, 1832.

103. Camus, *Journaux de voyage*, 51–52.

104. Camus, *Noces, suivi de L'été*, 179.

105. Ibid., 173.

106. Ibid., 175.

107. Ibid., 173.

108. Ibid., 182.

109. Ibid., 183.

110. Camus, *Carnets*, I, 94.

111. Camus, *Noces, suivi de L'été*, 86.

112. Camus, *Carnets*, I, 93–94.

113. Camus, *Noces, suivi de L'été*, 13.

114. Camus, *L'Envers et l'endroit*, 94.

115. Camus, *Noces, suivi de L'été*, 63.

116. Camus, *Carnets*, I, 70, 72.

117. Ibid., 218.

118. Camus, *Essais*, 1830.

119. Camus, *Journaux de voyage*, 41.

120. Camus, *Essais*, 1207–9.

121. Camus, *Noces, suivi de L'été*, 134.

# Albert Camus and North Africa:
# A Discourse of Exteriority                John Erickson*

> For Algeria . . . I have unbridled passion and I surrender to the pleasure
> of loving. Question: Can one love a country like a woman?

> Novel. "Somewhere, in a remote region of his soul, he loved them. They
> were really loved, but at such a distance that the word love took on a
> new meaning."[1]

For someone born in Algeria, who expressed frequently and fervently
his love of the country, Albert Camus disappoints the reader seeking in his
"North African" writings a telling encounter with the culture of the East.
The reader finds an engaging description of the physical landscape but of
its indigenous peoples, Berbers and Arabs, astonishingly little, and even
that little, disturbingly equivocal.

If the reader, seeking further, learns that Camus pointedly supported
the colonialist position in the Algerian struggle for independence, that he
refused to sign petitions favoring Algerian independence circulated by
French intellectuals in the late 1950s, he might well ponder. Did Camus,
for all his strident antitotalitarianism, hold the prejudices of many of his
fellow French-Algerians? From his outspoken defense of the rights of the
victims of extremist terrorism, whether Spanish Republicans, Jews,
Czechs, or Hungarians, did he exclude the Berbers and Arabs in his own
homeland?

It may seem somewhat incongruous to speak of the discourse of a
writer as being exterior to his place of birth. However, as a Frenchman
born in Algeria, a *pied-noir*,[2] Albert Camus undeniably inhabited a
country within a country and grew up within a culture and a language
superimposed from without upon another cultural-linguistic system.

Despite what several critics have argued, I view Camus's writings on
North Africa as belonging to an extended discourse of one culture on
another, more specifically, as joining the tradition of French Orientalism
and as such conveying not the insider's "truth" of another culture but a
representation of it from a position of exteriority. As Edward Said says,
"Orientalism is premised upon exteriority, that is, on the fact that the
Orientalist, poet or scholar, makes the Orient speak, describes the Orient,
renders its mysteries plain for and to the West. He is never concerned with
the Orient except as the first cause of what he says. What he says and
writes, by virtue of the fact that it is said and written, is meant to indicate
that the Orientalist is outside the Orient, both as an existential and as a
moral fact."[3]

*This essay was written especially for this volume and is published here for the first time
by permission of the author.

Albert Camus was not of course just another French writer or pilgrim traversing the North African landscape — in the succession of Chateaubriand, Nerval, Gautier, and Flaubert — but someone born and raised there. Several are the ways of defining a country or region, and those ways are integral to how we understand and speak about it. As a scion of the French Algerian working class and later a member of the French intelligentsia, Camus inhabited a defined realm, which, in relation to North Africa, can be described as a realm of superimposition: that of the French social and political system superimposed on the traditional ethnic systems, Arab and Berber, of the Maghreb. Writing out of the former system, Camus wrote necessarily out of a difference that reversed perspective by setting the writer apart from that about which he wrote. The object of this essay is to examine in what measure his North African writing was one of exclusion, superimposition, excision, in short, rewriting of the Maghreb in the language of the Other.

For Camus's supporters, the paeanism of his lyric essays on North Africa written during the 1930s and the sunwashed landscape of his novels set in Algeria in the 1940s bespeak a profound love of country. For the leftist intelligentsia, evidence enough of his disregard for the Algerians existed in his support of colonialist structures and objectives. But the truth was, in both cases, decidedly more complex.

Camus's much discussed relationship with North Africa and its peoples is in need of reevaluation, in terms not only of his political and philosophical thought with regard to the Third World but of the manner in which it informs and determines his literary works.[4] The more deeply we look into his prose fiction, aesthetic and political essays, and notebooks, the greater the jumble of ideas and attitudes towards North Africa presented to us. Their ambivalence resists a cohesive understanding of the role they play in his creative and intellectual production. Nonetheless, in his fiction set in Algeria — the novels *L'Etranger* (1942) and *La Peste* (1947) and his collection of short stories entitled *L'Exil et le royaume* (1957) — we sense an evolution in his representation of North Africa, an emerging and changing pattern at once in accord and at variance with his nonfictional writings.

The narrator of Camus's first novel, Meursault, lives in Algiers.[5] The opening episode relates his participation in the funeral of his mother, who has died at a home for the aged in Marengo, 80 kilometers from Algiers. The description of the events surrounding the funeral is fraught with images of heat and light. The warden tells Meursault, "she'd have to be buried mighty quickly because of the heat in these parts, especially down in the plain" (S, 8). On the morning following the all-night vigil, as the procession gets underway, Meursault notes, "Now, in the full glare of the morning sun, with everything shimmering in the heat haze, there was something inhuman, discouraging, about this landscape" (S, 18). During the procession, the oppressive heat and the "blue-white glare overhead" (S,

20) contribute to the extreme discomfort of Meursault and cause his eyes and thoughts to grow blurred.

The scene then shifts to Algiers, where the rest of Part 1 (which comprises almost exactly half of this two-part *récit*) occurs. After his return, Meursault's involvement in a quarrel between his friend, Raymond Sintès, and the brother of Sintès's Arab mistress, culminates in an episode on the beach where Meursault shoots to death "Raymond's Arab" (the brother).

Sun and heat images pervade Part 1, and the oppressive quality of the landscape, noted by Meursault at the funeral, plays a significant role in the murder scene. As Meursault meets the Arab, ". . . I saw him as a blurred dark form wobbling in the heat haze. . . . For two hours the sun seemed to have made no progress; becalmed in a sea of molten metal." As the Arab draws a knife,

> A shaft of light shot upward from the steel, and I felt as if a long, thin blade transfixed my forehead. At the moment all the sweat that had accumulated in my eyebrows splashed down on my eyelids, covering them with a warm film of moisture. Beneath a veil of brine and tears my eyes were blinded; I was conscious only of the cymbals of the sun clashing on my skull and, less distinctly, of the keen blades of light flashing up from the knife, scarring my eyelashes, and gouging into my eyeballs.
>
> Then everything began to reel before my eyes, a fiery gust came from the sea, while the sky cracked in two, from end to end, and a great sheet of flame poured down through the rift. (S, 75–76)

Meursault fires a shot. The Arab falls. "I knew I'd shattered the balance of the day, the spacious calm of this beach on which I had been happy. But I fired four shots more into the inert body. . ." (S, 76).

The Algerian sun serves as an integral factor in the act of murder which will lead, in Part 2, to the trial and impending execution of Meursault. It functions as an elemental motif in Camus's "Algerian" novels. Air and earth are subordinated to it; recurring images reveal its corrosive action on them: heat and parched earth. On the other hand, in Camus's Algerian landscape, water, usually in the form of the sea, figures as a benign element. The fact that the crime and consequent misfortune of Meursault occur on the strand—by its very contiguousness putting stress on that area which lies next to but distinctly *apart from* the sea—creates spatial support for the sun as a primary purveyor of discomfiture, unhappiness, alienation, and death. Though Camus, in his preface to the English-language edition, spoke of Meursault as being "in love with the sun which leaves no shadows," the text evokes another side. Only when the sun is of less intensity or wanes in the novel (at dawn or dusk) does the narrator feel contentment.

The stark contrast of this landscape dominated by the sun, moreover, is usually described in chiaroscuro terms that link otherwise dissimilar objects to the accompaniment of Meursault's journey from discomfiture to death: from the black accoutrements of the funeral procession ("It gave one a queer, dreamlike impression, that blue-white glare overhead and all this blackness round one: the sleek black of the hearse, the dull black of the men's clothes, and the silvery-black gashes in the road," S, 20) that result in Meursault's physical malaise; to the Arab on the beach whom Meursault glimpses first as a "blurred dark form" then as "the small black moving patch" (S, 74), and who becomes an accomplice-victim in the crime; then to the black robes of two of the judges who condemn Meursault (the third wears scarlet, color of the waning sun) after he tried incoherently "to explain that it [his crime] was because of the sun. . ." (S, 130).

To this point, the fact that Camus's "Algerian" novels depict a harsh landscape representative of the North African littoral is both obvious and tangential to the question of how he represented the Maghrebian East in his work. But two important facts have emerged: first, Camus's inordinate emphasis on the deterministic aspect of that landscape and, secondly, the manner in which he links it to the human element in his first published novel.[6]

In a May 1937 notebook entry, Camus wrote, "in our youth, we attach ourselves more easily to a landscape than to a man. It is because landscapes allow themselves to be interpreted."[7] Without probing the psychological import of that observation, we readily discern that in his "Algerian" novels the landscape does indeed dominate and, what is more, externalize the "causes" for the characters' actions — the sun, for example, as the motivating factor for murder. One notes, however, that, while the other Europeans in *L'Etranger* are largely flat characters removed to the background, none is fused with the physical landscape to the same degree as the Arabs. One example occurs when the brother of Raymond's Algerian mistress, ostensibly seeking vengeance for the beating of his sister, with his friends follows Raymond. As Raymond and Meursault, accompanied by Meursault's mistress, Marie, make their way to the beach, they pass the Arabs lounging near a shop: "I saw some Arabs lounging against the tobacconist's window [*un groupe d'Arabes adossés à la devanture du bureau de tabac*]. They were staring at us silently, in the special way these people have [*à leur manière*] — as if we were blocks of stone or dead trees. Raymond whispered that the second Arab from the left was 'his man' [*son type*], and I thought he looked rather worried" (S, 61). Meursault turns to look back, and sees the Arabs, "exactly as before, gazing in the same vague way [*avec la même indifférence*] at the spot where we had been" (S, 61).

The descriptive elements denoting the Arabs as mute and immobilized (*adossés à.* . . , "silently," still "gazing . . . at the spot"), their lack of proper names, the reference to them as a "group" and the third-person plural pronoun *leur* which fix them in a general category of differentiation — all function to fuse the Arab with the landscape through a process of depersonalization and objectification. In addition, the possessive pronoun *son* deprives the Arab of autonomous existence by making him live only through the European. An interesting linguistic transference operates here as Camus reverses through the descriptive matter the sense of the statement that the Arabs stared at the Europeans "as if we were blocks of stone or dead trees." For it is the Arabs themselves who are turned to stone, objects in the landscape, petrified by the Medusa-like gaze of Camus's perceiving subject.

From successive appearances of the Arabs evolves an ethical subnarrative leading from the benign figure of the nurse attending the funeral, first to the Arab as alien (Meursault's remark upon hearing the name of Raymond's mistress that she was a "Moor," their depersonalization and feigned "indifference"), then to the Arab as menacing object (the pursuit of Raymond), and finally to the Arab as aggressor identified with the severity of the sun (the Arab as "a blurred dark form," then as a "small black moving patch" reminds us of Camus's observation in his notebooks that Mediterranean peoples know the black side of the sun).[8]

The depiction of the Arab can be viewed wholly in terms of the exigencies of narrative logic. The actions of the Arab characters, beginning with the alleged infidelity of Raymond's mistress, integrally involve her, her brother, and his friends in the sequence of events leading to the commission of the crime. That Camus depersonalizes and objectivizes the Arabs should not surprise us. Nor should his tendency to exploit the divergences between the European and Arab cultures by casting the Arabs in an alien and antagonist role. For it is precisely through such means, through the merging of the Arabs with the landscape, that Camus makes them, like the landscape, interpretable in terms of the metaphysical notion of strangeness or estrangement.

That Camus in *L'Etranger* presents the Arab as a stranger in his own homeland accords with the nature of a representation of North Africa from a position of exteriority, with the "inside" position being that of French Algeria. One easily sees this "inside" position with respect to the events of Part 2 where Meursault is brought to justice. As Conor Cruise O'Brien has pointed out, the system of justice represented is not that of a French court in Algeria, for it does not ring true that a European would receive a death sentence for killing an Arab who had threatened him with a knife just after stabbing another European on the same beach (ACEA, 22). Omission of a plea for self-defense and a call to racial sympathy fully suggests the French judicial system operative not in Algeria but in Metropolitan France—*or in an Algeria reproducing the ideal of a French Algeria, in which Arabs have been fully assimilated and have ceased to exist as Arabs, where they have been subsumed into ground / landscape.* As O'Brien states, "by suggesting that the court is impartial between Arab and Frenchman, it implicitly denies the colonial reality and sustains the colonial fiction" (ACEA, 23).

Ultimately, the political, social setting of *L'Etranger* is unreal. While at moments the description in Part 1 conveys a convincingly realistic representation by depicting the Arab as he would probably be seen (or, more accurately, unseen), by the French Algerian (the Arab as Other, as specter), eventually this depiction, especially in Part 2, betrays itself as a novelistic refusal to confront the Algerian and goes so far as to defuse the sense of killing an Arab qua real-life human being by dehumanizing him. Even the bullets that enter his body leave no "visible trace" (S, 25). Estrangement of the Arab in this regard serves to conceal the underlying myth of a French Algeria that informs the representation.

One last observation regarding the depiction of the Arab in *L'Etranger*: the fact that Meursault is accused and condemned not because he killed an Arab but because he transgressed social norms, casts him in the very image of the Arab, for he too becomes reified, a "dehumanized" object, who functions out of a difference from Western society. Thus, the whole question of how Camus depicted the Arab reveals in a curious and important way how the Arab becomes a model for the protagonist himself. In other words, ethnic difference establishes the very model for the problematic of existential estrangement that Camus explores. In this light, Camus's relation to the Arab world relates centrally to all of his works.

The physical setting Camus chooses for his fictive account of the ravages of the Scourge appearing in modern times is the Algerian city of Oran.[9] He describes Oran as a city of striking "ordinariness," "a thoroughly negative place" (TP, 3, the French, *un lieu neutre*, suggests rather the Limbo-like quality of the city). His diction emphasizes deprivation and absence: "A town *without* pigeons, *without* any trees or gardens, where you *never* hear the beat of wings or the rustle of leaves" — in short, a proper place for a plague that will decimate the population.

That Camus ostensibly interests himself in the paradigmatic potential of the city of Oran is underscored by his comment in the same paragraph (TP, 3) that it resembles any other commercial center in the world.[10] Camus does single out one particularity of Oran, however, that suggests his preoccupation with it: he describes it as a city "so disposed that it turns its back on the bay, with the result that it's impossible to see the sea. . . ." This detail serves Camus's allegory of evil: Oran is a city turned away from the Mediterranean, turned inward on itself.[11] Given the fact that in Camus's Mediterranean cosmos the sea offers sanctuary and freedom, one is led to conclude that by turning away from the sea the fictional Oran symbolizes confrontation with misfortune and servitude.

The project of the novel might be described as showing how, with the plague as a catalyst stirring the awareness of men, the city will turn outward, towards the world, towards community. In a letter to Roland Barthes in 1955 Camus stated that, "Compared to *L'Etranger*, *La Peste* marks, indisputably, the passage from an attitude of solitary revolt to the recognition of a community whose struggles one must share. If there is an evolution from *L'Etranger* to *La Peste*, it was in the direction of solidarity and participation." He stressed that he was guided by "the desire to live through and for a community."[12] Most of his critics still take these words at face value, while failing to see the biting irony in the nearly total exclusion of the Arab from this community — a depiction even more radical in its effect and implications than that in *L'Etranger*.

The people of Oran are introduced in the opening chapter not as a collectivity but as a group of individuals fraught by ennui, mindless passion, and everyday concerns. When we look for Arabs among them, we find scarcely a trace. Early in the novel, the journalist Rambert inquires about the health conditions of the Arabs when speaking to Dr. Rieux, but the topic is soon dismissed and plays no role in what follows. In fact, thereafter we see not a single Arab, only their deserted quarters. (In one of few references to the existence of Arabs in the novel, the narrator alludes to a recent incident in Algiers, in which a young "commercial employee had killed an Algerian ["Arabe"] on a beach," TP, 51 — an autotextual allusion, of course, to *L'Etranger*.)

Given the conspicuous absence of the indigenous Algerian population, along with the fact that the characters' names are all European, one could (by setting aside the occasional allusions to the aridity of the landscape) replace the name Oran by that of any provincial city in Metropolitan France. At the time the novel was written, Oran was, in fact, the headquarters of a French department. The fictional Oran is culturally coded for a French audience.

Why, in a novel valorizing in the author's own words the notion of community, is the Arab so assiduously excluded — to the extent that we do not observe him even as a shadowy background figure as in *L'Etranger*?

In describing to Barthes the formulation in *La Peste* of the need for a community whose struggles we must share, Camus alludes to the German occupation of France, which forms the political-social backdrop for the allegory of the novel. As O'Brien has indicated, the suppression of the Arabs was necessitated by the fact that with their presence such an allegory was impossible, for the French themselves as occupiers of Algeria were to the Arabs what the Germans were to the French (ACEA, 55). The conspicuous expulsion of the Arabs from *La Peste* underscores the intolerability of their presence in an allegory condemning oppression while using a colonial setting and simultaneously denying colonial reality. Thus, an important question arises: why did Camus choose Oran in the first place? Why this insistence on a colonial setting in a novel evading the very question of colonialism? To dismiss these questions by observing that Camus chose a milieu with which he was familiar is too easy. Rather, the reason would appear to lie deeper — in the psyche of an author whose unconscious undercuts the very thesis sustained by his conscious articulation of an allegory of oppression. To follow this thread of speculation, however, carries beyond the immediate objectives of this essay.

One should note also, before turning from *La Peste*, that Camus considered the phenomenon of revolt to have no relevance at all in the Third World. In *L'Homme révolté*, he stated his belief that "The problem of revolt has meaning only within Western society." In viewing Eastern society monolithically as a society ruled by the sacred, he echoed Orientalist thinking, which characterizes Western thought as grounded in the material present, Eastern thought as passive, quiescent, eternal: "If, in the sacred world," he said, "we fail to find the problem of revolt, it is that in truth we find there no real problematic, all responses being given at once. Metaphysics is replaced by myth. There is no longer any questioning, only responses and the eternal commentaries which can then be metaphysical."[13] This provides one more reason why the passage in *La Peste* from solitary revolt to an active communal struggle for freedom involves only Europeans.

Before looking at Camus's collection of short stories, *L'Exil et le royaume*, which reveals a shift in his portrayal of Algerians, we might consider further why, with reference to his ideas expressed in his nonfiction, Algerians bear such importance in his "Algerian" novels that he must try to negate their existence as autonomous entities. That he was not insulated from Moslems and enclosed in a French Algerian cultural stratum is verifiable, for at the time he was writing *L'Etranger* in the late 1930s he was also writing for the newspaper *Alger-Républicain* a series of articles on North Africa, most of them protesting the French mistreatment of Algerians. Specifically, he wrote eleven articles discussing diverse aspects of life in the Berber Kabylia district as well as a series of articles in defense of ten Moslems imprisoned for having committed arson during a strike in February 1939.

Further explanation for his novelistic "silence" towards Algerians may be found in his theoretical ideas concerning art and in his social-political commentary. In his *Carnets*, kept from the age of 22, we discern how his artistic-intellectual development influenced his encounter with the Arab world. To begin with, we are reminded of how Camus characterized *L'Etranger* as an "exercise in objectivity." He consciously cultivated an objective attitude towards the world about. In speaking in 1937 of how the perfect actor sheds his personality, Camus stated: "If I had enough strength and patience, I know how completely impersonal I would become. . ." (N, 64). In the descriptive matter of his notebooks and his essays on Algeria (in particular, *Noces* and *L'Eté*), we find the same process of objectification or depersonalization at work that we find in his early novels.

Anyone reading in Camus's *Carnets* his description of the Algerian landscape cannot fail to be struck by the strength of his attachment to it, by how integral the sun, wind, stone-strewn earth, and sea were to his sense of existence. Sketching a fictional character, Camus described him thusly:

Perhaps never before had he been so aware of the harmony between himself and the world, of the rhythm linking his movements with the daily course of the sun. Now, when the night was overflowing with stars, his gestures stood out against the sky's immense and silent face. (N, 46)

We find little significant attachment between Camus and the Algerians in his *Carnets*. When he does describe them, they appear curiously like the self-descriptive passage above, elements fused with the landscape: "Villages grouped around natural sites, each living its own life," he writes,

> Men dressed in long white garments, making simple, precise gestures that stand out against the permanently blue sky. Narrow paths bordered with Barbary fig trees, olive, carob, and jujube trees. On these paths, you meet men with brown faces and clear eyes, leading donkeys laden with olives. And these men and trees, gestures and mountains, seen side by side, give birth to a feeling of acceptance mingled with joy and sadness. Greece? No, Kabylia. And it is as if suddenly, across the centuries, the whole of Greece had suddenly been set down between the sea and mountains, reborn in its ancient splendor with its laziness and respect for Fate hardly emphasized by the nearness of the East. (N, 71–72)

The process of depersonalization is complete as Camus puts the human element on the same level as the nonhuman ("men and trees, gestures and mountains") — a reductionism that returns the human to nonsentient existence. Any feeling, such as it is, comes from within the writer's mind — from an aesthetic and associative link "across the centuries" that displaces Kabylia by Greece. The reductive process ends by subsuming the very landscape, people, and beliefs into an ideal rebirth through which the Arabs are assimilated without trace into the Western world.[14] Nonetheless, the paradox persists that, at the same time that the Arabs are raised to the level of an ideal by becoming one with the founders of Western civilization, they disappear. Said's description of the Orientalist project applies here, for Camus reveals himself as concerned with the Algerians only as the first cause of what he sets forth — the ideals upon which Western civilization is based.[15]

Camus's techniques of depersonalization, linked to his Greek ideal, and of considerable influence in his depiction of Algerians, resulted in his being criticized for having gone too far in the "impassivity" of *L'Etranger* (N, 31). Though he defended himself, he eventually came to realize, after the appearance of his "Algerian" novels, that he had perhaps indeed gone too far: "One of my regrets is having sacrificed too much to objectivity." The year? 1949. The reasons he gives indicate the need he feels of being more direct in his response to social and political evils, but the question of character depiction is inextricably involved. It is perhaps no coincidence that his next fiction set in Algeria — certain short stories in *L'Exil et le royaume*, which appeared in 1957 — gives witness to a significant modification in his novelistic regard for the Algerians.[16]

In "La Femme adultère," a French woman accompanies her husband, a cloth merchant, on a selling trip by local bus to the interior of the country. The story focuses on their trip, their arrival in a village, and a visit by the couple during the day and later by the woman alone at night to the terrace of a fort overlooking the desert. The important events are, however, interiorized in the woman who commits a symbolic act of adultery. What interests us is that Camus chooses the figure of the Arab as an objective correlative for the inner movement of his main character, Janine. Though the figure of the Arab is transposed artistically, we encounter a dynamic evolution in his "portrait."

The initial encounter of the woman is with the Arab as an alien and subservient, if not servile, figure. The bus on which they ride is crowded with Arabs "who *pretended* to be sleeping, *buried* in their burnooses. Some had drawn up their feet on the seat and *oscillated more than the others* with the movement of the bus. Their *silence*, their *impassivity* ended by weighing upon Janine; it seemed to her that she had been traveling for days with that *mute escort*" (LEX, 10). When the bus is momentarily stalled, Janine spies shepherds on the embankment — "*draped forms* holding themselves still. *Under the hood* of their burnooses, and *under a rampart of veils, you saw only their eyes. Mute, come from who knows where*, they stared at the travelers" (LEX, 15).

The diction I have italicized delineates the silent, reclusive, impassive, originless, and vaguely menacing traits of the Arabs, who resemble phantoms. The incongruity of the words "come from who knows where" is enormous, for the female protagonist is a foreigner depriving the Arabs of an origin in their *own* birthplace.

On the bus Janine reflects on the North African coastal town from which she and her husband have come. She encounters an unexpected harshness in the interior; instead of the "smooth sand" she anticipated, she finds stone and rock. When they arrive in the desert village, she also finds the Arabs to be different. "She found in them, even when they bore rags, a proud air that the Arabs in her town did not have" (LEX, 20). As she stands in the street with her husband,

> From the other side of the square came a tall Arab, thin, vigorous, clothed in a sky-blue burnoose, wearing supple yellow boots, his hands gloved, and graced with an aquiline and bronze face. Only the *chèche* [scarf] he wore turban-like distinguished him from the French foreign affairs officers whom Janine had sometimes admired. He advanced straight in their direction but appeared to look beyond them, while unsheathing slowly one of his hands. "Well," said Marcel, shrugging his shoulders, "there's someone who thinks he's a general." Yes, all of them here had that arrogant air, but that one truly was exaggerating. (LEX, 23)

As the Arab reaches them, Marcel instinctively pulls his cane out of the way but the Arab passes without showing notice of them. "They believe everything is permitted now," he says. Janine resents the arrogance of the Arab and feels unhappy. The reason is not hard to grasp when we compare the portrait of her materialistic and pedestrian husband with the bearing of the Arab. Her unhappiness comes from her shame in regard to her husband.

From the fort ramparts they look out over the "kingdom of stones" stretching to "the immense horizon," beyond which lies "limitless space" (LEX, 25–26). Camels surrounding the tents of nomads near the oasis below appear to her like "dark signs of a strange writing whose sense needed to be deciphered" (LEX, 26).

> She looked at the encampment of the nomads. She had not even seen the men who lived there, nothing moved between the black tents and, nonetheless, she could only think of them, whose existence she had hardly known about up to then. Without houses, cut off from the world, they were a handful of men who wandered over the vast territory. . . . Since always, over the dry earth, scraped to the bone, of this enormous country, a few men ceaselessly wandered, who possessed nothing but served no one, destitute and free lords of a strange kingdom. (LEX, 23)

She is sad, thinks of how this "kingdom . . . had been promised to her but that it would never be hers, never more, except for this fleeting instant perhaps" (LEX, 27). She feels life to be suspended except for her inner feelings. That night, unable to sleep, she lies awake thinking about the nomads. She contemplates her marriage and suddenly feels the burden she has borne for 20 years. She wishes to be free. As she listens to the wind and rustling water in the palm grove, she imagines hearing "a mute call" (the adjective is paradigmatically linked to the Arabs). She rises, climbs to the terrace. Gazing at the night sky she feels in touch with "the most profound part of her being" (LEX, 34). She feels she has "recovered her roots." She feels exalted.

The act of adultery is no more no less than her congress in her thoughts with the exterior world of the Arabs and her own assimilation to that world. The portrait of the Arab has changed as Janine moves from the coast-exterior into the desert-interior. It is an infinitely richer portrait than that in Camus's novels, though we observe that it replaces one Western stereotype with another—the myth of the servile Arab gives way to an idealized Arab nomad.

In "L'Hôte," the Frenchman, Daru, is a teacher inhabiting a country schoolhouse on a barren hillside. A gendarme delivers into his charge an Arab accused of murdering his cousin. Daru is summoned to deliver the Arab to the authorities in the village on the following day. When he protests, the gendarme tells him that, owing to the impending revolt, all administrative personnel must consider themselves mobilized. Daru is angered for being involved in such affairs: "[He] felt a sudden anger against that man [the gendarme? the Arab?], against all men and their filthy wickedness, their unflagging hatreds, the madness in their blood" (LEX, 88). He warns the gendarme that he will not deliver the man, but the gendarme leaves him with the reminder that it is an order. Daru and the Arab spend the night together, Daru allowing him free movement, hoping he will flee. But the Arab is there when the morning comes.

Despite his anger, Daru feels a sameness existing between him and the Arab. He also was born there ("everywhere, however, he felt himself to be an exile," LEX, 84). He thinks to himself: "In this desert, no one, neither he nor his guest were anything. And, however, outside of this desert, neither the one nor the other, Daru knew, would be truly able to survive" (LEX, 91). Significantly, on the Arab's part also a feeling for the begrudging good will of Daru emerges, for he asks him to come with them if the gendarme returns to take him away. As Daru lies awake that night, he experiences uneasiness because of the presence of the Arab:

> But it made him ill at ease also because it imposed on him a sort of fraternity which he refused under the present circumstances and that he knew well: men who share the same rooms, soldiers or prisoners, develop a strange bond as if, their arms put aside with their clothes, they join each other in the evening, transcending their differences, in the ancient community of dream and weariness. (LEX, 95)

While put off by the Arab's crime, Daru refuses to dishonor himself by delivering him over to the authorities. The next day, he accompanies the Arab down the hill to where the path separates — one branch leading to the plateau where, as he tells the Arab, he can find refuge among the nomads, the other towards the village where the prison awaits. The Arab panics, but Daru tells him he must choose. Daru leaves him. When he arrives at the top of the hill, in the distance he sees, with disheartenment, the Arab trudging the path to the village. When Daru enters the schoolhouse, he finds written on the blackboard the message, "You have delivered our brother. You will pay." Daru stares into the distance. "In this vast country that he loved so much, he was alone."

In this story, Camus's depiction of the Arab undergoes a qualitative change. It is true that in "La Femme adultère," he focuses on the Arab much more intensively, and an intimate relationship arises between the Arab and the European. But it is equally true that he idealizes the former, makes him a mythic adjunct of emotional changes occurring in the woman.

To be sure, all along we have been bothered by the special diction allied with the figure of the Arab in Camus's work, which effectively builds into a metaphor of exclusion (words denoting silence, forms of the verb "regarder" — "to see" — that convey a sense of separation and alterity). Everywhere in Camus's work up to now we have encountered an exteriorization and hence a depersonalization of the Arab. He is an alien being, and we come to feel an insurmountable difference between races living side by side.

But "L'Hôte" suggests, as reflected in the ambiguity of its title (the title word in French can mean "guest" or "host"), the inseparability of the fate of a Frenchman and an Arab. Moreover, the "view" of the Arab is not purely the "point of view" or mental state of Daru (in the way the nomads are creations of Janine's desires). "Objective" narrative elements reflect the same feeling of belonging to a fraternity of the damned on the part of both men: in Daru's thoughts and in the Arab's words (his request for Daru to accompany him) and action (his decision to take the path to the village). The "honor" Daru feels prohibits him from depriving the prisoner of his liberty by collaborating with the authorities; it is ironically paralleled by the "honor" of the Arab who ostensibly feels obligated not to put Daru in jeopardy with the authorities by fleeing.[17] A parallel exists between their reactions to the obligations imposd on them—Daru resents having fraternity forced on him, the Arab panics at the "freedom" given him to choose. But the fact that they both put themselves in jeopardy shows that the "freedom" is only illusory—by their inseparable will and honor they are forced to act as they do. The irony of Daru being threatened with retribution for supposedly delivering the Arabs' comrade reenforces the metaphysical level of the story by indicating the essential unreason (existential absurdity) of the outcome.[18]

The fact that we find in the depiction of the Arab in Camus's later fiction a moving testimony to the possibility of individuals transcending the differences of culture and overcoming the gulf between their sense of self and other only underscores the deplorably tragic circumstances that shattered Camus's existence in the late 1950s. Those circumstances came out of the Algerian struggle for liberation. Camus went beyond a refusal to sign petitions supporting independence; he argued for a solution that would have denied it. In early 1958, in the preface to his *Algerian Reports* he wrote:

> I . . . cannot approve, either, a policy of surrender that would abandon the Arab people to an even greater misery, tear the French in Algeria from their century-old roots, and favor, to no one's advantage, the new imperialism [Communism] now threatening the liberty of France and of the West.[19]

Despite the few examples in Camus's later fiction that allow of the possibility of transcending cultural differences, Camus himself failed to do so. He was unable or unwilling to contemplate a non-French Algeria. The time, one will remember, was that of the Cold War and the bloody repression of Eastern Europeans by the Communists, a repression that Camus castigated in his political writings. Camus feared, as did many Europeans and Americans, a Communist encirclement and isolation of Europe by way of Africa. The most objective of writers under other circumstances, he acknowledged his own failure to think objectively in the face of the crisis occurring in Algeria.

Camus, an individual intensely sensitive to the human situation, who assiduously fought totalitarianism whether of fascist or communist origin, could not find it within himself to rise above his heritage as a Frenchman born in Algeria nor above his personal attachments to Algeria. These factors led him to see in the Algerian revolution not a national liberation movement with socialist leanings but a society duped by outside (Communist) forces. The dichotomy that we find in Camus, between his beliefs in the context of Western thought and his attitude towards the Third World, well illustrates a dichotomy common among contemporary left-wing or liberal intellectuals living in the colonies, torn between the demands and realities of two cultures. The Tunisian Jew Albert Memmi called this unfortunate individual, who objected to the conditions of colonialism while, largely unconsciously, sharing its basic premises, "the colonizer who refuses."[20] Paradoxically, those same traits that made Camus a "colonizer who refuses," that lay behind his discourse of exteriority on North Africa and his representation of the Arab, served as the model for the very problematic he explored — the state of the outsider.

## Notes

1. Albert Camus, *Carnets, janvier 1942–mars 1951* (Paris: Editions Gallimard, 1964). Citations in the text are drawn from the translation by Justin O'Brien, *Notebooks 1942–1951* (New York: Alfred A. Knopf). First extract, 15 January 1943, 54; second extract, October 1949, 219. *Notebooks* are hereafter referred to as N.

2. The term *pied-noir* or "black foot" was given to the early French settlers in Algeria by the indigenous peoples. It referred to the color of their shoes, to which Algerians were unaccustomed (or, as some claim, to the fact that the early settlers worked the land).

3. Edward W. Said, *Orientalism* (New York: Pantheon Books, 1978), 20–21.

4. Most critical commentary on North Africa in Camus's writings confines itself to his description of the physical milieu. Critics often fail to note or to account for the many discrepancies in his writings on Algeria. As with the otherwise useful collection, *Albert Camus' Literary Milieu: Arid Lands*, ed. W. T. Zyla and W. M. Aycock (Lubbock, Texas: Interdepartmental Committee on Comparative Literature, 1976), consideration of the physical landscape leads to a discussion of its metaphysical significance, which fastens on Camus's view of the human condition in general but overlooks the implications of Camus's regard for or disregard of the Algerian peoples and their culture. It is unconvincing to assert that "the Berber and the Arab never seemed 'strangers' to Camus," as does Germaine Brée, *Camus*, rev. ed. (New York, 1964). The most aware book on Camus and North Africa is that of Conor Cruise O'Brien, *Albert Camus of Europe and Africa* (New York: The Viking Press, 170), hereafter referred to as ACEA.

5. Albert Camus, *L'Etranger* (Paris: Gallimard, 1942). Citations in the text are drawn from the translation of Stuart Gilbert, *The Stranger* (New York: Alfred A. Knopf, 1946), and are hereafter referred to as S.

6. In 1971, Editions Gallimard published *La Mort heureuse*, which appeared the following year in Richard Howard's translation as *A Happy Life* (New York: Alfred A. Knopf, 1972). This narrative, written between 1936 and 1938, represents an early version of

*L'Etranger*. It is, however, much more autobiographical. And though it is set in Algiers, except for a long interlude when the hero travels to the continent, the setting has considerably less significance than that of *L'Etranger*. For the purpose of our study, it is virtually without importance. One might note in passing that the hero's name, Mersault, lacks the "u" of death of his counterpart in *L'Etranger*: the French suffix *Meur-* is a form of the verb "mourir," "to die," while *Mer-* suggests, appropriately, happiness by its reference to the noun meaning "sea."

7. Albert Camus, *Carnets, mai 1935–février 1942* (Paris: Editions Gallimard, 1962). English translation by Philip Thody, *Notebooks 1935-1942* (New York: Alfred A. Knopf, 1963), 34.

8. The other Arabs in the novel are insignificant, though we note a return to a certain benign aspect when an Arab in prison, knowing Meursault has killed one of his countrymen, offers him, like the nurse, advice, this time as to how to lay out his sleeping mat.

9. Albert Camus, *La Peste* (Paris: Gallimard, 1947). Citations in the text are drawn from the translation of Stuart Gilbert, *The Plague* (New York: Modern Library [Random House], 1948), and are hereafter referred to as TP.

10. In an essay on the "real" Oran, he felt the striking fact of its existence to be its banality. "The Minotaur, or Stopping in Oran," in *Lyrical and Critical Essays* (New York: Alfred A. Knopf, 1968), 109–33 – a translation by Ellen Conroy Kennedy of the original essay, first published in *Le Mythe de Sisyphe* (Paris: Gallimard, 1954). This essay, begun in 1939, records Camus's impressions of the city of Oran based on two visits there during the same year. He refers to Oran in several essays in *L'Eté*. The Minotaur of the title symbolized for Camus boredom: "The Oranais are devoured by the Minotaur: boredom" (*Notebooks 1935-1942*, 186).

11. In his *Notebooks 1935-1942*, Camus described Oran as "A town which turns its back on the sea and then turns on itself like a snail. You wander through the labyrinth, looking for the sea as for Ariadne's thread" (186).

12. Camus, *Théâtre, Récits, Nouvelles*, ed. Roger Quilliot (Bruges: Gallimard, 1962), 1973-75.

13. Camus, *L'Homme révolté* (Paris: Gallimard, Coll. Idées, 1965), 33–34.

14. The title of Camus's first essay in the series on Kabylia was "Le Grèce en haillons" ("Greece in Tatters"), *Alger-Républicain*, 5 June 1939. We might note as well that Camus was assiduously studying the classics at the time he wrote the passage cited on Kabylia (1937). In 1939, his long-awaited visit to Greece had to be canceled because of the war and he would not go there until 1955.

15. Camus extended his Greek ideal to a concept he called "Mediterraneanism." In 1937, for the opening of the Maison de Culture in Algiers, he delivered a lecture entitled "The New Mediterranean Culture," in which he called for a "nationalism of the sun." He contrasted the artistic genius, feeling for life, and ideal of beauty of the Greeks with the Roman genius for war and drive for power. Elsewhere in his work, he compared the Roman ideal with northern European political doctrine (born of Hegel, Marx, and Nietzsche) and the Greek ideal with the Mediterranean theorists. It should be stressed, however, that Camus did not equate the Greek ideal and the "New Mediterraneanism" (for one thing, the "disorder" of the latter contrasted with the Greek ideal), but the two are intimately related and equally opposed to the Latin ideal.

Camus characterized the Mediterranean peoples in the following way: "The Mediterranean, an international basin traversed by every current, is perhaps the only land linked to the great ideas from the East. For it is not classical and well ordered, but diffuse and turbulent, like the Arab districts in our towns or the Genoan and Tunisian harbors. The triumphant taste for life, the sense of boredom and the weight of the sun, the empty squares at noon in Spain, the siesta, this is the true Mediterranean, and it is to the East that it is closest. Not to the Latin West. East and West live close together. And there is, at this junction, little difference between the way a Spaniard or an Italian lives on the quays of Algiers, and the way the Arabs live around them. The most basic aspect of Mediterranean genius springs perhaps from this historically and geographically unique encounter between East and West." ("La nouvelle culture méditérranéenne," first published in *Jeune Méditérranée*, no. 1, Maison de la Culture, Algier [avril 1937]. English translation in *Lyrical and Critical Essays*, 194). In this same essay, Camus urges the need to rehabilitate the Mediterranean (at a time historically when the "Romans" under Mussolini and Hitler occupied Libya and Abyssinia).

16. *L'Exil et le royaume* (Paris: Gallimard, Livre de poche, 1966 [1957]). The English translations are mine. This work is hereafter referred to as LEX.

17. This is, of course, only one possible interpretation, which I base on the previous description of the Arab and his reaction toward Daru. Another possible interpretation is that the Arab takes the path to prison out of his fear of and servility towards the French authorities. Pessimistic as such an interpretation is, it is nonetheless a viable alternative reading both from literary and historical perspectives.

18. One critic states that "the story illustrates the lack of understanding of both sides, and the respective failure of Daru and the natives to communicate." If by the word "natives" we understand the anonymous Arabs seeking vengeance at the end of the story, perhaps, though the metaphysical properties of this "encounter" far outweigh any literal significance it might have; if we consider, on the other hand, the individual encounter of Daru and the Arab, I emphatically disagree. Georges J. Joyaux, "Albert Camus and North Africa," *Yale French Studies*, no. 25 (Spring 1960): 17.

19. "Algeria," In *Resistance, Rebellion, and Death* (New York: Alfred A. Knopf, 1961), 111.

20. Albert Memmi, *Portrait du colonisé, précédé du Portrait du colonisateur* (Paris: Jean-Jacques Pauvert, 1966 [1957]); trans. as *The Colonizer and the Colonized* (New York: Orion Press, 1965); cited by O'Brien, 10, 25 ff.; see also Henri Kréa and Pierre Nora, both writing on *L'Etranger* and Camus's unconscious attitude towards Arabs, in *France-Observateur*, 5 January 1961.

# Climates of the Mind:
# Albert Camus 1936–1940                    Germaine Brée*

I find Camus's "rebel" to be the ideal of Political Man in the modern world. (1978)[1]

. . . the social critic must have standing among his fellow-citizens. He exploits his connections as it were, not his disconnections . . . Camus was a connected social critic. (1984)[2]

The significance of *The Rebel* clearly transcends the political and historical circumstances of its gestation and the acrimonious polemics that accompanied it. (1985)[3]

A quarter of a century after Camus's death, "the profusion and chaotic proliferation of Camus studies coming out yearly," noted by Brian

*This essay was written especially for this volume and is published here for the first time by permission of the author. With thanks to Raymond Farrow III for his invaluable help in the preparation of the manuscript. All translations from the French are Germaine Brée's unless otherwise noted.

Fitch already in 1971,[4] have shown no sign of flagging. Around Camus's work, bibliographical listings are still accumulating, a testimony no doubt to its vitality — a testimony also to the quality of the academic scholarship, international in stature, that has worked toward its accessibility. In a short span of years, the bulk of Camus's writing has emerged from out of the turmoil, confusion, and obfuscation of a particularly contentious period in French history. By 1965, Camus's readers, those at least able to read French, could benefit from the two-volume edition of Camus's major — if not quite "complete" — works scrupulously edited by Roger Quilliot, rich in relevant documentation. In 1968, Brian Fitch, supported by an international team of young scholars — André Abbou, Raymond Gay-Crozier, and Peter Hoy among them — launched the "Albert Camus" series of the *Revue des Lettres Modernes*, still ongoing. Its bibliographies, reviews, critical "notes," and articles have provided the information, tools, and impetus for research and debate and for the related colloquia that have clearly underscored the continuing resiliency and resonance of Camus's work. In 1971, publication of hitherto unpublished, or only partly published Camus texts, were carefully edited by a team of dedicated scholars and published in an elegant format in *The Cahiers Albert Camus*. These texts, along with Herbert Lottman's biography,[5] have quite definitively altered the partisan approaches — often highly politicized — to Camus's work, which were launched from Paris even before Camus's death.

Of the three quotations used as epigraphs, the first and third, Norman Jacobson's and Raymond Gay-Crozier's, refer to the most controversial — to date — of Camus's texts, *The Rebel*, while Michael Walzer reexamines Camus's stance at the time of the Algerian war. Walzer and Gay-Crozier openly state their disagreement with the negative judgment of earlier critics: "I want to reconsider Camus's Algerian moment," writes Walzer, "to defend him from the bonds of myth" — the myth of Camus, the "hero," to be sure — but even more the myth of the "failed" Camus, dear to Conor Cruise O'Brien[6] and Simone de Beauvoir.[7] Supporting Gay-Crozier's evaluation of the significance of *The Rebel*, so often ridiculed, Edouard Morot-Sir, a philosopher, literary historian, and critic working within the broad framework of an investigation into the role of the essay as "genre" in French literature, concludes that with *The Rebel*, Camus "played a major role" in the intellectual evolution of the form. The essay, he argues, at least since Montaigne, has served as matrix for the elaboration of a "specific linguistic universe," an activity needed in times of change, harbinger of a "new order of language." This search for new forms of rhetoric, he claims, has been "overlooked or minimized by Camus's critics and "turned against him" by his adversaries "in the form of accusations of incompetence."[8] Camus himself had once remarked that "new epochs require, if not new words, at least new configurations of words."[9] It is just such configurations that Morot-Sir brings to light.

Clearly a critical revision is under way. The left-wing intelligentsia in the fifties and sixties tended to dismiss Camus's arguments in those later years as mere outbursts of "petit-bourgeois" self-interest or — in the Algerian debate — of personal nostalgia and bitterness. The so-called ideological controversy turned into a kind of protracted lawsuit with Camus cast somewhat in the role of Joseph K., the man under arrest in Kafka's *The Trial*. Since then, the ideological climate has changed in Paris more than once; it may well change again, given the volatile socio-political tensions of the day. But Camus's work, in its specificity and within its boundaries, seems to have reached the status of a "classic," at least as defined recently by Italo Calvino.[10] Of the fourteen related definitions proffered by Calvino, not without humor, two seem particularly apposite to Camus's status at present. "The classics," Calvino writes, "are the books that come down to us bearing upon them the traces they themselves have left on the culture or cultures they have passed through (or more simply, the language and customs)." And again, "A classic is a book which has never finished saying what it has to say." As things stand today, particularly in relation to Camus's narratives, *The Stranger* and *Exile and the Kingdom*, Calvino's definitions apply, so numerous are the "readings" proposed coming from widely different cultural areas. More recently, radically new readings of Camus's essays and articles are surfacing everywhere.

Taking into account these changes in critical orientation, I propose to examine briefly the contributions of the young Algerian reporter, Albert Camus, to the short-lived local daily newspapers, *Alger Républicain* and *Alger Soir*, between 1938–40, and more specifically, his report on Kabylia. They seem to me to provide a perspective on the formation of a point of view that furnished the matrix for his mature work and the unity that underlies its various modes. In a sense they may be seen as Camus's "Algerian moment" par excellence. This limited foray into Camus's early socio-political polemical writing is based on the texts collected in the two volumes of the *Cahiers Albert Camus III* (1978) under the title, *Fragments d'un Combat* (1938–1940).[11] These texts benefit from the meticulous notes of the two editors, Jacqueline Lévi-Valensi and André Abbou, who were thoroughly conversant with the Algerian situation in those years, an advantage not particularly common among the Parisian literati, whose abysmal ignorance on the subject of Algeria was noted as late as 1957 by the ethnologist, Germaine Tillion.[12]

Camus was not quite twenty-five when he was hired as assistant by Pascal Pia, a recently appointed journalist imported from Paris to launch *Alger Républicain*. The political climate of the governing circle in Algeria in 1938 was reactionary. Pia's aim was to keep alive the spirit and reforms of the Popular Front socialism of 1936, even while maintaining the strict independence of the newspaper. Its readership was never large. Camus's involvement in the Algerian Communist Party was over but he was and would remain a man of the left. His earlier political activities had given him a certain familiarity with the complexity of Muslim politics and in-fighting, reflecting the divergences of opinion among the literate Muslim French-educated elite, with some of whom Camus remained in touch all his life. Socially, although he had moved into a circle of young intellectuals gravitating around the university, it was with the "petit peuple" of Belcourt—the working-class section of Algiers—that he identified. Belcourt served as a kind of hinge between the Muslim section of Algiers, the Casbah—an ancient stronghold of the "Barbary" pirates—and the modern city, with its administrative and university section, and the residential quarters of Algiers. Camus thus belonged to two groups in Algiers society—the student world and the "world of the poor"—where the two populations—Muslim and non-Muslim—came into daily contact. As a journalist he was soon to discover other more dubious zones of reciprocity. But in his two first slim volumes of essays—the only literary works to be published until the forties—*L'Envers et l'endroit* (1937) and *Noces* (1938)—it is of Algiers only that he speaks, describing the Algerines of the working-class sections, and celebrating the beauty of its Mediterranean beaches and coastline.

Camus's world at the time was narrowly circumscribed. Its parochialism was apparent when in 1937 at the opening of the cultural center of which he was the director, he addressed the topic of "the native culture." Surprisingly, given the title, the word "Islam" was never pronounced. The "Arabs" were mentioned only once when the young lecturer, in a sweeping sentence, asserted their resemblance to the Spaniards, Italians, Maltese— to the "Mediterranean" type of which the Algerine was the exemplar. Clearly he had in mind the Muslim workmen of Algiers. The imaginary nature of his Mediterranean "type" is evident.

The young orator was at some pains to disengage the concept of a "Mediterranean culture" from its well-known earlier Western European versions, and to fuse into a single "signifier" its cultural, political, and geographical aspects. So, in a grand rhetorical gesture, he eliminated from that "homeland" the Romans, along with such "un-Mediterranean" types—in his eyes—as Mussolini and Franco. Geographically, the Mediterranean "patrie"—homeland—stretched along the two borders of that sea, north and south, from Genoa to Barcelona, to Algiers, but hardly to its eastern shores, from Greece to Tunis. Camus further defined his stylized projection into the future in broad and hardly original terms as that land where the Orient and the Occident meet. In doing so, he cleared the way for the living "turbulent" and free "new culture" in the making. Camus's Belcourt neighborhood quite recognizably typifies the "new culture" and his own political allegiance. With its projected antitotalitarian, democratic future, it is depicted in contrast to the monolithic, authoritarian society of the North. In that "new culture," the Westernized Arab and the Algerianized European would meet. "Lands without a past, lands of the imagination": this formula evoking the Mediterranean "homeland" caused some displeasure among the Muslims, well aware of their past. It rather aptly defines the myth that the small circle of talented young Algerines, still in their early twenties, had set up as a kind of password, whereby they proclaimed their independence from Paris while increasing their visibility.

I wish to pause here to consider a passage written two years later for *Alger Républicain*. Camus had been sent out to report on the condition of the Berbers of Kabylia — peasants living in isolation in the high lands south of Algiers — rumors of whose plight had reached Algiers. What Camus confronted there was in fact starvation. The "itinerary of famine" he travelled was no allegorical fiction. Condensed in an elliptical image it was the expression of a harsh reality:

> I had climbed with a Kabyle friend to the top of the hills that dominate the town. There we watched darkness fall. At that hour when the shadows which come down from the mountains over the magnificent land bring peace to the most hardened heart, I knew that nonetheless there could be no peace for those who, on the other slope of the valley, were gathered around a meagre loaf of spoiled barley. I knew too that solace which one can find by abandoning oneself to an evening so startingly grandiose, but I also knew that the misery whose fires were glowing across from us laid an interdict on the beauty of the land. "Shall we go down?" my companion said.[14]

In the light of starvation, the "Mediterranean" myth was dead. Camus had not before questioned the fine balance, in his own sense of reality, between poverty and beauty. Caligula's brutal rejection of the adolescent poet Scipio's lyricism is adumbrated here and the human deprivation manifest in the starving community of Kabylia is the first apparition of the word of *The Plague*. Kabylia jolted Camus out of his egocentric Algerine world. The positioning of the narrative "I" has changed, and with it, the perspective of the observer in a world where the lines are drawn absolutely — not in terms of race, ideology or class, but between those gathered around the fires, who have nothing to eat, and he and his Kabyle friend, who are going back down the hill to dinner. One of the fundamental structures in Camus's fictional works is the simultaneous presence of human worlds that overlap, whose boundaries cannot be crossed, but whose simultaneous existence can be sensed or perceived. This is, in fact, one of the major structures common to all the stories in *Exile and the Kingdom*. It places a restraint on facile concepts of universality and community.

It is my purpose here to trace certain of the rhetorical strategies adopted by Camus in those early years of his journalistic career, to which scant attention has been paid. Nor could those early pieces be taken into account before they were collected and their context clearly established, as has now been done. The content of the on-the-spot reports of daily events contributed by Camus to *Alger Républicain*, then briefly *Le Soir Républicain*, is well known. His articles offer a kind of kaleidoscopic view of the trouble spots in the functioning of Algiers' administration: labor disputes, municipal politics, rigged elections, and, on a somewhat larger geographic map, miscarriages of justice. His role as reporter for a politically committed, independent left-wing paper, and his personal convictions, quite naturally defined his role as trouble-shooter. He put to work certain strategies to alert his readers to the socio-political realities he observed, and in the process took on many masks and some pseudonyms. Here his love of the theater served him well, using mask, voice and semantic masquerades. Camus visibly enjoyed needling his adversaries, under his own name, but also under those of Vincent-Capable, Jean Meursault, Zaks, Liber, Nero, Irenaeus, until finally, with the report on Kabylia, he found his own, mature voice.[15]

## Journalism: The Making of a Writer

Whether one fights giants or windmills, Camus once remarked, matters little. For a couple of years, in his first journalistic skirmishes as "reporter-on-the-spot," those he fought were neither giants nor windmills, but the municipal and sometimes the regional Algerian authorities. *Alger Républicain*, a socialist, strictly non-Marxist daily paper, was dedicated to the "defense of the working-class" — that of Muslim workers among others. It had a few Muslim reporters on its staff, but typically, at the time,[16] the staff saw itself as a "watch-dog" group partly responsible for making public the illegal discriminations inflicted on the Muslims through the administrative-judicial power structure. By 1940, when *Le Soir Républicain*, the successor of the banned *Alger Républicain*, was banned in its turn, the latter was considered subversive, in part because of its antifascist, antiwar stance, in part because of its uncompromising defense of the Arab population. Camus, who in those two short years had become one of its most outspoken spokesmen, had to leave Algiers. But he had in the meantime acquired a valuable political experience and a realistic view of the complexity of Algeria. In the next five years and through the fifties, Europe was prominent in his preoccupations as newspaperman, although after 1945 Algeria gradually regained its central significance. Paradoxically, Camus's literary work throughout the period remained focused on Algeria, revealing the deeper sense of his double identity. In 1955, he proclaimed himself "French by birth, and since 1940, by deliberate choice." In 1956, as the crisis in Algeria worsened, his mood changed: " 'You must choose your camp,' shout those who are drunk with hatred. Ah! I have chosen my country. I have chosen the Algeria of justice where Frenchmen and Arabs will associate freely."[17] The "Algeria of justice," then, was the utopian home which would end a double exile, but for Camus it was an ideal which could turn into reality.

In the early reports of the apprentice journalist there is little, if any, awareness of the potential conflicts that could emerge from that complex identity. It was, it seems to me, Camus's work as an "on-the-spot" reporter that marked the transition from an unreflected to a reflected awareness of the presence of "others" on Algerian soil, a people whose existence had had no place in his Mediterranean myth. It was, as I shall attempt to show, his contact with the bedouins of Kabylia which opened his eyes to another reality, far removed from his highly romanticized "Mediterranean culture."[18]

It would be idle to attempt to survey all of Camus's newspaper contributions; they are uneven in the literary interest which I propose to underscore. *Alger Républicain* was not a "single issue" paper. It reported on local events, such as fires, on municipal meetings, elections, trials, and so forth—on the "news-in-brief"—and it kept its readers informed on European events. Camus's first assignments may be classified under "news-in-brief." They then became more weighty and significant, leading up to the eleven-article investigation of the famine in Kabylia. Camus enlivened reports of routine daily episodes by a lavish use of literary ploys: verbal caricatures of prominent political figures, caustic satire, cool tongue-in-cheek mockery, deliberately aggressive forms of writing. When writing serious pieces, such as the defense of the victims of injustice or the reporting of the famine devastating Kabylia, persiflage and facetiousness disappear. Camus speaks personally, eloquently, and one might say, "directly out of conviction and compassion." These two stylistic strains surface in most of his later fictional writings, informing their structures and the ambiguities of characters and perspectives.

Camus clearly relished the entertainment value of his satiric strategies. He addressed his readers under many masks: as "I" bemusedly observing some "amazing" happening; in the name of a righteous "we," implying readers' "consensus," or of a larger inclusive "*on*" (people). He introduced "other" diverse voices in his column, through the use of pseudonyms. Each embodied a "type" recognizable by his discourse: bland smugness, earnest puzzlement, self-righteous indignation. These classical stylistic games were well calculated to puncture complacency and win the complicity of readers by opening the text to laughter. Satire, irony, and parody turned the speaking subjects into figures of fun. "The Manifesto of Integral Conformism,"[19] subtitled "Yes, Yes, Yes," was a pastiche presented as an earnest declaration of loyalty to the authorities by a "group of conscious and determined citizens," a deadpan accumulation of more and more wildly absurd slogans. Parody, quickly veering to wild extravagance, was used by Camus in an item purportedly concerning a Nazi project to create an Aryan Bible.[20] It begins blandly enough but Camus soon introduces a telling adjective—"amazing"—a signal to his readers that it is a blatantly mocking invention:

> A new institute has just been created in Germany. Its task is to present a German Bible from which all Jewish influence will be expunged. . . .
> Even at this early date, we can reveal to our readers the main features of

this amazing project . . . the birth of Jesus will not be attributed to the
Holy Ghost but to the virile interventions of Siegfried.

The spoofing in both cases, extravagant as it is, serves a more serious
purpose — to disrupt the illusions of the conformist discourse and to point
to the absurdities of Hitler's anti-Jewish policies.

Elsewhere, Camus combines narrative and metaphor to transform
routine political procedures into grotesque masquerades with the purpose
of revealing the "true" implications behind words and gestures. A brief
glance at two reports reveals the patterns of a conscious rhetoric of irony
and distortion.

If one excepts prize-giving school ceremonies and the speeches of
Monsieur Rozis,[21] nothing is more dismal than a senatorial election. Yet
the two contestants made commendable efforts to be amusing. But
when they succeeded it was in spite of themselves.[22]

So begins one of Camus's earliest contributions to *Alger Républicain*. The
school metaphor appears at first to come into conflict with the image of
senatorial gravity and experience. But the "puerilism" it suggests injects
into that image the notion of senility and thence of irresponsibility, which
Camus underscores.

Contrary to all previsions, it was in a jovial mood that the municipal
council met last night. Not merely in a jovial mood but with a display of
the most subtle charm and juvenile improvisation . . . to be sure
Monsieur Rozis almost spoiled things at first by the visible exasperation
which marked his answers to the native councillors. But so light a cloud
was rapidly dissipated and it was smilingly that serious affairs were
considered. . . . Yet at first sight the situation hardly seems funny.[23]

So opens an account of the voting of the municipal budget. It is entitled "A
picturesque municipal council" ("The municipal féerie"). The "fairy-land"
image gives the report its rhetorical consistency. Camus, designating the
European-Algerian councillors by name, sketches in their attitudes, one by
one, in brief, graphic detail: doodling, kneading, and sculpting pieces of
paper; sending signals or notes "like butterflies" to persons at the back of
the room; chatting, yawning, making paper windmills as the reader of the
minutes drones on; until, in a grand finale, "the budget is voted"
unanimously. "With a last smile Mr. Rozis gives the signal that the session
is over while one of the native councillors is still speaking." The implications of the "féerie" metaphor are clear. But irony stops short as Camus
underscores the humiliating treatment inflicted on those "others," the
legally elected representatives of the Muslin population. Here the political
message is direct, not a matter for mockery. The ironic metaphors of
school and fairyland, even while trivializing the episodes and characters,
reveal Camus's urge to wrench an aesthetic shape out of what he had
witnessed, even for so ephemeral a genre as a newspaper piece. But the

game is over when the satirical gives way to the polemical, and Camus calls upon a "we" — his readers and himself — to pass stern judgement on the whole affair: "This judgement is ours, and with us that of the Arab population and the working-class in its entirety." As reporter, Camus was addressing the ills of his own society, a society which for him includes "le peuple arabe." Throughout, Camus avoids using the noun "Arabe," with its connotations of contempt — the contempt manifested in Mr. Rozis's behavior. For Camus, the Arab population shares in a community life, which the abuse of the mindless local politicians he lampoons threatens to destroy.

The report on Kabylia[24] strikes a different note. "This was not written for a political party, but for men. And if I wish to give the investigation the meaning that should be recognized, I should point out that it does not try to say 'See what you have made of Kabylia' but 'See what you have not made of Kabylia.' " Concluding his report, Camus speaks to a "you" of much greater scope than the local politicians of Algiers: the French colonial power, France itself.

> For if colonial conquest could ever find an excuse, it is in proportion to the help it gives the conquered populations to keep their own personality. And if we have a task to perform in this land, it is to allow one of the proudest and most human people in the world to remain faithful to itself and its destiny. I do not think I am mistaken when I say that this destiny is both to work and to contemplate, and thereby to give the troubled conquerors we are, lessons in wisdom.

The shift in the relation between the "we" and the "they," via the "you," is critical. The identification of the reporter with the "we" of the "entire Muslim population" has become impossible. Kabylia marks Camus's initiation to the reality of his socio-political status as one of the "colonizers." A question, which he reiterates in the conclusion, expresses his anguish: "What have we done for [Kabylia]? — What have we done, all of us who write or legislate and who, when we are back at home forget the misery of others?"

From the beginning, the text is meticulously documented: Camus gives stark, brief descriptions of the miserable conditions of life in Kabylia: housing, food, water, physical deterioration, illiteracy, disease, desperation, "insulting salaries," usury. His text is accompanied by photographs, proofs of veracity, so urgent is the writer's need to awaken the imagination of his readers to the "unspeakable." Such qualifiers as "unspeakable," "atrocious," "terrifying," introduce a second level in the text, a deeply personal reaction to what Camus reports, as he follows day by day "the itinerary of hunger," the "promenade through the suffering and hunger of a people." This metaphor of a double odyssey in an uncharted land — as witness and as "discoverer" — is discreet but central. An inner journey accompanies the outer one, leading through horror and despair to a new sense of responsibility and dedication. Thus, the conclusion: "That is where I recovered the meaning of my investigation." Having gone through anger, despair, and revolt, Camus, observer and narrator, ends with a positive message. Exactly as in *The Rebel*, the text twists back upon itself and projects the possibilities of constructive action in the future. Not a *political* action, but a practical one, unencumbered by ideology: "What is important is that people are dying of hunger and children are undernourished." What is needed is the "bread, wheat, help, a fraternal hand we must offer. The rest is literature." Camus's aggressive games with words have disappeared, as he proposes what could be done, practically, for a people of whom he speaks with great respect. His point of contact with those "others" is not the shared heritage of a common land, but the recognition of a shared human need and vulnerability. Kabylia is a first model of the Oran of *The Plague*.

Camus's readers can trace in his journalist apprenticeship the development of writing techniques which he will put to use in narrative and drama to create apparently autonomous characters. The most immediately obvious technique is the ambiguous use of a first-person, seemingly oral narrative, which gives his characters their limitations and strange impenetrability: Meursault, Jean Baptiste Clamence, the Renegade. Parody, pastiche, mockery, introduce forms of low or high comedy into the text, via the self-betrayal of word and gesture. The play-acting of the municipal council of Algiers is a precursor of the play-acting of the judges and lawyers at the trial of Meursault. On the other hand, the position and attitude of Rieux in *The Plague* is adumbrated in the position of the young reporter-witness of the suffering of the Kabyles.

Perhaps most important of all is that, with these articles a gap is filled in our sense of the shaping of a vision, through a traumatic experience. In 1945, when he returned to Algeria after World War II, what Camus stressed again was the specter of famine for the Algerian population of the interior. And it was the vision of the devastation of people and land that led him to his desperate efforts to intervene in the Algerian conflict by advocating negotiation, through mediation, of those "differences" he had experienced as inherent in human and group relationships. In this he seems rather more "modern" than his uncompromising, ideologically oriented critics. "By the end of the war," David Caute noted, "the FLN (Algerian Liberation Front) estimated Algerian deaths, including victims of starvation, at over one million out of a population of nine million. The majority of Europeans fled, and by the end of 1962 Algerian industry was at a standstill, the harvest had not been brought in, two million were unemployed and four million others were declared 'without means of subsistence': the Algerian government had no alternative but to remain dependent upon French economic and technical aid."[25] One may well wonder whether Camus's program for Kabylia — the "helping hand offered" — might not have been a feasible, less costly alternative solution.

However that may be, the years 1936–40, between Camus's twenty-third and twenty-seventh year, seem to have been crucial years that shaped both his sense of "reality" and his stubborn independence and originality as a writer.

## Notes

1. Norman Jacobson, *Pride and Solace: The Functions and Limits of Political Theory* (Berkeley: University of California Press, 1978), 157.

2. Michael Walzer, "Commitment and Social Criticism: Camus's Algerian War," *Dissent* (Fall 1984): 426–27.

3. Raymond Gay-Crozier, *La Revue des Lettres Modernes: Albert Camus, 12: la révolte en question* (Paris: Minard, 1985) 3; hereafter cited as *RLM* followed by page number.

4. Brian Fitch, *Albert Camus* (Paris: Lettres Modernes, 1972), 3.

5. Herbert Lottman, *Albert Camus* (Paris: Editions du Seuil, 1978; trans. Marianne Véron, Garden City, N.J.: Doubleday, 1979).

6. Conor Cruise O'Brien, *Albert Camus* (New York: Viking Press, 1969). For an appraisal of the book, see Germaine Brée, *Camus and Sartre: Crisis and Commitment* (New York: Dell, 1972; rev. ed., London: Colder and Boyars, 1974), 151–52, n. 2, 4, 6.

7. Walzer, "Commitment," 135–36. To this trend, Robert Greer Cohn's fine article "The True Camus" (*French Review* 60, no. 1 [October 1986]: 30–38) contributes much.

8. Edouard Morot-Sir, "L'Homme révolté: entre non et oui" in *RLM, 12: la révolte en question*, 35–64.

9. Albert Camus, *Essais* (in *Oeuvres Complètes*), vol. 2 (Paris: Gallimard, 1965), 267.

10. Italo Calvino, "Why Read the Classics?" *L'Espresso* (1981); trans. Patrick Creagh, *New York Review*, 9 October 1986, 19–20.

11. Camus published the Kabylia reportage (with some omissions) in *Actuelles III* under the title "Chroniques Algériennes" (1958). It was reproduced in *Essais*, vol. 2, by Bibliothèque de la Pléiade, Editions Gallimard, carefully annotated by Roger Quilliot, who further gives a full history of Camus's contribution to the two newspapers. See also Emmett Parker's excellent *Albert Camus: The Artist in the Arena*, a study of Camus as journalist (Madison: University of Wisconsin Press, 1968). One of the best brief and impartial statements is "Albert Camus' Algeria," which appears in translation in *Camus: A Collection of Critical Essays*, ed. Germaine Brée (Englewood Cliffs, N.J.: Prentice-Hall, 1962), 38–47.

12. For a reliable analysis of the complex social spectrum in Algeria in those years, see Germaine Tillion, *L'Algérie en 1957* (Paris: Les Editions de Minuit, 1957).

13. Camus, *Essais*, 2:1321–27.

14. Albert Camus, "Fragments d'un Combat: 1938–1940," in *Cahiers Albert Camus*, vol. 1 (Paris: Gallimard, 1978), 288.

15. Algeria was divided, for administrative reasons, into three departments; the territories of the South were under military jurisdiction. For a brief description of the distribution of authority between the native officials, established by the Arabs, and the French system, see Camus, "Fragments d'un Combat," *Cahiers*, vol. 2, 763–65.

16. For a discussion of the attitudes in those years of the intellectuals, both Muslim and French, see Bjornson and Mouroe's introduction to *Africa and the West* (New York: Greenwood Press, 1986; London: Westport, 1986), 10, and also in that volume, Victor Levine's chapter, "Political and Cultural Schizophrenia in Francophone Africa," 169–71.

17. Camus, *Essais*, 2:984.

18. In the mosaic of ethnic and tribal groups that were (and still are, though less

widely) scattered throughout the vast expanse of the Maghreb (West North Africa: Tunisia, Algeria, Morrocco), the term *bedouin* first designated the nomad "men of the desert"; its meaning then extended to the former nomads who had become farmers, as in Kabylia. Nomads and rural tribes are thus distinguished from the city-dwellers. The term *Arab* was broadly used to designate the Muslim-Islamic population as a whole, with no perjorative sense intended. The word took on derogatory implications in late Western use, "but it merely designates," as *Webster's* dictionary puts it, "a member of the Arabic division of the Semitic people."

19. Camus, *Cahiers*, vol. 2, 696.

20. Ibid., 686.

21. Rozis was the reactionary, pro-Franco mayor of Algiers, one of Camus's pet targets — the regrettable mayor of Algiers; the "provisional" mayor of Algiers, as Camus dubbed him.

22. Camus, *Cahiers*, vol. 1, 155.

23. Ibid., 161.

24. "Misère de la Kabylie," the series of articles that appeared in *Alger Républicain*, was published in Camus's *Essais*, 2:905–38, as the first item in "Chroniques Algériennes," with some minor variants from the original text that appears in full in *Cahiers*, 278–336.

25. David Caute, *Frantz Fanon* (New York: Viking Press, 1970), 56. Frantz Fanon developed a theory of "therapeutic violence" in the struggle against colonialism, which influenced anticolonialist French intellectuals — Sartre and Jeanson among them — and to which Camus was opposed.

# *Supplementarity* in Camus                    Hanna Charney*

Derrida devotes a chapter of *Of Grammatology*[1] to the *"supplément"* in Rousseau, which ultimately leads him to some crucial ideas on writing, absence, and the "trace." The noun "supplement" in English does not fully convey the double meaning; underlined by Derrida in *"supplément"* and *"suppléer à"*: something additional (added from the outside) or a lack that can be filled. A supplement to a publication would correspond to the first meaning; that kind of supplement resembles a surplus. A vitamin supplement, on the other hand, compensates a dietary deficiency. Derrida's concept of the "supplement" seems to throw light on repeated allusions, in Camus's writings, to "something else," that may take various forms. "Supplementarity" (by analogy with complementarity or other -arity suffix words) is proposed here to suggest these notions.

Interestingly and unexpectedly, affinities between Rousseau and Camus appear through Derrida's extraordinarily convincing analyses of "this dangerous supplement" in Rousseau. Although it is impossible to do justice here to Derrida's complex argument, ill-served by simplification, it

*This essay was written especially for this volume and is published here for the first time by permission of the author.

is worth noting Rousseau's ambiguous conception of nature as a full, beneficent, maternal presence and also as subject to a deficiency that can be "supplemented." Derrida's modulations on Rousseau seem to call forth Camus's double presentation of nature: mute and hard, or striking with the burning heat of fate (like the sun in *The Stranger*), or conciliatory and pacifying (as in the sea bathing in *The Plague*), tender and indifferent ("the tender indifference of the world") or cruelly deaf to all human suffering. A full presence, but not self-sufficient? What, then, is added?

"Never for me [can there be] an intermediary between everything and nothing" (DLG, 226). Derrida shows Rousseau's deliberate refusal of mediation in an "either/or" gesture. Here again, Camus seems close in his repeated affirmation of inalienable antinomies and paradoxes. Derrida restores Rousseau's context: "From then on, I was alone, for there never was for me an intermediary between everything and nothing. I found in Thérèse the supplement that I needed."[2] One conclusion Derrida draws is that this supplement is a function of reading. "The presumed subject of the sentence always [says], using 'supplementing,' more, less or something else than what he would like to say [or means]" (DLG, 226). The reason is that "the writer writes *in* a language and *in* a logic of which, by definition, his discourse cannot absolutely dominate the system" (DLG, 227). Eventually, "the concept of supplement is a sort of blind spot in Rousseau's text, the non-seen which opens and limits visibility" (DLG, 234).

"Everything simple is beyond us" Camus says,[3] as if to confirm Derrida's concept of a blind spot. The sentence could mean that everything simple is beyond us because it is simple, but it also seems to suggest other possibilities in its paradoxical opposition of *"simple"* and *"dépasse"*: "tout ce qui est simple nous dépasse." This is especially true in the context, in which Camus explicitly rejects other forms of "beyond," such as another life after death. And since the meditation revolves around death, life, and youth, we can hardly take Camus at his word that death is only one among other "simple" things.

Death becomes the major reality of epidemic proportions in *The Plague.*[4] In the first pages of the novel, the narrator describes Oran as a typical modern city in which people work hard and play hard against a harsh landscape without shade, trees, or pigeons. This may not be exceptional, we are told: after all, "all our contemporaries are like that. . . . But there are cities and countries where people have, from time to time, a hint *[le soupçon]* of something else. In general, that doesn't change their life. Only there has been the hint and that's that much gained" (P, 6).

This puzzling remark, "c'est toujours cela de gagné," lingers in the mind throughout. Certainly in the agonizing realities that soon begin to invade the city, in the black flood of death that will blanket Oran, there seems to be no room for the trifling *"soupçon"* of something else, much less for anything gained by it. Yet the motif of "something else" can be seen as recurring again and again; it may be part of a pervasive theme in Camus's work, with important variations in the economy of style and ethics.

The urgency of the war and the horrors of Nazi occupation in which *The Plague* is steeped allegorically define what is essential in contrast to all superfluous trivialities. All energies are concentrated on the fight against the plague, starkly and simply represented by the exhausting activity of Dr. Rieux. And yet Rieux is in a paradoxically privileged position. He does not need a moral or philosophical justification for this fight, which is futile in the sense that there is no cure for the deadly disease which kills mercilessly. Rieux does his work with the self-sacrifices it is bound to entail. For him, justification is a needless luxury—here, as elsewhere, political urgency in Camus is related to social habits. Rieux is a son of the working classes and easily distinguishes what is essential from what is not. Germaine Brée discusses the importance, in Camus's own background, of "those clear basic 'images,' as he calls them, that rise straight out of his childhood world."[5] She quotes Camus: "It is in this life of poverty, among these humble or vain people that I most surely reached what seemed to me the real meaning of life." Germaine Brée notes that these words from the *Notebooks* (1935) are repeated twenty years later in the Preface to *The Wrong Side and the Right Side (L'Envers et l'Endroit).*

Yet Rieux's dedication does not resolve the conflicts experienced by other characters, nor even his own, which are partly suppressed. There is always "something else" raising its problematic questions. One important theme is in the modulations of exile in *The Plague*. Rieux (who, as we later learn, is the narrator), suffers only the general exile of the inhabitants of Oran—"like everybody" ("comme tout le monde") in the recurring phrase of *The Stranger*. But the journalist Rambert, as well as other "lovers who are the most interesting" (P, 63) is in a different position. A stranger to the city, he initially tries to leave in order to go home and join the woman he loves. His exile is double, and those "interesting lovers" suffer increased anguish in that the natural consolations of the "external world" do not exist for them. But, in the irrepressible system of Camusian paradox, these exiles are also specially privileged. They have "something else," something irreplaceable, "images of a place where a certain light, two or three hills, the favorite tree and women's faces composed a climate that was for them irreplaceable" (P, 62–3).

This unique inner landscape, in the development of the crisis, will become as irrelevant as all other special privileges, but at the end Rambert does survive, and, on the train platform with many others, waits for "this form running toward him" who falls into his embrace. Rambert seems capable of cherishing only a temporary illusion of happiness, however, trying at that moment to believe that "the plague can come and go again without changing the heart of men." No doubt the plague itself will become for him that consciousness of "something else" which will remain, just as "the bacillus of the plague never dies nor disappears" (P, 254).

Rieux, amidst the interminable spectacle of suffering that he sees, abandons pity as useless: "One gets tired of pity when pity is useless" (P, 77). The notion of "useless" recurs in a crescendo: pity as useless; love as useless; knowledge as useless. But these statements are deceptive and partly belied by the events of the novel. As a specific psychological reaction, pity may have disappeared in Rieux's conduct. But his general compassion, his unshaken loyalty to his friend, Tarrou, stricken by the plague, his mute but faithful attachment to his mother, are pervasive values without which the novel would make no sense at all.

"Truth" is also revealed as an unacceptable luxury when Father Paneloux gives his momentous first sermon on the plague. In that sermon, Paneloux reverts to the old theological reasoning: the plague is the result of the people's sin. "My brothers, you are in misery, my brothers, you have brought it on yourselves" (P, 81). He reiterates the necessity of returning to what is "essential, to the truth: 'I want to lead you to the truth' " (P, 83). Paneloux's truth, however, turns out to be falsehood: the death of a child is the turning point of this fundamental change. That death is the fall of a sparrow (see Matthew 10:29), the catastrophe which destroys any possible system. This catastrophe may mark a general reversal, in Camus's novels, of the concept of truth in relation to that "something else," the light fall of a sparrow and no longer a *"soupçon,"* such as the comfort of shady trees or peaceful pigeons. In *The Fall*, the light noise of a splash in the river becomes a crucial moral indicator. Clamence, a lawyer who leads a successful, well-rounded life in which every act of charity or persuasion has its appointed place, upsets the whole construction by retiring to the mists of Amsterdam, preaching the gospel of his role as "judge-penitent." It is the splash in the water, the sign of his omission, that took him there.

In this respect (as well as in others) Clamence, perhaps, answers Meursault in *The Stranger*. Clamence has listened—albeit too late, but it is always too late—to the summons of that fall, to the (something) other that disrupts his existence. Meursault, in contrast, is integral in his life and fate. Robert Champigny convincingly describes this alienated character as a pagan hero,[6] existing in the completeness of each sensory moment, an overwhelming present which it is as absurd to leave as to cling to. When offered the possibility of a position in Paris, Meursault fails to see any need for a change in his humdrum life, since all amounts to the same thing. Love for Meursault is a term as meaningless as the concepts prevalent at his own trial, when he stands accused of a "crime" which he cannot see in the same terms as his judges. In prison, in the second part of the novel, the hero reflectively and thoughtfully reaffirms his values, although at the very end he sounds two new notes, "hatred" and "tenderness," which foreshadow *The Plague*.

As Germaine Brée points out, everything in Camus is a matter of style, morality perhaps most of all. Unquestionably, Meursault's truth—of which, in prison, he "gets hold as much as it holds him" ("je la tenais autant qu'elle me tenait") — gives a representative weight to his fate. And that truth seems to be in large part a sort of linguistic ethos, according to which the hero says no more than he knows, expresses no feeling that he does not know he feels. In the wake of Sartre's article on *The Stranger*,[7] critics have often analyzed the characteristics of the novel's language, the simple subordination in sentences that resemble, as Sartre says, balls of mercury which refuse to be linked in causal or other relations. This classical sparseness of style is also a moral refusal — a refusal not only of ornamentation, luxury, or superfluity, but, on the part of the hero, of repentance through justification and rationalization. Strict justice must prevail for him.

Meursault, to the extent that he is presented as a martyr of his truth, is a simple hero and martyr. Certainly *The Plague* is syntactically and otherwise very different from *The Stranger*, and *The Fall* is a new stylistic experiment again, a tour de force combining classical elegance and the cumbersome use of the imperfect subjunctive, as well as relentless analysis and obvious self-justification. A closer look at Father Paneloux's sermon might show how, in *The Plague*, style and truth or ethics are balanced. "My brothers, you are in misery, my brothers, you have brought it on yourselves." This initial sentence, we learn, is the substance of the sermon. What followed did not seem logically related. "It is only the rest of the speech that made it clear to our co-citizens that, through a clever orator's device, the Father had given at one single time, as you administer a blow, the theme of his entire sermon." (P, 81). The elaborate parables that Paneloux recounts do not seem to modify the meaning of his one exhortatory statement. Yet both the simple statement and the rest of the powerful sermon leave dubious effects on the population of Oran, and shortly after the pages on Paneloux's sermon, Rieux is shown in conversation with Grand, the writer endlessly dedicated to reworking his beginning sentence until it becomes perfect: "Understand me, doctor. You might say it is rather easy to choose between *but* and *and*. It is already more difficult to opt between *and* and *then*. The difficulty increases with *then* and *later*. . . " (P, 87). Grand's preoccupation is, to say the least, purely linguistic, while Paneloux's conviction may be deeply felt. Yet Paneloux, no matter how eloquent a speaker, turns out to be *wrong* in a sense that Grand can never be.

One key to the complex and often paradoxical role of style in Camus may be the fact that language or art is not conceived as a separate area of experience. The author often returns, in his essays as well as in short stories and novels, to the conflict between writing and action, an essential concern in the 1940s, still active in some of the literature of the 1950s. The solution that Camus repeatedly seems to envisage is a diachronic one, such as the one Rieux adopts. Rieux is presented as a character, a physician whose functions and activities are dictated by events. It is only toward the end of the work that he is revealed as the narrator who wrote his journal about the plague after the fact and after the emergency was over. Grand also hopes to write his "perfect" work after "all that" is finished.

In a way that may seem alien to present theory and criticism, Camus does not seem predominantly troubled by the epistemological status of language, as if the subtle economies of his classical style were a natural efflorescence of consciousness. He sometimes posits a perfect correspondence between the word and the thing ("I felt . . . what word? what disproportion? how to consecrate the harmony of love and revolt?" [N, 92]), and Rieux, when he considers it his duty to bear witness to the events of the plague, does not question the feasibility of his narrative undertaking. Writing, in Camus, can clearly be a moral imperative, at the right time. If Camus's ethical concerns, especially in *The Plague*, underlie his conception of writing, they may partly explain the "truth value," in Ricoeur's term, that Camus sometimes attributes to language. It may be unimportant, in *The Plague*, to know how sincere Paneloux is in his sermon, but it does matter (to him as well as to other characters and to the reader) that he is wrong. That kind of truth is of ethical rather than epistemological import.

But Paneloux's sermon, even (or especially) if "truth" falsely resounds in it, must be taken in a context considered by speech-act theorists, or, simply, in context. It presents itself rhetorically as expressing truth, but it *is* not truth. Rieux does not use such terms (like Meursault, he leans toward the concrete and the factual). Camus, nevertheless, often does. The use of the word "truth" (as by Paneloux) hardly establishes its reality but it is an important one in Camus. Here is one definition of truth: "everything that continues" (N, 72), a definition which contains an irreducible paradox, particularly in the light of what follows—truth as the present. The text speaks of the Tuscan painters, those "novelists of the body" ("romanciers du corps," N, 72–73), who "work in this magnificent and futile matter which is called the present" (N, 73). The present of the painters' art is the truth that lasts. That is the esthetic paradox that may correspond to the diachronicity of Rieux's role as physician-narrator or the synchronicity of Clamence's existence as judge-penitent.

The paradoxical cast of Camus's thought has often been noted, in its affinities with such works as Augustine's, Pascal's, and Malraux's. From the "absurd" to "revolt," throughout Camus's essays and fiction, the sharp edge of paradox brands the form of consciousness onto the indifference of the world. In theory, Camus's "either / or" is relentless and unmediated, although the author attempted to propose viable ethical imperatives, practical absolutes, so to speak, which, however, seemed to satisfy him as little as his Existentialist detractors. This brings us back to the matter of truth by way of ethics.

If the action of *The Stranger* takes place at high noon under the Algerian sun, in the mute and uncompromising justice of the principle, a life for a life, a death for a death (and every life for every death), in *The*

*Fall* the little *"soupçon"* of shade to which *The Plague* alludes is transformed into the pervasive mists of a setting which, as has been pointed out, resembles the circles of Hell as much as it resembles the city of Amsterdam. And that plunge into Hell has been wrought by the splash in the water, an additional, unexpected pseudo-event in the hero's life. These small additional events, this "something else" can be as paradoxical as the wide antinomies of the general theme. In *The Plague*, the first rat discovered in Oran also seems *"de trop,"* an inexplicable presence which the concierge of the building is quick to explain away. And the bacillus of the plague is a little organism hiding away in linen closets until it monstrously expands into a vast catastrophe.

Is there, then, something else than the something else? "One at least learns there [says Camus about Florence] to count on nothing and to consider the present as the only truth which is given us in 'addition' *[par 'surcroît']*" (N, 85–86). So the present is truth, but that truth is "par surcroît." How can that *surcroît*, that surplus, be circumscribed? How is it related to truth and ethics? Is it related to writing? If Camus seeds his texts with allusions to "something else" and repeatedly sends light signals, it must be because blind spots in artists tend not to be completely blind. As Derrida says, they "open and limit visibility."

Camus's lyrical Preface to the 1958 edition of *The Wrong Side and the Right Side*[8] may provide a full context for his own conception of a "dangerous" but vital "supplement." The author explains his earlier reluctance and later decision to republish these texts which date back to his youth. What is in question throughout is the relation between the power, for him, of the early images and scenes contained in these pages and a certain immaturity in the writer's craft. Against this underlying structure, themes and motifs play against each other. A recurring one is the unsatisfactory quality of any finished work. From the beginning, a back-and-forth movement is established — between the "two contrary dangers that threaten every artist, resentment and satisfaction"; between the return to a source ("I know that my source is in *The Wrong Side and the Right Side*, in this world of poverty and light," WS, 13) and the work of writing; between exile and a "paradise"; between resistance and freedom. The note of "resistances" is struck in connection with an artistic tradition, as if it were, in Pascalian terms, a "second nature" as powerful as the first:

> . . . there are in me, it must be repeated, artistic resistances, just as there are, in others, moral or religious resistances. Interdiction, the idea that "this isn't done," which is rather foreign to me as a son of a free nature, is present to me as a slave, and an admiring slave, of a rigorous artistic tradition. (WS, 30)

Camus admits that "The dikes I have erected, today still, are perhaps too high." There is an imagery of clarity, light, and certainty — Camus knows where his source is, where his love started — contrasted to vague threats of anarchy, violence, and despair. Allusions to a certain "stiffness" (*raideur*) reinforce the impression of constraint and artifice. Other classical words, familiar in Camus — "balance," "nature and art" — seem to conceal rather than reveal the nature of the conflict and the object of the writer's quest.

The purpose here is not to engage in a hunt for psychoanalytic clues, and even less to venture an interpretation of them. But Camus's own use of "little" signs resembles a gesture pointing to something like a Freudian slip, or a stylistic or other deviance that arrests one's attention. In *The Plague*, such signs — the rats, or skin eruptions that manifest the disease — describe a medical symptomology. In the Preface to *The Wrong Side and the Right Side*, psychoanalysis seems close. The word "resistances," somewhat surprising for Camus, is striking in its context. It appears when the author begins to treat the painful question of the revelation made known by art. Shortly thereafter comes an unexpected quotation from Stendhal — the only direct quotation from another author in this text: "Stendhal exclaimed one day: 'But *my* soul is a fire that suffers, if it doesn't blaze' " (WS, 31–32). Camus comments that the "cry" comes straight out of such a flame and "creates its words." This is what artists, "uncertain of being artists," wait for "day after day, in order to finally consent to live."

After this revelatory and bold image borrowed from Stendhal — a fire that suffers — the rest of the Preface seems to flow naturally to its end. It includes first of all the acceptance of silence: "It is thus today and I need not say any more" (WS, 32). After that, several strong motifs mark the path of a smooth creative movement: "waiting"; "this long advance" ("ce long cheminement"); "the detours of art"; "my work is not even begun." All these motifs are under the sign of the dream. "Yes, nothing prevents us from dreaming, at the very hour of exile" (WS, 33). The dream is finally stated here — "to rewrite *The Wrong Side and the Right Side*." To wait for words to be created out of that "cry" in the flame and to set out for the "long advance" through the "detours of art" in order to find the origin of love (in "two or three simple great images") is the undertaking equated with "consenting to live." Freud's *Beyond the Pleasure Principle* speaks in similar terms of the "detour" ("*Umweg*") of life and of the text itself, with death always in sight. Likewise in Camus, but this time, the end is a beginning — "my work is not even begun." The return to the beginning is a movement of life because what Camus is describing is a harmonious blending of life and art in which the two have become inseparable. In that sought-for place, this "quiet homeland," words and silence become interchangeable — "death itself is a happy silence."

Undoubtedly the dream, pursued in the detours of art, is no trifling matter — it is not a "*soupçon*" of something half dismissed, which in any case changes life very little. It seems to make exile bearable and hold out a promise if not of continuation, at least of repetition and return. Exile and "homeland" seem to merge, or perhaps the "*cheminement*" of art is the bridge that links the two. In this state of things, which is also a process and a movement, the present must be redefined. Indeed, the Preface explains: "this is to be, to be capable of everything ('tout pouvoir en même temps'). In art, everything comes simultaneously or nothing comes; no lights without flames" (WS, 31). Could it be true that the present is no longer itself the "*surcroît*," the supplement, as it was in *Nuptials*, but is in turn supplemented? Certainly the return to the images of a beginning constitutes a new kind of present, one in which what is "always already" there calls for renewed beginnings. As in Derrida, the "addition" does not add anything. But the substitution of *being* for the *present* makes possible possibility itself, which is synonymous with the power of art.

**Notes**

1. Jacques Derrida, *De la Grammatologie* (Paris: Minuit, 1967). The translations are the author's. Hereafter referred to as DLG.

2. That "*supplément*," for Derrida, delays mediation and finally becomes a chain of substitutions.

3. Albert Camus, *Noces* (Paris: Gallimard, 1950). All translations are the author's. (*Nuptials*) Hereafter referred to as N.

4. Albert Camus, *La Peste* (Paris: Gallimard, 1947). All translations are the author's. (*The Plague*) Hereafter referred to as P.

5. Germaine Brée, *Camus*, rev. ed. (New York, Chicago, Burlingame: Harcourt, Brace & World, 1964), 77.

6. Robert Champigny, *Sur un héros païen* (Paris: Gallimard, 1959).

7. Jean-Paul Sartre, "Explication de *L'Étranger*," in *Situations I* (Paris: Gallimard, 1947).

8. Albert Camus, *L'Envers et l'Endroit* (Paris: Gallimard, 1958). All translations are the author's. (*The Wrong Side and the Right Side*) Hereafter referred to as WS.

# Existential Exile and a Glimpse of the Kingdom
## Diana Festa-McCormick*

Camus, like Flaubert, Zola, and Sartre himself, came to write short stories after having already mastered the technique of the novel or, at any rate, of the "récit." He had waxed impatient as if burdened by too long and too monotonous a self-imposed task while he was composing *The Plague*. As a relief and until he could withdraw to the relative seclusion of his retreat in Southern France, he wrote several stories between 1955 and 1957. One of them, *The Fall*, became too long to be included with the other six and was published independently as a complex and ingeniously

*This essay was written especially for this volume and is published here for the first time by permission of the author.

wrought monologue. None of the stories gathered in *Exile and the Kingdom* reaches the same perfection of craftsmanship or offers revelations of the same order on Camus's own inner struggles. Two or three have psychological depth, social impact, and promise to remain as masterful examples of evocative, restrained prose: "The Renegade," "The Host," "The Adulterous Woman." They are likely to be for some time included in anthologies of modern French stories and be the first introduction to Camus for many students.

The title adopted by Camus for his collection is a felicitous one, mysterious and admirably fitting the lifelong concerns of the Algerian writer who never ceased feeling like a stranger in France. Several of the stories are laid in an exotic and African scene—one of them in Brazil whose forests, rivers, and inhabitants strongly impressed Camus when he visited the country briefly in 1949. Only one, "The Artist at Work" ("Jonas" in the French title), bears traces of the author's residence in France, where he found himself, as a successful and famous personality, oppressed by professional and social engagements and deprived of leisure for meditation and self-renewal. Camus's ambivalence as a man residing simultaneously in the public domain and in the necessarily private one of the artist is suggested by the word "exile." He felt exiled from his Mediterranean origin and the intoxicating North African landscapes. In Tuscany, where he travelled in a rapturous mood, and more particularly in Greece, he felt more at home. He hailed the light, "the noontide of existence," stressed by the Greeks, as offsetting the darkness dear to Western Europeans.[1] He upbraided the moderns for having exiled Helen, the personification of beauty, while the Greeks had taken up arms for her. Rashly he prophesied the eventual return to beauty in a world yearning for the lost kingdom. In his stories, the Renegade and Daru have allowed themselves to be exiled from their kingdom, from that larger communion with man and place for which D'Arrast longs when taking over the burden of his Brazilian friend. Inevitably the word kingdom also suggests the solemn declaration of Christ confronting Pilate: "My kingdom is not of this world" (John 18, 36). The true kingdom for Camus is likewise not anything of this world but an arcane entity residing within man himself. Without being a preacher, Camus is a moralist in the tradition of Descartes, Pascal, Rousseau—not concerned with metaphysical, ultimate, and insoluble questions but with man's behavior toward his fellow man.

The six stories that make up Camus's last volume reassert the author's perception of morality as a loose blend of personal experiences and needs, of struggles which allow resolutions to emerge from a welter of uncertainty. Singular experiences either strengthen characters into a new cohesiveness or shatter their whole beings. The moral message that may be read between the lines of these stories is not reached through intellectual commitments or deliberately made choices. It may not be unjustified to characterize Camus's perspective as that of a reflexive moralist distrustful of the intellect — distrustful even more of Manichean oppositions between right and wrong. Nowhere does Camus offer a dogmatic judgment or propose uniform solutions to complex issues. He sedulously eschews the conventional technique of the short story that works toward a climax and a dénouement contriving a surprise effect. He likewise refrains from allowing similarities or parallels to creep into the varied tales.

Each story offers a fresh start and each has its original tone. "The Artist at Work" resorts to the third person narrative. "The Silent Men" (more impressive in its French title, "Les Muets," suggesting speechless, embarrassed men, and not just silent) is also set in a realistic frame. "The Renegade" reads like a horrifying monologue, placed boldly in the mind if not in the mouth of the tortured missionary. "The Guest" is steeped, with moving restraint, in the social and political climate of the Algerian war. "The Growing Stone" hesitantly carries symbolic meanings without imposing them to skeptical readers. "The Adulterous Woman" successfully blends elements of poetry in the evocation of the Algerian desert with the creation (unique in the whole range of Camus's fiction) of a real, anguished, unfulfilled female character. A note of dissatisfaction with their prosaic fate, of rebelliousness against the exile to which they are doomed, and of yearning for an imaginary kingdom, discreetly rings through the very diverse tales. None of them really involves a multiplicity of actors, but each focuses essentially upon one character. In this, Camus respects the primary rule of the genre, that of concentration.

The first story (composed in 1952 and first published in Algiers in 1954) is half-ironically entitled "The Adulterous Woman." The central character is an altogether believable woman accompanying her husband, a prosaic salesman, in a trip to Moslem villages on the border of the African desert. She is forlorn, bored, alienated from her middle-class existence, patient with her uninspiring mate, but hardly likely to confide her thoughts and longings to him. Listless, passive, she is barely aware of other passengers, of silent, dignified Arabs in their burnooses. She registers sensations of estrangement without analyzing them as the wind blows clouds of sand over the desert. She faintly recalls her past, the everyday struggles, her acceptance of monotony with no prospect of change. There is no urge to revolt in her, no dream of escape. She is a disinterested vagabond in an alien world, prisoner of her burdensome body and heavy soul. A thought painfully crosses her mind, "She was going to die in truth, without having been liberated."[2] But at night, obeying a mysterious call, she sneaks outside in the cold splendor of the African desert and climbs to a tower she had seen in the day. In a flitting moment of pantheistic communion with nature,  her back pressed against the parapet, she reaches toward the sky that bends over her. From her briefly visited kingdom of beauty she returns to her exile. "It's nothing, dear it's nothing," she replies to her awakened husband. Her adultery has been symbolic, her tears are only the mirror of the liquid beauty she had embraced in her glimpse of eternity.

It was bold of Camus to bequeath to us the image of a woman who makes love to the stars and who, for the fraction of a moment in the span of time, breathes in primordial oneness with the cosmos. His technique is to switch back and forth between a realistic setting and the heroine's inner disarray. Descriptions in the story are incorporated in Janine's experience, the elements of nature and people become selected frames in her world of sensory perceptions. From the opening lines, the third person narrative projects at the same time external events and Janine's personal apprehension of them. "A housefly had been circling for the last minutes in the bus, though the windows were closed." Immediately after, an absent narrator observes, "An odd sight here, it had been silently flying back and forth on tired wings." But to the impersonal voice of the narrator a more direct perception is added, that of the heroine: "Janine lost track of it, then saw it light on her husband's motionless hand." The focus is subtly enlarged, and from this point on all contingencies in Janine's foreign landscape become the center of a wider search. If her quest remains caught in uncertainty at the end, she does nevertheless regain sight of an initial wholeness lost in the quandary of bourgeois existence.

This first story holds a premise to which the others adhere in varied degrees—that in a society fragmented by contradictory impulses man has lost his sense of cohesiveness. The recovery of harmony can hardly be gained deliberately through intellectual notions, however. The only possible rescue from social disarray rests with man's surrender to a privileged moment, in which natural and vital forces surge anew. The stories in *Exile and the Kingdom* may be said to fall into two groups: the first one allows man to recapture his wholeness, placed in a larger sphere of existence. Along with "The Adulterous Woman," "The Growing Stone," and "The Silent Men" would belong there. "The Renegade," "The Guest," and "The Artist at Work" would appear to make the broad assumption that man founders when he submits to artificial, borrowed concepts that stand at odds with his deeper nature.

The second story in the collection, "The Renegade," is the most striking and perhaps the most artistically composed. Much has been written on this remarkable tale of hallucinating cruelty, where pride and the urge to dominate wage unremitting war to charity and humility. The protagonist of the story obeys the imperatives of dogmatic beliefs and turns prey to a hatred reminiscent of the Nazi's cult of supremacy and of destruction. The crispness of its language contrasts with the lyrical prose of Camus's early essays on Algeria. It is a violent story of grim brutality and images of unbearable pain, with a quick tempo that projects hidden regions of lust and sadism. A missionary, recently converted from the Protestant to the Catholic faith, defiantly embarks on a mission to redeem from utter evil a tribe of men dwelling in a land of implacable sun upon a mountain of salt. Taghasa is the name of that inferno that all charity and fraternity have shunned. The Renegade finds that the obscene force of evil triumphs over his God of love, that the Idol venerated in this land of apocalyptic atrocity is the strongest and the only reigning God. The Calvary he had proudly sought for his mortified senses is now a source of hatred. He is forced to witness hideous sights of rape, and "screams of pain and possession" become his daily *via crucis*. The Sorcerer is master here. Then one day an idol-like girl tantalizingly proffers her nakedness to him. Hell ceases to be a concept at this point and becomes a lived experience. The men of Taghasa beat him mercilessly, grip his jaws, open his mouth, tear his tongue which was to bring his Christian message. He becomes the martyr he had once dreamt of being. Finally conquered by hatred, the Renegade basks in its power. He dismisses all thoughts of love and waits in the unflinching desert sun for the arrival of the new missionary, whom he will kill. But total evil proves as theoretical a machination of the mind as total goodness had been. Irrepressibly, a voice within him clamors for a new kingdom of hope. In the darkness of approaching death, the Renegade is adrift in uncertainty.

Readers are left with a sense of awe after this journey in the bleak recesses of the mind with its graphic illustration of evil. No didactic element or message has infiltrated the tale of sheer horror. Yet Camus seems to hint that the Renegade had wrongly searched for an ideological absolute, lying to himself and denying the kingdom of a natural, sensual life. Symbolically, the Renegade utters no words but only inarticulate "gra gra." From those guttural sounds of mental anguish and burning pain images will have taken shape, bidden from an obsessive memory of unrequited yearnings. Those images spread before the mind's eye and recreate for the reader a story of passion and tragic fault.

Camus did not attempt to repeat this masterpiece of nightmarish cruelty. The next story, "The Silent Men," does not have the hectic pace and obsessively recurring images found in "The Renegade." It opens on a more idyllic note: "It was the dead of winter and yet a radiant sun was rising over the already active city. At the end of the jetty, sea and sky fused in a single dazzling light. But Yvars did not see them" (EK, 62). The brevity of the sentences creates the effect of frames distilled from wide spaces and objects, each self contained and a microcosm of the large whole. The frames thus evoked by Camus's masterly prose remain separate. They encompass a view of the sky and of the distant city, of the nearby jetty and vast sea, and of the man held captive of his unresolved emotion. The sentences are brief and jerky, the whole produces a sense of isolation.

The story gets its title from a small group of men back to work in a cooper's yard after an unsuccessful strike and their silent confrontation with the owner of the place, symbol of their oppression. There is rancor in them and scant hope in their hearts. Yvar begins his day in despondency, alienated from man and nature. But the code of silence to which he clings with his coworkers brings a sense of solidarity. When they learn that the boss's child is gravely ill, resentment grudgingly gives way to compassion. At the end, when Yvar is back home with his wife, on the terrace facing the sea, reconciliation takes place: "The sky was becoming transparent; over the wall the soft evening sea was visible" (EK, 83).

The story is quite short but it manages to convey the problems of the passing of years and aging and the helplessness of dedicated craftsmen whose security is increasingly menaced by the inroads of industrialization. Not much happens here, there are no dramatic turns or violent confrontations. The tone is restrained and it translates a more optimistic and sentimental side of Camus. A sense of regret vaguely fills the air at the end, as Yvar muses that aging prevents him to start anew "across the sea." But with regret one senses simple acceptance. No ideology or intellectual interpretation is allowed, no polemical argumentation such as was, in the nineteen fifties, rife among Existentialist circles in Paris.

"The Guest" may be read as closer to presenting a dilemma and the necessity for a tragic choice to some of the Existentialists. It is also a more gripping story in its conciseness and its avoidance of all melodrama. It probably remains one of the most widely read and anthologized of the six tales and, a quarter of a century after the Algerian war and the fierce debates that it aroused in the French intelligentsia, it stands as one of the most deeply touching literary pieces on that war. The chronicles that Camus gave in the very same years to the press on the Algerian dilemma testify to his loyal efforts to do justice to the two sides — that of his mother, as he called it, and that of the Algerian Arabs with whom he had played and studied in his youth.

The story is set in the Algerian countryside in a school where the master, Daru, teaches Arab children, understands their language and needs, but still feels socially and culturally an exile. Written in 1954, just as the Algerian rebellion began in the Eastern part of the country, the story reflects the difficulty encountered in all efforts to communicate and the impossibility to win the confidence of the population for a teacher who appears as a symbol of colonization. One day a French gendarme brings a prisoner whom he entrusts to the reluctant guard of Daru, who is in turn to take him to jail some miles away. Daru is revolted by the brutal murder the youth has committed. Still, he treats him with kindness, shares his food, makes his bed and, on the next morning, instead of surrendering him to the police, offers him two options — he may escape and join the Nomads or he may walk toward the police station. The prisoner utters few words and clearly does not understand the "existential" choice that confronts him. He hardly knows why he had killed ("He ran away, I ran after him") and has probably been touched by Daru's manifested trust and generosity. "Come with us," he begs, naively thinking perhaps that Daru may join the rebel Arab forces. When he is left at the bottom of the hill to fend for himself, he probably only tries to guess what is expected of him. The look on his face is blank. "Listen," he pleads. But Daru's is the discourse of the deaf, one is tempted to conclude, the clumsy language of words divested of inner echo. He does not explain, he does not "listen." The youth stands motionless until his host disappears over the hill and then he takes the road to prison.

Daru is treated with sympathy by the author. But that does not diminish the fact that he has betrayed his mission as teacher by not conveying to the young criminal the importance and inviolability of freedom, by not attempting to communicate, either in pedagogical or in human terms, abhorrence against murder and prison alike. Trapped in his own alienation in a land he loves but that rebuffs him, he stands condemned. Silently he watches the Arab walk to his surrender. When he returns to school he finds scribbled on the blackboard a message of hate, "You have surrendered our brother. You will pay for this." The rapture he had momentarily experienced in the contemplation of the sky and the desert is gone. All is opaque now, held in a pall of sadness. With no display of imagery, no attempt at poetry, no intrusion of ideology, the story of "the Guest" (the French "L'Hôte" designates a guest, but also and primarily the host) is one of the most restrainedly moving in *Exile and the Kingdom*.

"The Artist at Work" ("Jonas" in the French title) was first published in Algiers in 1953 under the title "La Vie d'Artiste," and then reprinted to be a "mimodrama." The theme of the artist held in social and family clutches had been uppermost in Camus's mind since 1951, when he had been catapulted into notoriety and celebrity by the success of his work and the violence of his public debates on philosophical and political subjects. His notebooks, his correspondence,[3] disclose Camus's quandary and growing anguish. He yearned for solitude, so as to focus undisturbed on his writing, and yet he needed companionship, the stimulation of talk, the tribute of admirers, the presence of women. Literary creation required a selfish banishment of all distracting activity and he began to doubt that he had the moral strength to live and work in voluntary exile. He also realized that to be popular meant to be both misunderstood and betrayed, and to be praised for one's superficial virtues at the expense of more deeply felt commitments.

The Jonas of the story is a successful painter. Dealers, would-be collectors, disciples, friends, and potential rivals flock to him. The demands made by his wife and children increase. Only too late does he attempt to renounce the turmoil brought by fame and to withdraw into a flimsy studio erected over his living quarters. But he is by now obsessed by fear of sterility, much as Baudelaire and Mallarmé had been, as was Camus himself. He works feverishly for days on end, believing he has regained his old fervor. But when he collapses at the end, only a few letters are found painted upon the blank canvas. They spell "solitary," or perhaps "solidary." The two words, which appear interchangeable, show indeed the two self-excluding choices confronted by the artist. He can either be solidary, and receive from the world around him social comfort, or he can be solitary, and allow his innermost self to feed his creative imagination.

"The Artist at Work" is perhaps too laden with irony verging on satire. The banal circumstances of Jonas's life may have been stretched beyond plausibility and the characters may not always appear fully convincing. But the strength of the story lies in the overall impression it leaves with the reader, in the picture it draws of the artist's plight in modern society. Theories, schools of thought, are indirectly shown to have little or no relevance to creativity. For Jonas, they prove a destructive intrusion upon his natural gift, and his ability to paint in direct communion with beauty becomes thereby contaminated.

The twin themes of solitude and the groping for fraternity are at the core of the last story, initially entitled "Iguape" and later "The Growing Stone." The French title contains an untranslatable ambiguity in the verb ("La Pierre qui pousse"), which means both to push and to grow. The stone in question may be seen as a symbol of the cross, the unbearable weight which, sustained in superhuman effort by a man in an act of love, brings redemption and fraternity. Alone among Camus's writings, the story is laid in a setting of the New World, in the wilderness of Brazil, among simple villagers whose Christian faith is imbued with pagan traditions, rites, and superstitions. The tale, quite long and strange, was written after a short trip by Camus to Brazil in 1949.[4] The by then celebrated French author was invited to lecture there. He fretted at the official character of his visit and escaped when he could to the poorer areas of the country, among simple people, who talked and danced with abandon, whose superstitious beliefs were a bewildering Afro-Catholic mixture of fear and faith. The descriptive passages of the tale convey the impression of the strangeness Camus must have felt at the sight of the tropical jungle and watching the customs of the natives.

The central character is a French engineer, D'Arrast, who has come to build bridges over untamed waters. He observes the inhabitants with curiosity, then with a growing sense of sympathy, and he realizes that his work for them and among them will forge bonds of fraternal support. He feels drawn by the passion of their wild dances and naive beliefs. "Yonder in Europe, there was shame and wrath. Here, exile or solitude, among these listless and convulsive madmen who danced to die" (EK, 198). A native by the name of Socrates has explained to the agnostic foreigner that a stone had been found in the river on "the day of the feast of good Jesus." Fishermen had placed it in the grotto and they came periodically to cut off pieces from the hard block as talismans. Yet the stone kept on growing. Every year pilgrims march in procession to celebrate the miraculous event. A cook, who serves as D'Arrast's guide, has made a vow to carry the hundred pound stone to church. But he is too weakened from a night of orgy to fulfill his vow and grows desperate. In a sudden impulse, D'Arrast takes on his head the heavy burden that was crushing the penitent cook. Tired, encouraged by the admiring natives, the new Sisyphus enters for a fleeting moment the kingdom of fraternal love for his fellow beings. "The sound of waters filled him with a tumultous happiness. With eyes closed, he joyfully acclaimed his own strength; he acclaims, once again, a fresh beginning in life" (EK, 212).

"The Growing Stone" is rich in scenery, in images of crowds, of people milling, swaying, dancing and, while D'Arrast is the central character, there are others whose personalities are sufficiently well drawn. The story is quite long and could easily have been worked out in a "récit" or short novel. Its painterly quality conveys to D'Arrast's subjective experiences an enlarged focus—his loneliness, his sense of discovery, and his broadened identity are visually communicated to the reader, so as to become to a degree the reader's own experience. The ferocious sensuality so intermixed with cruelty and repression one found appalling in "The Renegade" has been transmuted here in images of strange appeal, where the grotesque appears both bewitching and human. "Their heads would wag backward and forward literally separated from a decapitated body. At the same time all began to howl incessantly with a long collective and toneless howl, apparently not pausing to breathe or to introduce modulations—as if bodies were tightly knotted, muscles and nerves, in a single exhausting outburst. . ." (EK, 194–95). The pagan flavor of the scenes exerts a magnetizing force whose appeal to the senses is urgent. Camus, who had granted scant attention to the Moslem rites and to the Catholic liturgy amid which he had grown up in Algeria, imparts to his character D'Arrast—and through him, to his readers—an almost rapturous thrill of physical and spiritual bliss drawn from a more naive cult.

The enigmatic title *Exile and the Kingdom* endows the stories there assembled with a unity of purpose. Camus not only did not fear monotony, he praised it as the chief virtue of what he called "classicism." "To be classical is to know how to repeat oneself" and to achieve "a passionate monotony."[5] The ambiguity or the dilemma suggested by the two nouns in the title, the oscillation between absurdist pessimism and "Mediterranean" faith in the life of the senses, and the communion with beauty in nature endow the stories with an affecting vibration. One likes to think that the author would have composed more stories had he lived after the publication of that last volume for they seem ideally fitted in their brevity to illustrate one of his strongest beliefs, "Life always favors those who love it."[6]

Along with the underlying unity, which under varied impersonations imprints Camus's long standing concerns as an imaginative moralist upon the six sections of *Exile and the Kingdom*, a diversity of tone and of technique impresses the reader. The six tales are not equally successful but none of them yields to facile virtuosity with effects of surprise, clashes of characters, or unexpected dénouement. Theatrical effects are avoided by the novelist who was, in the years when he composed his stories, tempted by the dramatic form. Indeed, he proves more effective in discreet, evocative pieces such as "The Adulterous Woman" and "The Guest" than he was in his plays, where he laboriously contrived effects of surprise and offered hardly disguised didactic messages. The tension that makes stories like "The Renegade" and "The Growing Stone" moving remains inward and subtly restrained. The prose, variously descriptive and colorful at times, is evocative of the Algerian countryside, the desert and luminous sun, the Brazilian jungle, rivers, and mysterious sounds. It is invariably free from rhetoric and sentimentality. The display of oversimplified syntax and the masterful manipulation of expression that characterized *The Stranger* are almost absent from *Exile and the Kingdom*. So is the dryness that the novelist had intentionally achieved in *The Plague*. But nowhere has Camus come as close as in these stories to his cherished aim of finding "the exact appropriation of form and matter, of language and subject."[7]

## Notes

1. See the interview with Emile Simon, first published in *La Revue du Caire*, quoted here from Albert Camus, *Essais* (Paris: Bibliothèque de la Pléiade, Editions Gallimard, 1965), 379. See also in the same volume "L'Exil d' Hélène," 853–57.

2. Albert Camus, *Exile and the Kingdom*, trans. Justin O'Brien (New York: Knopf, 1974) 29; hereafter cited as *EK* followed by page number.

3. See a particularly revealing letter by Camus to a friend, Pierre Berger, who had complained to the suddenly famous author that he no longer had any time for friendship. The letter is dated 15 February 1953 and appears in Albert Camus, *Théâtre, Récits, Nouvelles* (Paris: Bibliothèque de la Pléiade, Editions Gallimard, 1962), 2061–63.

4. For further light on the subject, see the extracts from Albert Camus, *Notebooks*, ed. Roger Quilliot (Paris: Bibliothèque de la Pléiade, Editions Gallimard, 1962).

5. See the essay published by Camus during the war in *Confluences*, included in *Problèmes du Roman*, ed. René Tavernier (Lyon: René Tavernier, 1943), 220.

6. Camus's beloved teacher, Jean Grenier, states that his pupil remained faithful to that belief. See the introduction to Camus, *Essais*, xix.

7. Ibid., interviews of 1945, 1427.

# Intertextuality in Albert Camus    Jeanine Parisier Plottel*

Albert Camus's account of his personal history was rooted in error. Whereas he believed that his father's family emigrated to Algeria from Alsace after 1871, the French public records office, the Service Central de

*This essay was written especially for this volume and is published here for the first time by permission of the author.

l'État Civil in Nantes, found data showing that the first known member of the Camus family to live in Algeria, Claude Camus, Albert's great-grandfather, was born in Bordeaux in 1809. He migrated to Ouled Fayet, a village near Algiers in the earliest years of French colonization.[1] An American reader may fail to perceive any notable difference between Alsace and the Bordeaux region, or even Marseilles, the birthplace of Claude's son, Baptiste Jules Marius, the "Alsatian" ancestor Albert had in mind. In a French-Algerian context, it is likely that a recent Alsatian extraction would carry a higher status than the more common meridional lineage of an ordinary French colonist whose ancestors had been share-croppers. *Alsatian* conveys the connotation of all the positive traits of a Germanic heritage: seriousness, integrity, conscientiousness, hardworking, pragmatism, honesty. Furthermore, French patriotism impregnates all these virtues. The implication is that the family chose France over Germany and sought to remember all the indignities of the Franco-Prussian War. The stereotypes of a Bordeaux or Marseilles provenance usually suggests more easygoing, less educated ways.

The genealogy of Albert Camus, not necessarily his actual genealogy but the genealogy he imagined, may be compared to a treasure chest containing a stock of riches to be drawn upon for the purpose of creating an image of the self he would present in his writing. It is easy to suppose that the Spanish side, the cruel strong grandmother and the silent, maimed mother of *L'Envers et l'endroit* contributed a sense of alienation, aloofness, pride, boredom. The Spanish sense transmitted to his work some of the traits that make us perceive the author as a Mediterranean man. According to Salvador de Madariaga, the Spanish writer who was Spanish Ambassador to Washington before Franco came to power, Camus is one of a small handful of French writers to have really felt Spain, not merely a writer who used Spanish texts, but a writer who was able to effect a synthesis of the real Spain and the Spain of the literary imagination.[2]

The Alsatian element, pseudo though it was, translated itself into rigorous moral values and flawless ethical positions. Much like the name of *Alsace* in books Camus must have read as a child—I am thinking, for example, of the 19th century books by Emile Erckmann and Alexandre Chatrian, who wrote about Alsatian customs under the name Erckmann-Chatrian—his own name has become synonymous with ideals of modern French liberalism and humanism. France had been ravaged by war, but during the war, from the *France d'Outre Mer*, a writer emerged in the tradition of its greatest moralists, a writer who was ranked with La Rochefoucauld, Mme de La Fayette, and La Bruyère, the French counter-part of Ignazio Silone, Salvador de Madariaga, and Arthur Koestler. Algeria, the country that had become Camus's land, takes on the shape of sun, light, water, beaches, exotic semitropical landscapes, pretty girls, and the dandy who is their rival.

My fanciful representation may not be entirely accurate. Accuracy in linking what we know of a writer's background with his work may have more to do with our own perception of the self in the work than with any verifiable truth. The Albert Camus I have constructed from my reading of his works and of the works about him may be far removed from the Albert Camus made of flesh and bones, to use Miguel de Unamuno's expression. But that is also true of how we define anybody's self at all. Family? Occupation? National origins? Physical attributes? Sex and gender? Publications? Religion? Clubs? Such are but some of the categories that may be chosen, and it all depends on the context.

The point I want to make in this essay is somewhat different, however. Just as I can construct a model of the textual self out of the author's genealogy, so this genealogy can lead me to imagine a paradigm for the textual production of this textual self. In such a framework, texts may be analyzed as if they embodied the written representation of the author's life, thought, or experience sifted through the amalgam of all the texts he has ever read. In short, the treasure chest is turned into a branch library of Jorge Luis Borges's library of Babel, the library containing all the books of the universe; it becomes the local intertextuality from whence the writer's own productions will develop. If I examine Camus's intertextuality in this spirit, and if I consider that his genealogy is a metaphor that can be used to define his uniqueness, I can expect to discover that the intertextuality he imagined—the literary tradition he set forth for himself—will have the same characteristics as his genealogy and the same tenuous connection with reality.

Which books and authors did Camus consider his forebears? André de Richaud's *La Douleur* was the book he claimed gave him the confidence that he too had something to express. Jean Grenier, André Gide, André Malraux, and Henry de Montherlant are the contemporary French writers he avowed for his masters. Herman Melville, Franz Kafka, Fyodor Dostoyevsky, Leo Tolstoy, and Friedrich Nietzsche were the foreign names towards whom he admitted a debt.[3] Max-Pol Fouchet's list of his friend's preferred texts added the *Bible*, Henri Barbusse, *La Nouvelle Revue Française*, and *Europe*. Claude de Fréminville included populist literature and Katherine Mansfield's *Journal*.[4]

This partiality for the "best" writers or for writers of correct social persuasion is comparable to Jean-Baptiste Clamence's fondness of elegant language, "le beau langage," for the imperfect subjunctive, for example. The list is carefully chosen and all the items have what I should like to call a Sunday-best appearance. Camus surely believed that these lofty figures were indeed his textual mentors and friends. He sought to write novels that would be like those of Melville, "whose admirable books are among those exceptional books that can be read in different ways, mysterious and obvious at the same time, with the obscurity of the full sun, and the transparency of deep water."[5] He was drawn to Gide insofar as he was the

master of modern classicism, the Gide who was the author of *Prétextes*. "I
know the anarchy of my nature, and in art I need to give myself barriers.
Gide taught me to do so. His conception of classicism considered as a
romanticism that is tamed, is also my conception."[6] Yet the impression is
that Camus wears such writers and themes as if they were designer's labels
meant to enhance his own value in the eyes of his audience. Let me give
some examples.

Critics have paid considerable attention to *The Fall*'s possible
sources.[7] An article by a close friend, Jean Bloch-Michel, "Une littérature
de l'ennui," deals with the tradition of the monologue between one's self
and an interlocutor who remains silent: Dostoyevsky, Balzac, Musset, and
Cocteau. Bloch-Michel cites *Krotkaia*, a short story by Dostoyevsky in the
work translated into French as *Journal d'un écrivain*: "Sometimes the man
is talking to himself, and sometimes he is addressing an invisible auditor, *a
kind of judge*."[8] René Micha's remarkable essay, "L'agneau dans le placard," examines the links between *The Fall* and Stavroguine's confessions.
For example, Stravroguine's description of Claude Lorrain's painting
*D'Acis et Galatée* that he calls "L'Age d'Or," "The Golden Age," has much
in common with the painting Jean-Baptiste Clamence calls *L'Agneau
Mystique*. An exceptional article by Léon-François Hoffmann in *Revue
d'Histoire de la France* analyzed some similarities between this novel and
Jean Lorrain's, *Monsieur de Bougrelon*.[9] The connections between *The
Fall* and the Camus / Sartre polemic in *Les Temps modernes* were examined
at length by Roger Quilliot in the April 1960 issue of *Preuves*. I suspect
that Camus would have approved the representation of such genealogies
for his work. The implication is that the company they keep qualify his
books as "Great Books." Even Jean Lorrain — but I am unsure about this —
might have appealed to his "dandy" side, because a little decadent spice
here and there is desirable in modern classics.

In fact, there is little intertextuality at work here. What has been
borrowed are technical processes and devices. Furthermore, Camus was a
great imitator. His notion was that the classics endlessly repeat the same
themes: "Etre classique, c'est en même temps se répéter et savoir se
répéter."[10] Camus mastered this technique to a very high degree. He played
on a certain conception of man and humanity expressed by the writers of
Great Books, and produced his own up-to-date versions. His virtuosity in
the assimilation of styles and techniques probably earned him his present
position in French literature. While the works that Camus drew upon may
be considered to be his sources, in the sense that traditional criticism gave
to this term, perhaps we should discriminate between chance encounters,
sources, imitation, and intertextuality. Recent critical literature has been
engaged in the coining of terms that will elaborate on some of the
distinctions that should be drawn. Rather than participate in the proliferation of nomenclature, I should like to keep these terms and try to clarify
some of the issues. At the risk of being simplistic, I will postulate that a

source is the author's conscious, or at the very least semiconscious use of another work; imitation is the attempt to represent by copying; intertextuality should be reserved for borrowing that is unconscious, that is to say, repressed. Other coincidences will be dismissed as chance encounters. For example, everyone in America uses the greeting "Hello." Hemingway cannot be deemed a source for Salinger merely because characters of one and the other often say "hello" to each other. These are expressions and words that are used by every writer of a given time and place.

I shall not deal with the topoi of *imitation* in Camus. Many authors have already written about this, and there is a large bibliography devoted to Camus and Melville, Camus and Dostoyevsky, Camus and Gide, Camus and Bernanos, Camus and Stendhal, Camus and Montherlant, and so forth. I am more interested in less obvious intertexts, in authors who do not rank among the great classics. Not that all the names that come to mind made any significant contributions in this respect. Although Henri Barbusse, for example, has been cited as a source for Camus, albeit a superficial one, I doubt whether we are dealing with either sources or intertextuality. Both authors often wrote sentences that bear the stamp of their time and that sound like sentences in the public domain. For example, the following sentence from Barbusse's *L'Enfer* (1908) is quite typical: "Et moi? Moi, je suis un homme comme les autres, de même que ce soir est un soir comme les autres." [And me? Me, I am a man like other men, the same as this evening is an evening like other evenings.][11] Camus wrote many similar sentences, but so did many film writers of the early talkies. It is more a question of a technique widely used to convey a sense of solidarity, and it is doubtful that this has much to do with either sources, imitation or intertextuality. Camus considered that literary techniques were just so many tools to be used when needed for whatever purpose a writer had in mind. "Personally," he said in an interview, "all techniques interest me, but none interest me for themselves."[12] For instance, the linking of the present to the past by referring to common weather conditions, was a device Camus handled particularly masterfully. I have in mind a sentence such as "En sortant du Palais de justice pour monter dans la voiture, j'ai reconnu un court instant l'odeur et la couleur du soir d'été."[13] Barbusse uses the same device: "Le lendemain, l'après-midi fut encore une fois ensoleillé et brûlant. Je me rappelai des après-midi pareils, il y avait bien des années, et il me sembla vivre à cette époque disparue, — comme si l'éclatante chaleur effaçait le temps, étouffait tout le reste sous sa couvée." [The next day, the afternoon was again hot and full of sun. I recalled similar afternoons many years ago, and it seemed to me that I was living at that time, a time that has now disappeared — as if the dazzling heat erased time, and stifled everything else under its hatch.][14]

It was surely appropriate for a young militant writer of the thirties, whose family origins were quite humble, to allow himself the spiritual patronage of Henri Barbusse. He had not only been one of the first French writers to depict the special horrors of modern warfare, but he was a staunch pacifist and the founder with Romain Rolland of the Anti-Fascist 1932 Congress, *Congrès contre la Guerre et le Fascisme*, and of the *Association des Ecrivains et Artistes Révolutionnaires*. Although Camus may well have shared the enthusiasm of both World War I veterans and antifascists, the aesthetic affinities to be found between the works of these two writers remain quite superficial. In fact, it is quite likely that if a source exists for this technique, that source was Victor Hugo. Camus may not have cited Victor Hugo among the writers to whom he was indebted, but like most other French writers, he imitated him more than he imagined.

A number of scholars have indeed noted that Hugo's novel *Le dernier jour d'un condamné* may be a source for *L'Etranger* and *Réflexions sur la guillotine*.[15] It is the story of the impressions of a man sentenced to the guillotine. For example, as he is returning to court, his attention to the state of the elements—a device meant to provide a contrast between freedom and imprisonment—is very much like Meursault's notice of the outside world:

> Nous traversâmes une cour intérieure. L'air vif du matin me ranima. Je leval la tête. Le ciel était bleu, et les rayons chauds du soleil, découpés par les longes cheminées, traçaient de grands angles de lumière au faîte des murs hauts et sombres de la prison. Il faisait beau en effet.

> [We crossed an inside court. The lively morning air revived me. I raised my head. The sky was blue, and the hot rays of the sun, cut out by long chimneys traced large angles of light above the high and dark walls of the prison. It was really a beautiful day.][16]

This is not an isolated instance: the intrusion of the outside occurs many times during the trial:

> Un air chaud, mêlé de bruit, vint me frapper au visage; c'était le souffle de la foule dans la salle des assises. J'entrai [. . .]
> Les fenêtres étaient ouvertes; l'air et le bruit de la ville arrivaient librement du dehors; la salle était claire [. . .]
> En face de moi, une fenêtre était toute grande ouverte. J'entendais rire sur le quai des marchandes de fleurs; et, au bord de la croisée, une jolie petite plante jaune, toute pénétrée d'un rayon de soleil, jouait avec le vent dans une fente de la pierre.
> Comment une idée sinistre aurait-elle pu poindre parmi tant de gracieuses sensations? Inondé d'air et de soleil, il me fut impossible de penser à autre chose qu'a la liberté;

> [Warm air, mixed with noise, came to hit me in the face; it was the breath of the crowd in the courtroom. I walked in [. . .]
> The windows were open; the air and the noise of the city came in freely from outside; the room was bright [. . .]
> In front of me, a window was wide open. I heard the flower

vendors laugh on the quay; and, in front of the window, a pretty yellow plant, completely filled with the rays of the sun, played with the wind in a crack of the stone.

How was it possible for a sinister idea to sprout in the midst of so many graceful sensations? Drowned in air and in sun, it was impossible for me to think about anything else except freedom.[17]

I agree with Marie Naudin that Camus borrowed from Hugo here, and I disagree with Fernande Bartfeld's conclusion that Camus's reading of Hugo did not have any substantial impact upon him because he viewed matters differently.[18] It is hard to believe that this is a case of a chance encounter. Camus is said to have researched his positions thoroughly, and in France, Hugo's novel is one of the best-known books against the death penalty. Because almost every French-speaking writer read Hugo as a child, and we often repress the reading of our childhood much as we repress its memories, the work of this greatest of writers — and André Gide's "hélas" is beginning to seem old-fashioned — may be the most consequential intertext of all. Is it possible that Tarrou's tale about going to hear his father plead in court for a prisoner's death and his deep disgust at the whole procedure was motivated not necessarily by Camus's mother's story that her husband had become ill after watching the beheading of a criminal, but by reading *Le dernier jour d'un condamné*?[19] What prompts my question is that Camus ignored Hugo when he wrote against the death penalty. For example, his *Réflexions sur la guillotine* recounts several anecdotes about heads that continue to breathe and stare after their bearer has been guillotined. Hugo gives many more such examples, but Camus carefully cites Roger Grenier's *Les Monstres*, and carefully omits any reference to Hugo, except to say: "Il ne s'agit pas de céder à quelque imagerie conventionnelle et d'évoquer les bons forçats de Victor Hugo."[20] In fact, Hugo's anecdotes are so horrible — they go beyond the conventions of melodrama — that it is not inconceivable that they might convince a child of the evil and horror of the death penalty and lead him to develop a lifelong aversion to it. I suppose what I am suggesting is that it is quite plausible that Camus' story of his own father's vomiting and illness after attending an execution may have been become incorporated with vague recollections of reading about such scenes in *Le dernier jour d'un con-damné* and perhaps other books. A very close reading of these texts might confirm my hypothesis, but then again it might lead to nought. It all depends on the perception of the reader. This reader believes that there is a link, albeit a tenuous one, between Hugo and Camus's construction of the paternal imago.

The question is what is the textual consequence of such discrepancies between myth and reality. If you believe that your grandfather came to Algeria from Alsace after 1870, but in fact this grandfather was born in Marseilles, the son of immigrants to Ouled Fayet, does the error of chronology and place matter? Does it matter that Victor Hugo may actually be the intertext of a story attributed to your father? In a sense Patrick McCarthy may be right when he states that because Camus believed his father to have come from Alsace Lorraine, then it is as if his father had indeed come from there.[21] Is this also the case for Camus's literary genealogy? Perhaps. Yet, it is a well-known psychoanalytic dictum that repressed material often returns in inverted form. In a Lacanian perspective, the unconscious is the chapter of my history that is a blank, or that substitutes a lie for the truth. It is the chapter that is censored. The truth may be written in another text, perhaps in heroic and enhanced versions of family traditions and legends that are interwoven in my individual history. The truth may be found in the traces canned within the distortions that come about when the adulterated parts are reintegrated in the chapters that frame it, the meaning of which my exegesis will restore.[22]

If we consider the heroic versions of the Camus genealogy that were circulated by him and his family, what appears to have been censored was what Lacan called le "Nom-du-père," the Name-of-the-Father, that is to say the presence of the Father's Name, both mortal and divine. In so-called "real" life, Albert's father died on 11 October 1914, following shell wounds[23] shortly before the baby's first birthday. We are told that nobody ever spoke of him. But many of Camus's critics have written at length about the absent father in his work.[24] The truth that has been restored may be found in the heroic transformation of ordinary relatives into noble descendants of Alsatian patriots, who chose France over Germany when called upon to do so, and became pioneers in a frontier-like country. In other words, Camus gave his father a Name by inventing him. The various versions of the father's reaction to capital punishment, an incident that haunted the son, and its possible links with Victor Hugo, whose name came to be a symbol of all that was most noble in the Third French Republic, suggests how textual repression operates. Another example, one from *The Fall*, will explore further the transformation of repressed material at the textual level. The sentence I propose is the following one:

> J'étais d'une naissance honnête, mais obscure (mon père était officier) et pourtant, certains matins, je l'avoue humblement, je me sentais fils de roi, ou buisson ardent.[25]

> [I was of respectable but humble birth (my father was an officer), and yet, on certain mornings, let me confess it humbly, I felt like a king's son or burning bush.][26]

At first glance the reader perceives a trite portrait put together by a string of clichés: "naissance honnête, mais obscure," "fils de roi," "buisson ardent." Closer scrutiny reveals a logical incompatibility between the various elements. Take the word "naissance." In French, "naissance" refers to one's family, and "un homme de naissance," a man of birth implies high rank, and possible nobility. An obscure birth, "naissance obscure," an echo of Racine's *Iphigénie*'s "triste naissance" suggests illegitimacy, but such an interpretation is contradicted by the adjective "honnête." It would hardly be inconsistent for a "man of birth," an "homme de naissance" to feel as though he were a "fils de roi."[27] Using the adverb "pourtant," ("however") stresses the incongruous aspects of Jean-Baptiste's lineage, an incompatibility reinforced further by the disjunctive conjunction "ou" linking "fils de roi" and "buisson ardent." "Buisson ardent," ("burning bush") refers to the bush in Exodus 3:2 that was on fire but was not consumed, and also to the shrub the Robert *Dictionnaire* characterizes as being Mediterranean.[28]

The meaning of the sentence for me, — and perhaps also for Michael Riffaterre's arch reader — is revealed in an intertext in Chapter 2 of Arthur de Gobineau's *Les Pléiades*. Conrad Lanze, a young German sculptor, Wilfrid Lore, a young Englishman who has lived in the Middle East, and Louis de Laudon, a young Frenchman who has all the faults Gobineau found in the French people, meet in Switzerland. They are particularly drawn to each other, and they proclaim themselves sons of kings:

> We are three calenders, [mendicant derviches] sons of kings; you would be offending me to a considerable extent if you were reluctant to accept this truth. The fact that we also have a blind right eye is also undeniable; my fear is that we are even completely blind, and that is something we'll know with certainty only towards the end of our existence, if only we acquire the critical sense that is sorely lacking in all of us up to now.
> — I allow your fable, replied Laudon; I know only too well how much I miss my right eye; but as far as being a king's son, that's another business, and I see little likelihood of it.
> — That is because you have examined only one side of this question, answered Nore in a lively voice, and that side is precisely the most insignificant one. When the Arab storyteller lends his voice to his hero and begins his tales by making him pronounce these sacramental words: "I am a king's son," less than once in a hundred times the character who is being presented is only a poor devil that fortune has treated badly. He may be either a dervish or a castaway dying from hunger; or sometimes, as in the present case, a cripple. There is never, never, I repeat, never a question of an unknown Highness to whom the character might owe his birth, regardless of how the business at hand turns out. But why then, do you think this character should be made into a king's son. Such a calling grants him nothing from his father's inheritance; neither palaces, nor pompous gardens planted with giant rose bushes and plane trees; neither Khorasan rugs, nor craquelé Chinese vases; neither horses harnessed with gold and turquoise nor a harem of Mingrelelian women. [. . .]
> The explanation is that by uttering the magic words: "I am a king's son," without having to detail his thought, the first words of the narrator establish that he is gifted with special precious qualifications that naturally lift him above common people. "I am a king's son" doesn't in any way mean: "My father isn't a merchant, a military man, a writer,

an artist, a banker, a boiler-maker, or a station-master . . ." Who asks him for news of his father about whom nobody in the audience cares anything at all about — everyone is interested only in what he himself is? It means: "I have a generous and daring temperament, one that is alien to ordinary suggestions of natural commoners. My tastes are not those of fashion; I feel for myself and I neither hate nor love according to suggestions I find in newspapers. The independence of my mind, the most absolute liberty in my opinions are unflinching privileges of my noble origin; Heaven granted them to me in my cradle just like French princes were knighted with the blue ribbon of the order of the Holy Ghost, and I shall keep these favors all my life. Finally, the logical consequence of these premises is that I am unhappy with what is good enough for the plebs, and in the treasures Heaven has placed within reach of men, I don't seek the jewels that infatuate them."[29] [ . . .]

Jean-Baptiste Clamence's words following the confession that he feels like a king's son are but an echo of Gobineau's pages. Let us now place the Camus sentence back into its context in *The Fall*:

To tell the truth, just from being so fully and simply a man, I looked upon myself as something of a superman. I was of respectable but humble birth (my father was an officer), and yet, on certain mornings, let me confess it humbly, I felt like a king's son or a burning bush. It was not a matter, mind you, of the certainty I had of being more intelligent than everyone else. Besides, such certainty is of no consequence because so many imbeciles share it. No, as a result of being showered with blessings, I felt, I hesitate to admit, marked out. Personally marked out, among all, for that long and uninterrupted success. This, after all, was a result of my modesty. I refused to attribute that success to my own merits and could not believe that the conjunction in a single person of such different and such extreme virtues was the result of chance alone. This is why in my happy life I felt somehow that happiness was authorized by some higher decree. When I add that I had no religion you can see even better how extraordinary that conviction was. Whether ordinary or not, it served for some time to raise me above the daily routine and I literally soared for a period of years, for which, to tell the truth, I still long in my heart of hearts.[30]

Further confirmation of the connection between the two texts occurs through the word "buisson," shrub. Modern society, says Nore, has begun its sabbath. Yet at the bottom of the abyss, some were able to survive:

Quelques-uns se sont rattrapés, lentement, lentement, aux anfractuosi-tés du roc, aux touffes d'herbes, aux branches des buissons.

[Some were slowly, slowly able to hold on to the anfractuosities of rock, to tufts of grass, to the branches of shrubs.][31]

So we understand the connection between being a king's son and a burning bush. The suggestion is that the utterer of such words, an

Algerian storyteller, an Albert Camus close to the Arab narrators of ancient oriental tales, may be counted among the slaves and sons of slaves imagined by Gobineau who returned to the "earth's surface, tainted and battered," a beggar and a king's son.

But what if the king's son was not truly a king's son, but part of the mass described by Gobineau's Wilfred? At the head comes the tribe of idiots: "They lead everything, carry keys, open doors, invent sentences, weep that they were mistaken, claim that they would have never believed. . . ." The second group comprises what Gobineau calls "les Drôles," the buffoons, the fools: "They are everywhere, on the flanks, in the front, at the end; they run, they become agitated, they get excited and their only care is preventing things from settling down and stopping before they are also seated." Finally, we have the brutes. Imbeciles have let them loose, and fools push them.[32]

Even if one's father was not what he seemed, one could still be a king's son. But one could also be ranked among the idiots, the buffoons, or simply the brutes of this world. Jean-Baptiste Clamence is all of these things, of course. A slight shift in the intertextual looking glass has provided the breach, the gap that may open up not only the text's unconscious, but a repressed ideology as well.

Gobineau lays bare Camus's desire. Just like the king's sons of the Orient, the humble "pied-noir" from Algeria who won the Nobel Prize for literature knew he was one of the chosen few, a Dr. Bernard Rieux, but also a part of the common populace, an ordinary man who, like Meursault, was at once an idiot, a fool, and a brute. An Alsatian, but also an Algerian whose ancestors had come from Bordeaux and from Spain. An outsider, a king's son.

## Notes

1. Herbert R. Lottman's introductory chapter of his superb biography, *Albert Camus* (Garden City, N.J.: Doubleday, 1979), carefully records his research of the origins of the Camus and the Sintès families. The information he collected "simply overturns the myth of Algerian ancestors," and we know more about these ancestors than did Camus himself. My information is drawn entirely from chapter 1, "The First Man," 5–13.

2. Salvador de Madariaga, "Un des nôtres," in *Preuves* no. 110 (April 1960): 10–13.

3. See Gabriel D' Aubarède, "Rencontres avec Albert Camus," *Nouvelles littéraires*, 10 May 1951, in Camus's *Essais* (Paris: Bibliothèque de la Pléiade, Gallimard Editions, 1965), 1338–43; "Dernière interview d'Albert Camus," 20 December 1959, in Camus, *Essais*, 1925–28.

4. Roger Quilliot in his notes to Camus, *Essais*, 1171.

5. Albert Camus, "Herman Melville," in *Théâtre, Récits, Nouvelles* (Paris: Bibliothèque de la Pléiade, Editions Gallimard, 1962), 1899.

6. D'Aubarède "Rencontres avec Albert Camus," in *Essais*, 1340.

7. See *A Critical Bibliography of French Literature*, ed. Richard A. Brooks, vol. 6, part 3 (Syracuse, N.Y.: Syracuse University Press, 1980), 1618–25.

8. Jean Bloch-Michel, "Une littérature de l'ennui," *Preuves* no. 131 (January 1962):14–23.

9. Léon-François Hoffman, "Albert Camus et Jean Lorrain. Une source de *La Chute*," *Revue d'Histoire Littéraire de la France*, no. 100 (1969):69–93.

10. "L'intelligence et l'échafud," in Camus, *Théâtre*, 1890.

11. Henri Barbusse, *L'Enfer* (Paris: Albin Michel, 1985).

12. D'Aubarède, "Dernière interview d'Albert Camus," in Camus, *Essais*, 1927.

13. Albert Camus, *Romans* (Paris: Bibliothèque de la Pléiade, 1967), 1192.

14. Barbusse, *L'Enfer*, 50.

15. Marie Naudin, "Hugo et Camus face à la peine capitale," *Revue d'Histoire Littéraire de la France* (March–April 1972); Marianna C. Forde, "Condemnation and Imprisonment in *L'Etranger* and *Le Dernier jour d'un condamné*," *Romance Notes* (Winter 1971); Fernande Bartfeld, *Camus and Hugo: Essai de lectures comparées*, no. 156 *Albert Camus 3* (Paris: Minard, Archives des Lettres Modernes, 1975).

16. Victor Hugo, *Le Dernier jour d'un condamné*, in *Oeuvres Complètes de Victor Hugo, Romans 1* (Paris: Librairie Ollendorf, 1910), 626. The translations are mine.

17. Ibid., 626–27.

18. Bartfeld, *Camus and Hugo*, 33.

19. Albert Camus, *The Plague*, trans. Justin O'Brien, in *The Collected Fiction of Albert Camus*, 214–15; *Réflexions sur la guillotine*, in Camus, *Essais*, 1022.

20. *Réflexions sur la guillotine*, 1055.

21. Patrick McCarthy, *Camus* (New York: Random House, 1982), 11.

22. Jacques Lacan, "Fonction et champ de la parole et langage," *Ecrits* (Paris: Seuil, 1966), 259.

23. Lottman, *Camus*, 18.

24. One of the largest and best articles on the subject is Jean Sarocchi's "Albert Camus: père manqué, oeuvre ouverte," in *Albert Camus: oeuvre fermée, oeuvre ouverte?* Acte du colloque du Centre Culturel International de Cerisy-la-Sale, 1982, *Cahiers Albert Camus 5* (Paris: Gallimard, 1985), 37–53.

25. Camus, *Théâtre*, 1488.

26. Camus, *The Fall*, in *The Collected Fiction*, 262.

27. José Barchilon, "Les jeux du narcissisme," *Cahiers Albert Camus 5*, notes: "Mais que veut-il dire par naissance obscure? Ne sait!" 22.

28. Arthur de Gobineau, *Les Pléiades* (Paris: Gallimard [Le livre de poche], 1960). All translations are mine.

29. *The Fall*, in *The Collected Fiction*, 262.

30. de Gobineau, *Les Pléiades*, 32.

31. Ibid., 33.

# Two Faces of Terrorism: *Caligula* and *The Just Assassins*

Rosette C. Lamont*

In *The Rebel*, Camus's study of the problematics of metaphysical and historical revolt and revolution, the author indicts his century for having severed the roots of the spirit of rebellion, depriving it of what he calls "concrete morality."[1] As a result, we are left with only the following alternatives: individual terrorist acts or the all-powerful terrorism of the state. According to Camus, both of these stem from a rejection of the natural order, as exemplified in the writings of the Marquis de Sade, the poet Lautréamont and the young Rimbaud, and the philosophy of nihilism as it arose from the regicidal lucubrations of one of the most consistent and self-destructive makers of the French Revolution, Saint-Just. With the death of God, following that of his representative on earth, man is condemned to making his solitary way through History. It is a path strewn with the corpses of the contestants in the Hegelian Master / Slave duel to the death. The perversion of the thought of Nietzsche, Hegel, and Marx led inexorably to the ruthless orthodoxies of fascism and Stalinist communism. Camus's view that our society does not "recognize any other norm than violence"[2] is prophetic. In this light his plays that deal with the philosophy of terrorism, *Caligula* and *The Just Assassins*, speak to us with renewed vigor.

Hijackings of airplanes and ships, the blowing-up of public buildings and private business concerns, the taking of hostages, murders of the aged by housebreakers, rapes in public spaces—alley ways, parking lots, subways, rooftops—random maiming and killing, constitute the regular fare of newspaper readers and T. V. watchers. We move every day in a climate of irrational violence. Terrorism, however, must be distinguished from the terrors of modern living. It is a philosophy that can be defined as the relentless pursuit of an arbitrary ideal of justice peculiar to an individual or a group. By crossing the tenuous borderline between the idea and the act, the terrorist assumes his own being as appointed, or self-appointed avenger. Moreover, he enters the metaphysical dimension by coinciding with Non-Being as he affronts the death he so readily imparts, but which he also is ready to receive, either at the very moment of killing and destroying, or later, if caught and condemned. Individual terrorists, or terrorists as a group, wish to impose their will upon people, a people, a whole civilization, future generations. They do not think of themselves as murderers but as vindicators.

There are also terrorist governments guilty of crimes against humanity. They impose upon their own citizens an official, rigid state philosophy supported by an enslaved intelligentsia. Under these circumstances the

*This essay was written especially for this volume and is published here for the first time by permission of the author.

concept of individual freedom and the desire for free expression constitute heinous crimes to be punished by imprisonment in high security jails, slave labor camps, or psychiatric clinics.

The psychology of terrorism, whether on an individual level or on that of a government or state, stems from the desire to exercise absolute control at the price of one's own life or of the apocalyptic end of one's own nation. Terrorists wish to destroy society, which they hold responsible for their failures and frustrations. Once unleashed, this mechanism can no longer be stopped. Carried to its logical extreme, annihilation is supposed to englobe all of humanity.

In its transcendent goals, terrorism is a perverse mystique. The terrorist is led by an "ideal" that remains out of reach. He reaches only his victim or victims and this violent act puts him, he feels, in touch with himself. Moreover, a kind of fraternity is established between the killer and his victim as though the blood shed flowed from the body of the murderer. The terrorist act is a ritual of violence and death, a sacrificial ceremony played out for a visible or imagined audience. In fiction no one described it more vividly than André Malraux in the opening chapter of *The Human Condition*. Tchen, the revolutionary hero, is alone at night in the hotel room of the man he is supposed to kill. The silence of the room where the potential victim lies asleep under the protective gauze of mosquito netting is contrasted with the throbbing sounds of the city. Tchen knows that he must pierce the man's heart in one quick, unfailing gesture. Yet, before proceeding to do so, he jabs the knife into his own arm as though to mingle his blood with that of his enemy. At this moment no one is closer to him than the living creature he must sacrifice.

In "Revolt and Revolution," a chapter of *The Rebel*, Camus analyzes the terrorist's complex psyche:

> The destruction of man is still an affirmation of humanity. Acts of violence and death camps are the means, extreme though they may be, whereby the terrorist escapes from his solitary condition. He quenches his thirst for unity within the mass grave. . . . By destroying the other, terrorists in some way also kill themselves. Yet, they also bring proof of their inability to exist apart from other human beings; in this way they assuage their frightful hunger for fraternity.[3]

The fraternity Camus evokes here is that of Cain and Abel. Eugene Ionesco, a writer who spent every effort denouncing violence, seems to echo Camus when he writes in *Fragments of a Journal*:

> The greatest crime of all is homicide. Cain kills Abel. That's the crime *par excellence*. And we keep on killing. I have to kill my obvious enemy, the one who is trying to put me to death, in order that he shall not kill me. In killing him I find relief, for I am obscurely aware that I have killed Death. . . . By killing I exorcise my own death; the act of killing is part of a magic rite.[4]

In *The Rebel*, Camus also states that we are witnessing today an infinite multiplication of murderous acts. Irrational crimes have now been replaced by crimes that pretend to have a rational basis. The brotherhood of henchmen constitutes a new kind of consanguinity.

There is, however, another kind of fraternity, that which binds together co-conspirators who share an ideal, but are not willing to indulge in random assassinations for its sake. In January 1948, Camus published in *La Table Ronde* an article entitled "Les meurtriers délicats." Later he incorporated this piece into the section on "Historical Revolt" of *The Rebel*. The essay deals with the small group of revolutionaries who belonged to the *Combat Organization*, a group formed in 1903 within the Socialist Revolutionary Party. Led by Boris Azev, the double agent who, as a member of Plehve's secret police was able to orchestrate the latter's 1904 assassination by Sazonov, this cell planned the murder of the Czar's uncle, the Grand Duke Sergei. Not one among the co-conspirators realized that Azev had been diligent in furnishing to the police the names of radical plotters *after* an operation had been carried out. For the most part, the young revolutionaries of Azev's cell were members of the intelligentsia, high-minded rebels who hoped to alter once and for all their government's repressive system.

Camus calls them "delicate murderers" because they did not carry out their orders blindly. Ethical considerations were never set aside. Thus, their act against the Grand Duke was delayed because, on the chosen day, the Czar's uncle did not ride alone in his carriage; he was accompanied by two children, his nephew and niece. Kaliayev, one of the two appointed bomb throwers, finds that he is unable to take the lives of two innocent children. By postponing his act, he knows that he places in jeopardy the group's enterprise. Yet, faced with this unexpected development, the conspirators support their "brother" in his last minute decision. Dora Brilliant, the group's bomb-maker, states that "the Poet" (Kaliayev's nickname) was right. Two days later, when the Grand Duke sets out alone in his carriage, he will be killed by the same Kaliayev.

The revolutionary brotherhood constitutes, as Camus writes, a chivalric order. Each and every one of them is ready to pay with his or her life for the life they take. In a statement that is the obverse of the *lex talionis*, the companions of the *Combat Organization* embrace a doctrine of self-sacrifice whereby, as Camus explains, "murder is identified with suicide": "Our life for that of the enemy." They believe that new values are bound to arise from this double holocaust. Camus emphasizes the fact that "they place no idea above human life, although they themselves are ready to kill for an idea."[5] They find their justification for this act in their becoming the incarnation of an ideal to the extent of accepting to die for it. This throws a religious, or at least a metaphysical cast, upon the enterprise of these proclaimed atheists. They are the opposite of unbelievers, being men and women of conscience. Savinkov writes about Dora Brilliant: "Terrorism weighed upon her like a cross." When, upon his second attempt, Kaliayev succeeds in throwing the bomb made by Dora for this purpose, the young woman cries out to Savinkov: "We killed him. I'm the one who killed him!" "Whom did we kill?" questions her companion, assuming her to mean Kaliayev who will now be caught and brought to justice. "The Grand Duke!"[6] Dora whispers with awe and horror.

Later, at his trial, Kaliayev declares: "I consider my death to be the ultimate protest against this world of blood and tears."[7] Given the chance of a full pardon at the price of disassociating himself from his companions and repenting publicly, the young man is adamant in his refusal. His death will be the final gesture of solidarity with his associates. Nor will he let himself be swayed by the moving visit in his cell of his victim's grief-stricken widow, a woman of exceptional gentleness and piety.

Kaliayev's sacrifice illustrates the extraordinary devotion of each member of the organization to their common cause, and to one another. The tie that binds them is sacred in character; it is the oath of their chivalric order. Camus writes:

> Huddled together within the huge Russian nation, this small group of men and women chose to become executioners, an undertaking for which they were totally unfit. They lived out a paradox: imbued with a deep-seated respect for human life, they seemed to scorn their own, offering it as a supreme sacrifice. . . . Boldly putting their own existence at risk, their attempts upon that of others were carried out with the utmost punctiliousness.[8]

It is for this reason that Camus describes the 1905 terrorists by an oxymoron that conveys their paradoxical attitude, "les meurtriers délicats" ("murderers with delicate feelings"). They are martyrs or priests of a new religion. Yet their faith does not give them peace of mind; they are bound to suffer the inherent contradiction of their beliefs. Ever full of philosophical doubt, they are not prevented by it from taking action. Camus admires them for transcending History and triumphing over the spirit of nihilism.

*The Rebel* and *The Just Assassins* were born simultaneously, issuing from the same inspiration. If in *The Rebel* Camus attempted "to give an account of the reasons which led him to take the position he took with regard to the political ideologies of our time, and more particularly Communism,"[9] a move which brought about a public break between him and Jean-Paul Sartre, the play demonstrates how a noble ideal can become vitiated. Kaliayev and his friends hope to create a better world, yet one can glimpse the seed of the greater destructive forces to come. Ideologies, Camus believes, are essentially murderous. The "noble" murder, the generous sacrifice of one's own life for some distant future good, lead to tyrannical regimes which do not hesitate to sacrifice the present generation for some nebulous utopia. The dream becomes the nightmare.

Grounded in Camus's precise historical research on the subject of

Russian terrorism, *The Just Assassins* cannot be considered as historical drama. It is Camus's attempt to write a classical tragedy in the spirit of Corneille's *Polyeucte*. The play is divided into five acts, according to the tradition of French neoclassicism. Each act brings out an important point, often argued between two characters, so that, as in Sophocles's *Antigone*, "the center of gravity does not lie in one person but between two."[10] It was also Camus's intention to introduce a love scene into his play, one that would demonstrate the possibility of a normal relationship between Dora and Kaliayev, had they not dedicated their life to the revolution.

In a lecture delivered in Athens in 1955, "Sur l'avenir de la tragédie" ("On the Subject of Tragedy's Future"),[11] Camus defined with clarity and elegance his ideas as to what constitutes the tragic genre. His main point is that "the forces which clash with one another within the tragic universe must be equally legitimate, equally grounded in reason."[12] Tragedy is "ambiguous" whereas drama is "simplistic."[13] The example he offers is that of Creon and Antigone ("Antigone is right, but Creon is not wrong").

According to this definition, Camus's own play is closer to drama than to tragedy. Although the sequences in every act are beautifully argued, there is little room for shades of meaning, for nuances, except perhaps in the deeply moving scene between Kaliayev and the Grand Duchess (Act 4). There is however a loftiness of intention and a nobility of tone which had not found their way onto the modern stage since Claudel. It is obvious that Camus intended to recapture the passionate involvement with the theatre which characterized the age of Pericles, or the court of the Sun King. In a 1958 interview granted to *Paris-Théâtre*, Camus stated unambiguously: "Theatre is the highest of literary genres . . . *The Misunderstanding, The State of Siege, The Just Assassins*, are the different approaches I used in my personal exploration of modern tragedy."[14]

Camus was certain that the time was ripe for a new Renaissance of the art of tragedy. In his Athens lecture, he explained that the tragic genre arises in the Occident whenever society finds itself precariously poised between the sacred and the man-centered universe. His epoch seemed to him to be characterized by a transformation of individualism under the pressure of History. Man could no longer believe, as he had in the Age of Enlightenment, that the individual could remodel the world through the judicious exercise of reason. Indeed, the world as it appeared to modern man was monstrous in its boundless worship of rationality. History, Camus explains, has assumed in modern times some of the aspects of destiny. Since man is no longer in control of his destiny, all that is left him is the nobility of his questioning mind, torn between hope and doubt. "Modern man lives in a tragic climate,"[15] Camus stated forcefully in his Athens talk. To reflect faithfully this situation, the dramatist must forge a new language, "hieratic and familiar, . . . mysterious and clear, lofty yet full of human pity."[16]

It is this critic's opinion that Camus succeeded in this purpose, particularly in *The Just Assassins*. But what is perhaps more important still is that he brought to the modern stage "the metaphysical dimension"[17] which would dominate both the tragic and the comic genres throughout the second half of the twentieth century.

In an interview given to *France-Soir* in 1958, nine years after the premiere performance of *The Just Assassins* (15 December 1949) at the Théâtre Hébertot, Camus defined the parameters of his dramaturgy by setting himself against realist drama and the light comedy of the Boulevard:

> I have no interest whatsoever either in the bedchamber or the bedroom closet. We must put an end to derision on the stage, we must transcend it. Our theatre ought to be one of confrontation. Its dimensions should be those of the world, allowing for the dramatization of life's struggle for greater freedom in the face of a difficult destiny. . . .[18]

The individual terrorists of 1905, grouped under the fraternal leadership of Boris Annenkov, are convinced that every one of their acts is to be played out for the future of humanity. As Kaliayev exclaims, addressing Dora: "We kill to build a world in which no one will have to kill again! We accept to become criminals so that the earth may be covered by innocent people at last."[19] Kaliayev admits that he is kept awake by the thought that social conditions have turned him and his friends into assassins, but he adds: "Then I think that I'm going to die, and my heart grows quiet again. I smile, and fall asleep like a child."[20]

Kaliayev is not only a revolutionary but a poet. This earns him the suspicion and dislike of Stepan, who had rejoined the group after escaping from Siberia and a period of exile in Switzerland. The others, however, do not doubt the courage and determination of their companion. They know that the same exalted impulse that drives him to consign his thoughts and emotions to paper will carry him through his demanding assignment. His sensitivity and imagination are not liabilities in an undertaking that must mobilize a man's passions. Kaliayev is both a writer and an actor—like Camus—and he puts these personal gifts to use by assuming various disguises and personalities, by blending into the crowd in order to secure information. To Stepan's somber: "I don't trust you!" he has the following answer: "I love life. I'm never bored. I entered the revolution because I love life."[21] He expands this statement when talking to Dora, the woman he loves: "They see me as a little crazy, too spontaneous, and yet I believe in the idea just as they do. Like them, I want to sacrifice myself. I can also be skillful, silent, secretive, efficient. But life continues to strike me as marvelous. I love beauty, happiness! That's why I hate despotism. How can I explain this to them? Revolution, of course! But it must be a revolution for life, to give life a chance."[22]

By stressing in the above speeches the fundamental oneness of *eros* and *thanatos*, Camus sets the metaphysical level of his drama on the highest plane. His protagonist's exultant affirmation of life is true *eros*, in the ancient Greek sense, since it transcends personal existence. Embracing not only the future generations, but the entire planet, it envisions the earth as renewed by the idealist's sacrifice. It is a *renovatio* of cosmic dimensions. By offering himself as the sacrificial victim on the altar of society, the hero breaks the cyclical repetition of History, taking Man into mythical time.

Camus does not stop there in his evocation of the power of renunciation. Kaliayev speaks of insuring the success of his terrorist act by throwing himself with his bomb, *kamikaze* style, under the horses' hoofs; thus he will die together with his victim. However, Dora suggests that there is still "a greater form of happiness": to die "on the gallows."[23] As soon as the young woman voices this thought, Kaliayev embraces it, making it his own: "Yes, I have thought of it. To die at the moment of the attack leaves something unfinished. Between the act and the gallows, however, lies an eternity of time, perhaps the only form of eternity known to man."[24] We recognize here an echo of Camus's *The Stranger*. Like Meursault, Kaliayev will refuse at the end the succor of a priest. In the last hours left him, Meursault has no time "to waste on God."[25] As for Kaliayev, he realizes that the terrorist act must be followed by a time of reflection in which the killer peers into the abyss of Non-Being and offers his own life in exchange for the one he has taken. Dora, who has thought this through, states with a strange kind of calm: "To carry out the act and then ascend the gallows is to give one's life twice. Then we will have paid more than we owe." Kaliayev echoes: "Yes, to die twice! Thank you, Dora."[26]

Camus did not wait till the end of the play to write for his lovers a duet of love and death, a dirge which is an anticipated farewell and the most intimate expression of spiritual union. Dora and the "Poet" will not be lovers on this earth, but they will be joined in death, joined also in their uncommon aspirations. As an epigraph to his play, Camus chose an eloquent line from *Romeo and Juliet*: "O love! O life! Not life but love in death" (Act 4, scene 5).

Not everyone in *The Just Assassins* is a "murderer with delicate feelings." Stepan, who has emerged from the hell of Siberia, is a revolutionary whose sense of outrage leaves no room for finer feelings. For Camus, he represents the mentality the writer feared the most, an ideological rigidity. When he hears that Kaliayev has not followed through on the original plan because of the two children in the Grand Duke's carriage, he states with profound bitterness: "Children! That's all you know. Don't you understand that because Yanek failed to kill these two, thousands of Russian children will die of hunger for many years to come? . . . Do you live for the moment only? Then choose charity and heal the maladies of the day. The revolution wants to cure all ills, present and future."[27] In Act 5 Dora will express a deep-seated anxiety: "When I listen to Stepan I am full of fear. Those who will come after us will use us as an example to kill but they won't pay with their life."[28]

In structuring *The Just Assassins*, Camus lived up to his dramaturgic principle of mixing the noble rhetoric of tragedy with more familiar, sometimes coarse forms of exchange. In this, he is closer to Shakespeare than to Corneille and Racine.

Act 4 is the perfect example of this amalgam. Kaliayev's conversation with a fellow prisoner who has been sent in to sweep his cell owes as much to Dostoyevsky as it does to Shakespeare. Foka, the alcoholic who has killed three people when drunk, reminds us of some of the minor characters in *The Idiot*, or *The Possessed*, a novel Camus adapted for the stage in 1959. A simple peasant, Foka has no interest in the other prisoner's idealistic intentions for the Russian masses. Since the man is a "barin" ("a member of nobility"), he will no doubt be released soon ("The earth is made for the barins").[29] However, when he finds out that the nobleman's victim was the Grand Duke, he backs away in horror, not on account of the crime itself, but because as the jail's executioner, he will be required to hang this talkative young man. With each hanging, Foka's sentence is reduced by one year. Kaliayev, who voices here Camus's own horror of capital punishment, exclaims: "To pardon your crimes they force you to commit others." The peasant's answer is not unexpected: "You can't call these crimes. They've been ordered."[30]

This exchange is followed by the arrival of the director of the police department, a cynical, elegant bureaucrat who hopes to shame or frighten his prisoner into divulging the identity of his accomplices. The dialogue is patterned on the *agon* between Creon and Antigone, with Kaliayev in the role of Antigone, ready to defend his revolutionary faith at the price of his life, and Skouratov, a Creon, representing order and logic.

As in the theatre of Sophocles, the *agon* brings out two contrasting ways of life, two divergent personalities in confrontation with one another. However, the oratorical jousting which constitutes the *agonic* architecture of Act 4 of *The Just Assassins* suggests Euripidean tragedy with its emphasis on the social sphere, and its fearless, realistic baring of what Aristotle called the "revolting" *(miaron)* aspects of life.

Skouratov's carefully selected words paint gory images that force the young idealist to recreate in his imagination the consequences of his act: the Grand Duke's head, torn from his body by the explosion, was projected out of the carriage; what was left was a headless, mangled, unrecognizable mass of torn, bleeding flesh. The urbane administrator then shifts his tone to a scornful sneer, dismissing the whole enterprise as "the job of amateurs."[31] Snakelike in his insidious approach, Skouratov suggests that his "prisoner of war"[32] (Kaliayev insists on being defined as such rather than being referred to as "the accused") may believe to have wreaked this horror for the sake of a noble idea, but that the flesh and blood reality has an eloquence of its own ("Ask the Grand Duchess. There was blood, a great deal of blood."[33]). There is nothing abstract about blowing a human being to smithereens.

Deeply shaken by this description and the devastatingly ironic tone of his visitor, the revolutionary can only counter by reaffirming his hatred of the tyrannical regime which Skouratov serves with apparent devotion. When the young man calls him "a valet," the head of the police department bows ceremoniously ("At your service"),[34] only to remind his prisoner that they may not be as unlike one another as he imagines: "I wouldn't get on my high horses, if I were you. One starts by thirsting for justice and ends up by organizing the police. . . ."[35] Ideals sour into ideologies as aging Antigones grow into Creons. This is the author's own aside, his warning to the deluded.

If idealism proved to be the most pernicious of illusions, then, Skouratov suggests, Kaliayev would do well to turn in his co-conspirators "for their own good, to prevent them from getting into more trouble and hanging for it."[36] Adamant in his refusal, the terrorist cannot avoid the moral sting inflicted on his conscience by his clever interlocutor: "Don't forget the Grand Duke's head. If you were to hold it in mind, all your ideas would be of no avail. You'd be ashamed of what you did instead of feeling proud."[37] Skouratov's final torture, however, is waiting in the wings: he has acceded to the Grand Duchess's wish to visit her husband's assassin in his cell. Their dialogue constitutes the second stage of the *agon*.

The woman who steps in is heavily veiled in black. Her first gesture is to lift the veil to reveal a tear-stained, tormented face. After this, words are almost unnecessary; yet the Grand Duchess, kind as she is, can turn speech into a knife.

It is never quite clear, not even to herself, why the Grand Duchess has wished this encounter. She says that she finds it unbearably painful to be alone with the horror of this act. She is unable to share her grief with anyone, except perhaps with the murderer himself. They are linked by this bloody deed.

Kaliayev has killed a name, a symbol. As he says to Dora in Act 1: "I will not be killing a man, but despotism."[38] The Grand Duchess shows him the man, his qualities and human weaknesses. She tells the prisoner that her husband loved the Russian people, that he was at ease with the simplest ones among them, often drinking with the peasants. Then she describes a man peacefully asleep in his armchair, his feet propped upon a facing chair, two hours before setting out for the theatre, for the death planned for him by the terrorists. The image of the sleeping man touches Kaliayev to the quick. Perhaps at this moment he recalls his conversation with Dora in Act 1, when the young woman wondered whether he could bring himself to throw the bomb were he to catch sight of his victim sitting in his coach: "He may have gentle eyes, full of pity. Or you'll see him scratch his ear, smile happily. Maybe he'll have a slight cut from his razor on his cheek."[39] Having seen the human side of a man, you can no longer destroy the symbol of injustice. Men are not symbols.

As to the children Kaliayev spared, the Grand Duchess reveals that they are lacking in generosity and kindness. "My niece is heartless. She refuses to bring her alms to the poor for fear of coming into contact with them."[40] Perhaps more than any other statement this one visibly shakes Kaliayev's faith. He begs to be left in peace to think of his impending death. The Grand Duchess seizes this opportunity to suggest that they pray together, joined in a love and mercy greater than human conflicts. The young man refuses; to pray would be to betray, to be untrue to his cause and his friends. Only one love will fill his heart at the foot of the gallows — the love he was never able to know fully in his short lifetime. He explains to the Grand Duchess, who wonders about the nature of such a desperate affection: "Imagine two beings who have renounced the possibility of happiness and can only love one another in a universe of pain, join one another in suffering, could one say that they are united by the hangman's rope?"[41] It should be noted that Camus's original title for *The Just Assassins* was *The Rope*. Indeed, at the very end of the play, Dora, who has requested to be allowed to throw the next bomb, longs for that union on the gallows: "A cold night, and the same rope! It'll be easier now."[42] These are the final words of a play which, although classical in structure and tone, is one of the last modern Romantic dramas.

Traces of Camus's meditation on state terrorism can be found in his *Notebooks (Carnets)* as early as January 1937 when he outlined the canvas of a four act play, *Caligula or the Meaning of Death*. The death of the emperor's sister / lover Drusilla, which, in the 1941 version, as well as in the finished work, precedes the action and precipitates the crisis, is mentioned only at the end of Act 2, but the play's conclusion suggests already Caligula's dying words: "I'm still alive!"[43]

In the initial version, Caligula was supposed to step out from behind the curtain, after it had fallen on his assassination, to address the audience:

No, Caligula isn't dead. He's here, and there. He's in each one of you. If you had power, or boldness, if you loved life, you'd witness the wild unleashing of this monstrous or angelic creature. Our era is perishing because it had faith in a system of values, because it believed things could be beautiful, that they could cease being absurd. Farewell, I am about to enter history where those who fear excess of love have locked me up.[44]

As James A. Arnold traced in "La poétique du premier *Caligula*," this Nietzschean *Ubermensch* will suffer a complete metamorphosis during the years of war and occupation, the years when the author entered the Resistance movement. Arnold concludes: "We find ourselves facing a rare phenomenon: a writer who undertakes to think and write against himself because he perceives and fears the probable perversion of a truth he still values."[45] This truth is the Absurd, a dangerous philosophic apprehension at a time when Nietzsche's subtle and complex thought was being twisted out of shape and used for propaganda and the elaboration of a racist myth.

Drusilla's death leads Caligula to the full realization that "men die and are not happy,"[46] and to the decision to enact the truth of the Absurd. Possessing absolute power, he is able to order random executions, particularly those of the fathers and sons of his closest friends; to seduce or rather rape the wives of his senators forcing the latter to give up their exalted rank to serve him at table. He suggests to the wealthy citizens that they disinherit their progeny in favor of the state and his person, and, in a grotesque, sacrilegious piece of theatre within the play, he offers himself for religious adoration, dressed as Venus, the goddess of love.

This brilliant stage image of state terrorism constitutes a metaphysical tragicomedy. Although Camus differentiated sharply between state and individual terrorism, Kaliayev, the prime example of the noble individual terrorist, is not unlike Caligula; both exist on a plane which is not that of the average human being—the metaphysical plane. Caligula and Kaliayev can be viewed as "images of revolt."[47] Their existences were devoted to history to the point of being willing to die for an idea, yet, at the moment of death, they transcended history, became mythic figures.

With growing maturity, Camus came to realize the dangers of "démesure" ("boundlessness"). The Dionysian spirit he had studied in Nietzsche was seen by him as responsible for the wars and holocausts of his era. It is in *The Rebel* that we will find his conclusion: "The true madness of boundlessness dies or creates its own sense of measure. It does not kill others to seek an alibi. . . . Measure is not the opposite of rebellion. It is revolt which is the true measure; it orders, defends, recreates measure throughout history and its disorders. . . . We bear within us our penal colonies, our crimes, our devastations. But our task is not to unleash these upon the world, but to fight against them within ourselves and in others."[48]

## Notes

All quotations from the works of Albert Camus have been drawn from the two-volume edition of the Bibliothèque de la Pléiade published by Gallimard. Volume 1 is entitled *Théâtre, Récits, Nouvelles* (Paris: Editions Gallimard, 1962). In the individual notes the title of the work referred to will appear in French, followed by the English translation, and an abbreviation for the volume. Volume 1 will be abbreviated as *TRN*. In subsequent notes (after the initial mention), the title of the work will appear only in English. Volume 2 is entitled *Essais* (Paris: Editions Gallimard et Calmann-Lévy, 1965). It will be abbreviated as *E*. Here also, in the initial note the work will be mentioned in French, followed by the English translation. Subsequently, the title of the work referred to will appear only in English. The quotations have all been translated by the author of this essay.

1. Albert Camus, *L'Homme Révolté (The Rebel)* in *E*, 540.

2. Nicola Chiaromonte, "Sartre Versus Camus: A Political Quarrel," *Camus*, ed. Germaine Brée (Englewood Cliffs, N. J.: Prentice Hall, 1962), 32.

3. Camus, *E.*, 649.

4. Eugene Ionesco, *Fragments of a Journal*, trans. Jean Stewart (New York: Grove Press, 1969), 92.

5. Camus, *The Rebel*, 575–76.

6. Albert Camus, "Les Meurtriers Délicats" (this text, originally published in January 1958 in *La Table Ronde*, was reworked by Camus and incorporated into *The Rebel*). It can now be found in the Appendix to *TRN*. The quotation comes from p. 1822.

7. Camus, *The Rebel*, 577.

8. Ibid., 574.

9. Chiaramonte, "Sartre Versus Camus," 32.

10. H. D. F. Kitto, *Greek Tragedy* (Garden City, N.Y.: Doubleday, 1955), 130.

11. Albert Camus, "Sur l'avenir de la tragédie," in *TRN*, 1699.

12. Ibid., 1703.

13. Ibid.

14. Camus, *TRN*, 1714.

15. Ibid., 1707.

16. Ibid.

17. E. Freeman, *The Theatre of Albert Camus, A Critical Study* (London: Methuen and Co., 1971), 10.

18. Camus, *TRN*, 1710.

19. Albert Camus, *Les Justes (The Just Assassins)*, in *TRN*, 322.

20. Ibid., 323.

21. Ibid., 320.

22. Ibid., 322.

23. Ibid., 324.

24. Ibid.

25. Albert Camus, *L'Etranger (The Stranger)*, TRN, 1208.

26. Camus, *The Just Assassins*, 324.

27. Ibid., 337.

28. Ibid., 384.

29. Ibid., 361.

30. Ibid., 363.

31. Ibid., 367.

32. Ibid., 366.

33. Ibid., 367.

34. Ibid., 365.

35. Ibid.

36. Ibid., 368.

37. Ibid.

38. Ibid., 326.

39. Ibid., 325.

40. Ibid., 373.

41. Ibid., 376.

42. Ibid., 393.

43. Albert Camus, *Caligula*, *TRN*, 108.

44. Camus, *TRN*, 1733.

45. James A. Arnold, *Les Cahiers Albert Camus* (Paris: Gallimard, 1984), 173.

46. Camus, *Caligula*, *TRN*, 16.

47. Camus, *The Rebel*, 579.

48. Ibid., 704.

# The Fall: The Flight                    Maurice Blanchot*

Clamence, the man so named in *The Fall* — though he is nameless (a voice crying in its own wilderness) — is talking *sotto voce* with someone whose face we do not see, whose replies we do not hear. A "solitary dialogue," it is not Oedipus' tragic dialogue with the silence of the gods, the solitary man's utterance, divided in itself and actually split in two because the heavens which it strives invincibly to engage are mute; because for Oedipus, from whom both gods and men have turned away, divesting him of his glorious appearance, this void into which he must now speak, questioning his unjustifiable fate, is not a void but rather the sign and the depth of divinity, suddenly revealed to him through the misery of knowing.

It is true that the man who speaks here has somewhat the outward appearance of Oedipus. He, too, has reigned over himself and others; king in appearance, as befits a kingdomless era, king in the minds of men, but fallen from this semblance of glory, satisfaction and virtue of which, for a time, it had been permitted him to make a solid reality. And why has he fallen? For the same reasons as King Oedipus, about whom it has been said, in a verse borrowed from the madness of Hölderlin, that he had "one eye too many perhaps." Lucidity prevents a king from reigning for long in innocence.

But this other king is not talking with the gods, nor even with the remoteness of the gods who have turned from him; he is talking simply with the shadow of a chance acquaintance, invisible behind a curtain of silence, his double, perhaps, but also anyone at all, the casual individual whose fitful attention and vague presence allow the well-formulated language which tries to reach him to fall constantly into unreality. The kind of sober malediction with which the story confronts us is contained in this partitioned word. A dialogue enclosed in a monologue. Reflective minds will not fail to comment on the different ways in which *The Stranger*, *The Plague*, and *The Fall* accommodate the needs of the

*Reprinted from *L'Amitié* (Paris: Gallimard, 1971), 228–35. © Editions Gallimard 1971. Translated by Alba Amoia.

confidential recital — and on the fact that the stranger, speaking of himself and saying I, is speaking with the impersonality of a He already a stranger to himself; that, in *The Plague*, the central character, the teller of the story, uses the third person to relate events which nevertheless concern him directly, because, in the community of anonymous misery, it would be unsuitable to invoke the intimacy of one's own recollections. And here, in *The Fall*, where the one who is speaking speaks only about himself, deviating at times, but apparently without reticence, and using all the marvelous rhetorical resources of the successful barrister that he is, we soon realize that he is not talking about his own life, but about the life of all of us, that this life is without content, that his confidences reveal nothing, just as the interlocutor to whom he turns is nothing but a wall of fog in which his words bury themselves, unheard and as if they had not even been pronounced.

What is left? Irony.

What will undoubtedly be sought in this recital is the rugged movement of a satisfied man who, by lending himself a virtuous and happy ego, in the end gives in to that power of discontent and destruction that also exists in the ego. It is dangerous to pay too much attention to oneself. Such attention is at first a spontaneous and contented acceptance, forgetful of everything, of others and of oneself; but this attention gives way to reflection; the pleasant, self-caressing look becomes a wary look; one is wounded where one thought oneself loved; the wound is alert to see everything that wounds; and everything wounds. Finally, lucidity comes into play. It judges everything and condemns everything — ironically, without gravity and without rest, with that cold flame it has kindled in the ego.

My reading of *The Fall* is quite different, however, from this narration inspired by the psychology of La Rochefoucauld. Even less do I believe that it is intended to teach us discontent, the uncomfortable truth and necessary disquiet. First of all, it is careful to teach us nothing. Such is the mercy of irony: it gives us only what it takes away from us; if it affirms, the affirmation is a hot seat from which we are in a hurry to escape. Irony sometimes becomes heavy. Its weight is also its lightness: for it is humorless.

In this engaging story, I see the traces of a man in flight, and the attraction of the story, strong and without content as it is, lies in the very movement of flight. When did he flee? From what was he fleeing? Perhaps he doesn't know, but he does know that his entire personality is only a mask: from his borrowed name to the trivial episodes in his life, which are so little individualized that they could pertain to anyone. His confession is nothing but a calculation. His tale of a guilty man is based on the hope of believing himself guilty, since a real transgression would be a certainty on which he could base his life, a solid reference point which would enable him to demarcate his course. Similarly, when he seems to be reproaching himself for his selfish existence, when he says: "I, I, I is the refrain of my whole life and it could be heard in everything I said" [as translated by Justin O'Brien, *The Fall*. New York: Penguin Books, 1957, p. 37.], this is strange, for each time he says I, no one answers; it is only a call that echoes and re-echoes, an ironic reminiscence, a recollection that he does not recall.

If he is a masked man, what is behind the mask? Another mask, Nietzsche said. But the cold and passionate brilliance which announces his appearance and allows us to follow him through the meanderings of interrupted confidences, digressions intended solely to prompt his refusal and nevertheless to drag us along with him, convinces us of his presence, like some bright light over a moving expanse of water. There is, certainly, in him and about him, a strong dose of absence, but this void, this distance, is only a hideout, a means of concealing himself, of constantly moving further on, if necessary, and of leaving for the person who seizes him nothing but a semblance and cast-off clothes. This is an example of how Albert Camus uses classical art for a completely non-classical purpose. The impersonality of traits, the generality of characteristics, the details which do not refer to anything unique, and even the scene of remorse, which seems to have been taken bodily from a letter of Stendhal, this "scornful confession" in which nothing is confessed that is recognizable as a living experience, everything which, in classical discretion, is used to depict man in general and the fine impersonality of all, is used here only to bring us into touch with someone who is almost no longer anyone, an alibi in which he tries to entrap us even while he is escaping.

The movement of the story is constantly paralleled by a quasi-nocturnal progress — even when it takes place during the day — through the sunless and unsmiling flatland of some northern country, through the gray labyrinth of its waters, a wet desert in which the man without refuge has his base in a sailors' bar, hangout of men who have little respect for the law. This second progress is essential to the story, and the landscape is not simply a stage setting. On the contrary, it contains all that is real. The narration behind which the man hides, and which is almost painfully empty and unreal, finds there its modicum of truth and its moving end. Something is alive here that is real, it draws us into reality, we know that someone could be there, moving to and fro, looking at the brightness created in the sky by the wings of some still invisible doves (perhaps they are gulls), a derisive prophet calling down judgment on himself and others, so that the judgment may take hold of him and stop his fall. Vain hope. He must simply flee, helping to sustain this great, universal flight which involves everyone, unbeknown to all, but of which he has become aware and of which he is the bitter, avid conscience, sometimes almost cheerful, a bit drunk.

But what is he fleeing from? What is this flight? The word can scarcely please. Courage lies, however, in the acceptance of fleeing rather than living peacefully and hypocritically in false refuges. Values, morals, fatherlands, religions, and those personal convictions which our vanity and our self-complacency generously bestow on us, are just so many deceptive stopping places furnished by society for those who think they can thus stand propped up or relaxed among stable things. They know nothing of the immense rout in which they are caught up, ignorant of themselves, to the monotonous rumble of their ever more rapid footsteps, which move them along impersonally in a vast immobile motion. Fleeing to escape fleeing. Clamence is one of those who, having had the revelation of the mysterious drift, no longer can bear living amid the subterfuges of permanence. At first he tries to take advantage of this motion. He would like to withdraw personally. He lives apart. In the grand army's retreat, he plays the sniper, that human species which malicious spirits generally condemn in terms reserved for runaways from battle. But this approach does not produce the desired results. The petty, debauched life that he leads gives some satisfaction, but not that of being discredited and rejected at large. Virtue continues to protect him with its appearance. He who carries the banner of evil ought not to have learned fancy language and good manners. Meursault, though innocent, had been condemned to death because a slight difference set him apart — an apartness which was his own fault. This one cannot allow himself to be considered guilty, because whatever he does to set himself apart is only one form of the general discordance. It is said that, in a vacuum, heavy and light objects both fall at the same speed and, consequently, do not fall. Perhaps that is what the fall is: that it can no longer be a personal destiny, but the fate of each one, as part of everyone.

Believers will say that Clamence is simply running away from God, just as humanists will say that he is simply running away from mankind. Each of them will thus express himself in his own language of flight. There is an unusual page in the book. Evoking his life as a self-satisfied man, the narrator says to us, to our surprise: "Indeed, wasn't that Eden, cher Monsieur — no intermediary between life and me? Such was my life," and again: "Yes, few creatures were more natural than I. I was altogether in harmony with life, fitting into it from top to bottom without rejecting any of its ironies, its grandeur, or its servitude." [Translation by Justin O'Brien, pp. 22–23] This is a strange confidence, for the man who is speaking, or at least the personage that he borrows to speak through, is a man of vanity and self-esteem, to whom natural spontaneity is completely foreign, and the very way in which he confides without confiding anything, by a movement of irony and ruse, heightens still further our impression of affectation or artifice his character wants to give us. How could we possibly believe that he had ever been in harmony with life? Or should we believe that the masked man is now unmasking himself? That he will betray someone else? I would not like to suggest that Albert Camus suddenly thought of himself, the natural man that he was fortunate enough to be—and that he would no longer be, since a man who writes must first, like Oedipus, have "one eye too many perhaps." But it is true that both *The Stranger* and *Noces* had allowed us to experience the pleasure of life in its immediacy. The stranger was a stranger even in that respect, because of a simplicity and innocence so certain that they could only render him guilty. It is as though the deformed, bitter, shifty man of *The Fall* opened up onto another man and onto another life which he evokes like the pagan dawn of creation. The fall, then, would only be mistrust with respect to happiness, the need for being not merely happy but justified in being happy. The search is a dangerous one. There is no justification without transgression. One becomes guilty through the same happy sentiment that was originally the substance of innocence. One was happy, therefore innocent. One is happy, therefore guilty, then unhappy and still guilty; finally, never guilty enough in light of this lost happiness which was without authority and without justification. The search for the transgression becomes, henceforth, the whole of life, a transgression one would like to share with everyone in a community which only enhances one's solitude.

But this way of looking at things is only a temporary bearing which, in terms of the endless motion of the fall, has no real value. We are falling. We find consolation in imagining the point when we began falling. We prefer to be guilty rather than to be tortured without having transgressed. Suffering without reason, exile without a kingdom, flight without motive are intolerable. Imagination comes to help fill the void in which we are falling by establishing such and such a beginning, such and such a point of departure, which in turn give rise to the hope of reaching such and such a point of arrival, and even though we don't really believe in them, we are comforted by being able to establish these momentary points of reference. And then we talk about them. The most important thing in all of this is to talk. The word in itself is without end, like the fall. It is the sound of the fall, the truth of this mistaken motion which it seeks to make audible and perpetual, revealing without betraying it. Rather than the monologue of a man fleeing from the world, from fake consideration and false virtue, from happiness without happiness, what I hear is the monologue of the fall, as we might be able to sense it in advance if only we could stop the idle chatter of the routine lives in which we are holed up out of sheer necessity. The character who speaks would willingly take on the guise of a demon. What he is so roughly grumbling about, behind us, is the space in which we are invited to perceive that we have been falling since the beginning of time, without respite and without our even knowing it. Everything must fall, and everything that falls must drag along with it, in an ever-increasing progression, everything that claims to be permanent. At times, we realize that the fall is much greater than our own measure and that in some sense we must fall even further than we are capable of. Then can the dizziness begin by which we double ourselves, becoming for ourselves the companions of our own fall. But sometimes we have the good fortune to find close to us a real companion with whom we talk eternally about this eternal fall, and our conversation then becomes the modest abyss in which we also fall, ironically.

# The Compulsion of the Minimal:
# The Aesthetics of *La Chute*    Michael Bishop*

Across the noisy, smoke-filled room of Amsterdam's *Mexico-City*, the dazed, stultified barman looks out upon his clientele and concludes, vaguely but shrewdly, so at least Jean-Baptiste Clamence would have us believe, that "Something is out of kilter amongst men."[1] Indeed! . . . Hélène Cixous, Mary Daly, or Benoîte Groult might exclaim, and no doubt because everything has been circulating for all too long amongst men exclusively: the inclusion of a feminine principle and practice might well have transformed a vicious circle into one of harmony and balance. And, indeed too, Clamence / Camus renders clear — for the above is not a mere whim, nor a gratuitous digression calculated to please fifty-one percent of the readership — the vitiated "circumstances" in which "events," mind, and aesthetics unfold with the gradual deployment and creation of *La Chute (The Decline)*. All ultimately swirls in the only apparently Dutch, but really at once Camusian, French, and universal atmosphere of facticity and disequilibrium inevitably generated by a "male" substance, a "male" optic, and as we shall see, a "male" aesthetics inextricably bound up with the latter.

This, of course, is neither a criticism addressed to Camus nor a statement of absolute conviction or reductive categorization. Still less is it a "criticism" or simplification addressed to what, in effect, will principally hold our attention here — namely the interiority of *La Chute*, its inner aesthetics, laid down line by line, though elliptically and parabolically, in the *univers imaginaire* it at once constitutes and, metalogically, as Ponge might say, autodetermines via the intermittence of a self-analytical, and a self-synthetical, *mise en abyme*. The aesthetics I shall elaborate thus belongs to a mind-set and a reality that, entirely fictitious, tend to escape the grasp of any existential limitation or valuation: fiction and aesthetics,

*This essay was written especially for this volume and is published here for the first time by permission of the author. All translations are the author's.

buried deep within their non-space and non-time, generating each other reciprocally. *Et pourtant*, thrusting dizziness aside, and plunging into the vortex of *La Chute's imaginaire*, where we can catch up with its nonexistent life (and consequent non-values) — and in the hope of returning, like Orpheus, to "the true life" where textual shadow and ontic light are reconciled — let me seek within the (play of) the text itself the stark and central logic of my initial apparent reduction. To do this, and to better sense the "framing" of *La Chute's* aesthetics, let me delve briefly, but more intently, into the "substance" and the "optic" this "male" novel ceaselessly creates.

That something is "out of kilter" in the exclusively male exchanges and perceptions informing the declining world of *La Chute* is made manifest throughout the novel. Everywhere reign ambivalence and ambiguity. Our approximateness, so warmly, passionately sung by Tzara, here dogs our every ambition of transcendence. "Nous ne sommes qu'à peu près en toutes choses" (LC, 13), Clamence proclaims. Furthermore, not only are we incomplete, partial, but we are divided in what remains to us, Janus-like (LC, 15, 41, 57), fraught with doubt, hesitation, contradiction, paradox. In this, Clamence's natural affinity for what he calls "life" (LC, 35) can be seen as a hindrance and noncreative instinct, rather than a force compelling regeneration and spiritual/ecological harmony. It speaks, indeed, more as a confirmation of the gap, in Clamence's self-made and projected world, between belief, thought, appearance, and the truth of being (LC, 24 and passim). Indeed, rather than presence and affinity, what characterizes Clamence's life and, further, his conception of life unfolding about him, is its ghostliness, its deep, puffed up emptiness. "I would play at being effective, intelligent, virtuous, civic-minded, indignant, indulgent, supportive, edifying. . . . In short — I won't go on — you've already grasped that I was just like my dear Dutchmen who are there without being there: I was absent at the very moment I took up the most room" (LC, 102). Essence, in effect, in this Dutchmen's world, is always hazy, murky, basically unplaceable, "here" and yet "elsewhere" (LC, 18), unstable, almost fatuously — and, only partly anguishingly — unnameable. Without wishing to plunge into the endless nuances required to articulate the notion fully, we can surely sense here a fundamental divergence from the passion, the desire for clarity, the refusal of play and the opting for the "transcendence" of love, humility, and ephemeral simplicity that, in such varying ways, are conveyed by the work of, say, Marceline Desbordes-Valmore, Simone Weil, Marie Noël, Andrée Chedid, Claire Etcherelli, Marie-Claire Bancquart, and so many other women, including Simone de Beauvoir, Benoîte Groult, Hélène Cixous, Annie Leclerc. Let it again be understood that this is neither a criticism nor a purely arbitrary division. But if there is androgyny in *La Chute's* fictional universe, it is surely held firmly in check by a vision only minimally resilient, minimally resurgent, minimally governed by altruism, desire for reform, transcendence, "aquarian" revolution. The "fall" that occurs, of Clamence and the world as he sees it, involves a collapse of such a vision into the baselessness of its negativity and intransitiveness. For the ultimate "refrain" of life, such a vision repeatedly affirms, is self (LC, 58 and passim). Love always unmasks itself as self-love (LC, 41), as a plunging back into the empty security of our isolation, a jettisoning of the risk and joy of the other. Women, and men, in this perspective always fall prey to those dictates of hubris, maya, and fear that La Rochefoucauld has so deftly, all too tidily, thrust upon "man," "all men"—dictates which, in reducing significantly the meaning and gravity of "human affairs," (LC, 101), tend equally to reify and objectify the actions, sentiments, and aspirations of all those caught in *La Chute*'s (fictional) net(work). Where dismay and upset might have led to remedy and reversal, the power of the absurd thrusts the mind within the novel down into cynicism and irony, play (LC, 57, 70) and theatricality, (LC, 11), indifference (LC, 123) and yet the urgency of immanent self-salvation in conscious duplicity (LC, 161–63 and passim).

The aesthetics proper of *La Chute* might reasonably be said to anchor itself in a fundamental divorce separating language from reality and leaving articulation—speech, literature, linguistic communication in all its forms—stranded upon the exterior enveloping membrane of life. "I thus moved forward," Clamence tells us, "upon the surface of life, in words, you might say, never in reality" (LC, 60). Existence thus plunges one not just into the *difficulté d'être* that Cocteau evokes, but into the difficulty of naming what flickers across the screens of the heart, the mind, the soul (LC, 80), already in themselves disturbed, uncertain, muddied. In principle, of course, nudity and rawness seem self-imposing means of securing absolute contact. "For the statue to be naked, fine speech must disappear" (LC, 81), Clamence maintains. In principle, there is always the possibility of "saying" what "is" (LC, 151, and passim). In principle, saying will flee simple "pleasure" and self-gratification, just as it will avoid the ubiquitous trap of speaking "so as to say nothing" (LC, 152). In principle, the "orientation" of saying will be dictated by a purity, a transcendent logic, however unnameable they, too, may remain (LC, 152).

And yet, writing, speech, and the aesthetics that underpins them, are bedevilled by various "impurities" and impediments. If Clamence can feel at a given moment that his elaborations are about to place him "at the heart of things" (LC, 19), we can not overlook the constant reminders of the ambivalence, ambiguity and, indeed, sheer inauthenticity that filter into every word, every act, every mental maneuver in and around him, penetrating his *récit*. Rather than lament the "duplicity" of the language and gesture his *récit* constitutes, and not unlike Ponge or certain exponents of the *nouveau roman* and its subsequent avatars with their stress upon an "evacuated" fictional interiority, Clamence installs himself within this very duplicity (LC, 163), opting for a kind of aesthetics of "[the intoxication] of bad language" (LC, 166). "And my stories," he argues, "true or false, do they not all tend towards the same end, do they not have the same meaning? Well then, what does it matter whether they're true or false, if, in both cases, they point to what I have been and what I am" (LC, 140). Thus is it that truth becomes indistinguishable from falsehood in the logic of the saying of *La Chute* and that saying what "is" becomes clouded with a mixture of impotence and indifference, simple acceptance and nonchalant playfulness. Just as Clamence does not hestitate to set himself up under another name in moving from Paris to Amsterdam (LC, 160), so does he not balk at the idea of moving freely from real to invented, "true" to "false" in the selection of those "names" that found his *récit*, in his "relating of himself" (LC, 23).

Thus is it that the text itself suffers from the same problem besetting the perception of reality: its essence is equally "unplaceable." Of course, the one complements the other; they are mutually justifying in a sense. And, of course, the aesthetics of Clamence's *récit* is based upon a seeming, at least intermittent, need to "confess all one's lies" before death (LC, 105), and before the *récit* reaches its close, and its more complete "publicity" (LC, 161). Of course, too, the aesthetics of confession avoids coarseness and thus chooses "seemliness," propriety, and simplicity over exaggeration and imperfection. But, as Clamence makes clear, his "style" is, in effect, more elusive: "I navigate with suppleness, I am given to nuance, and digression, I adapt my language to the listener" (LC, 161). A complete rhetoric of subtle persuasion thus comes to light in the midst of this aesthetics, a rhetoric that, like all rhetorics, is implicitly geared to other ends than truth alone. Intrigue, seduction, play, may, in fact, jostle for equal attention. In speech, in the deployment of *récit*, as in the endless exchange of daily life, Clamence is apt, as he says, to "light apparent fires," plunging joyously, and to the applause of his listeners / readers, into the bantering, shimmering style that (ill-)defines him, that of the *maître-comédien* he prides himself upon being (LC, 57). Whilst it is true that such a *pointing* to the manner and "how" of the articulation of Clamence's *récit* remains, like the admission of the blurring of the frontiers between truth and falsehood, a significant feature of the aesthetics at hand, it is equally true that in the realm of mask, deception, and seduction one can never be sure whether the pointing is straight, or, indeed, if it is directed to anything at all. That such a problematic lies at the heart of *La Chute*'s aesthetics as well as its ontology can not be lost from sight without risk.

In effect, to opt for an aesthetics of theatricality is, ineluctably, to succumb to that "weakness for fine language" (LC, 10) which Clamence recognises from the outset of his "discourse." Such a temptation is, of course, the temptation of style itself: the avoidance of content, meaning, substance; the decision to opt for the dazzle of form, pure aestheticism, *obgame* and *obplay* as Ponge again might say, to the detriment of any real contact with the object. Just as certain "things" may be omitted from the *récit* (LC, 37), leaving it holed, imperfect, half-forgotten (LC, 59) and chosen as partial, so the entire *récit* may risk evacuating itself, its "object," in centering upon the shimmer of its surface, its *passage* rather than its *profondeur*. The rhetoric of "demonstration" and "method" (LC, 16) thus always treads a thin line between sheer autonomy of text / *parole* and deep, even if vitiated, purpose, between tautology and true ontic urgency and at least possible transitivity. Whilst such a discourse continues to self-correct (LC, 148), it tends to fall into the trap of its own self-veiling, the endless intermittences (LC, 52: "I even have trouble turning my sentences. I don't speak as well, it seems to me, and my speech is more hesitant"), digressions, *flottements* and symmetries that feed its relentless unwinding. If, thus, the sleight-of-hand aesthetics utilised may have the root of its logic in the preservation of self and, simultaneously, the protected condemnation of all others, it is equally an aesthetics constantly turning in upon itself, conscious of the ruin of its own interiority, aware of the hollow defeat of self at the very moment of the latter's declared and subtle superiority.

A number of other factors remain to be focussed upon before moving to an elaboration of the, for me, residual, undeniably central character of the aesthetics of *La Chute*. Firstly, and on the "positive" side, the latter rests upon a need for contract, exchange, self-exorcism and even, Clamence tells us from the outset, the giving of oneself, the "service" of one's *récit*, tattered but beautiful, to others (LC, 7). If, then, the discourse of Clamence tends towards the double narcissism of egocentricity and pure, hygienic, "symbolist" aestheticism — interlocking black holes speaking of a double absurdity — we cannot neglect a certain "movement'" within the aesthetics that brakes and restrains its self-centering proclivities.

Secondly, the aesthetics subtly aims to center the discourse of Clamence's *récit* upon a coincidence of self and other (LC, 161). Whilst it is true that such a convergence, such a "self-recognition," is fabricated by means that are constantly held to be intrinsically suspect, not to say deceitful and, in a sense, quite "unreal," it surely cannot escape the listener / reader — the other — that only in projection, even experimentally and "inauthentically," through the force, the nuanced "coercion" of rhetoric, can the other — we, ourselves — hope to sense in some obscure way the mode of being of what and who we are not — whose relevance to us, and even partial presence within us, we might all too gladly overlook. In short, the aesthetics of *La Chute*, despite everything, thrusts us up against our secrecy, our hiddenness, our darkness. It reminds us of our provisional, circumstancial mode of being, and the fictions that can lurk within our separateness.

Thirdly, *La Chute* offers an aesthetics of tension. As Clamence narrates "[his] career as a false prophet crying out in the desert and refusing to emerge" (LC, 135, 169), he lays bare / veils over a discourse *divided* between an aesthetics of prophecy and communion, evangelicism, and potential revolution, and one that prefers to contradict and deny the value of its (fore)telling, one that chooses resignation, withdrawal, and nonchalance where transformation and some Rimbaldian "future Vigor" might just have been chanced. If there is no idle idealisation here, there is a sense of static impotence, even of ideal idleness, a surrender, not without anguish, but not without indulgence — and surely we can see ourselves in such a mask! — to the logics with which Clamence has surrounded himself. There may, indeed, in *La Chute*, be a speaking from knowledge (LC, 162), but equally there is, as with all of our *récits* of the self, a walling-in of the self within the aesthetics / ontics we create for ourselves.

"It's sheer overflow," Clamence admits toward the beginning of his confessional *récit* that Camus will call *La Chute*, "as soon as I open my mouth, the sentence flows" (LC, 17): thus, in an odd way, factors of excess, overflowing, join those of minimality, aridity, nonchalance, and consciously tensional compulsion in an aesthetics that on the surface appears to shift radically away from the "aphasia" of *L'Etranger* but which in effect maintains considerable furtive contact with the latter's paradoxes. "Style," Clamence himself owns, "like poplin, often hides eczema" (LC, 10). But, as I have tried to show already, the presence of such a scabbed sub-reality should not lead us to believe that there is no heart, no soul, no significance, still further below, and, indeed, mingled with the oozing matter so stylishly draped. Whilst the aesthetics of *La Chute*'s discourse argues the frivolity of the serious (LC, 101), let us not overlook the reverse perspective it equally proposes. Nobody, Clamence maintains, is hypocritical in his or her pleasures (LC, 77), and, thus, a whole wave of "authenticity" sweeps back over the bared shore of Clamence's pleasurable textual-confessional play: through a typical legerdemain we suddenly find ourselves talking about an aesthetics of the seriousness of frivolity. Can such a reversal of the equation really be, we ask; is it intellectually, emotionally, spiritually feasible? One feels giddy with this theatrical shifting of the ground. What seems to be on the one hand — like Clamence's *micro-récit* of the traffic incident, and as he himself continually inclines us to believe with respect to the *macro-récit* — "[a] story of no importance" (LC, 63), with its aesthetics of play and pleasure *in* "false prophecy," *in* a residing within the "desert" of life-time "career" withdrawal (LC, 169) — this we are implicitly asked to view as subtly meaningful, as it were "absurdly significant." An aesthetics of the insignificant, though hardly that elaborated by a Michel Deguy, say, or an André Frénaud, or even a Marguerite Duras — such an aesthetics, with its various noted slacknesses, suddenly seems to be drawn tight, its minimality more sharply and compulsively delineated, its potential fatuity arrested at a critical moment.

If, in fact, it is difficult to deny what I have characterised at the beginning of my argument as the "maleness" of the aesthetics (and ethics) underpinning *La Chute — amour-propre*, nontranscendence of the self, fear, hubris, indifference, cynicism, and the ultimate opting for a theatre, a play, an irony, a "style," a minimality "one refuses to step out of" (LC, 169), all of which confirm the role of hubris in the generation of the *récit* — then, at least we can make ourselves available, *beyond all judgment*, moreover, to the force and claim to legitimacy of that powerful minimum compulsively cried out to us from its desert — and that makes *La Chute* a moving, meaningful, even if ambiguous testimony to the passing amongst us of a man named Albert Camus. Such a compulsion tinges the aesthetics of the minimum, on which Clamence's *récit* rests, with the wryest of wry smiles. We do not reproach, even *in* judgment, a *moliéresque* twinkle, nor even the "style" of *l'absurde*. To be "taken at one's word" would, it is true, imply a number of things for Clamence — as indeed it would for us all! — and the prospect is dismissed with mock horror. Yet would anything really change? Do we not already live and breathe, as only we can via the discourse of *La Chute*, fictitiously, theatrically, assuming the minimality, assuming the compulsion, too, of its *chiaroscuro*. Living the ambivalences of our species, the otherness we oddly need to embrace, the tense love of what we are not, the smiling gravity of an impotent revolt yet crying out to each of us.

## Notes

1. Albert Camus, *La Chute* (Paris: Gallimard, 1956), 9. Hereafter referred to as LC.

# The Ethics of Albert Camus    Serge Doubrovsky*

For Sartre, Mauriac, and many others who may or may not have written, the deep shock felt, at Camus's death, combined with personal sorrow, is the feeling of a work suddenly stopped in full momentum, mutilated. As Malraux said long before, through Moreno in *Man's Hope*, "The capital thing about death is that it renders irremediable all that which has preceded it. . . ." For the writer, however, all the effort of writing is directed, before death, at escaping death. The author dead, the work continues; it lives. It can not progress, but it can be enriched. It could not be modified, but through its relation to new minds it can be renewed. . . .

During Camus's lifetime already, in order to neutralize his message, attempts were made to ossify his work, to disarm it by means of one or two often repeated epithets. At first, the word was "existentialism." Camus protested in vain on many occasions against the appellation and the

*From *Preuves*, no. 116 (October 1960): 39–49. Translated by Sondra Mueller and Jean-Marc Vary. Reprinted by permission.

affiliation, going so far as to attack by name the philosophy that was attributed to him: to no avail. One can still consult several manuals, especially the Anglo-Saxon ones; there lies Camus under the heading "existentialism." But this is not really troublesome; and existentialism is a scarecrow only for imbeciles. Although it is, in fact, an error in classification, it wrongs no one. More serious, is the stereotyped image: Camus, the moralist par excellence of the immoral twentieth century; the austere, just, righteous preacher. We need only consult the obituary notices. Some congratulate him for it, others detest him for it. His will to be ethical, his moralism is praised or denounced: it is none the less an established fact. Some people do not hesitate to speak of "Jansenism" and Camus, like Racine's Phèdre, becomes a Christian without grace. Or again, Camus is not a believer and that is just the point: a professor of ethics, he knows only a professor's ethic, two or three abstract notions which he exalts. There again, in spite of his protestations, Camus had been witness to his metamorphosis. "Like everyone, I tried as best I could, to correct my nature by means of an ethic; that is, alas, what cost me most" (*L'Envers et l'endroit*).

Morality? What morality? That is what we should like to examine here. When re-reading Camus, we are struck by the repetition of a certain number of terms that seem to come out of a course on ethics: justice, happiness, revolt, etc. These words reoccur repeatedly, like a call to order, in the editorials of *Combat* and in the polemical exchanges with his contradictors. In his personal and philosophical essays they are constant themes of meditation, focal points of his thought. All Camus may seem to be contained in his choice of a particular glossary. Yet, and this is remarkable, these key words are never rigorously examined and really given a definition. It might be objected that the words "absurd" in *The Myth of Sisyphus*, "revolt" in *The Rebel*, are analyzed at length, and often in an authoritative way. But the analysis is, so to speak, horizontal rather than vertical, proceeding by extension rather than by inclusion. Revolt leads back to the original emergence of value, the emergence of value to the consciousness of evil, the consciousness of evil to the inverse affirmation of happiness and justice. But what of happiness, justice? The contents of these concepts, their immediate and far-reaching implications, the dialectic of inclusion or exclusion that relate them are all latent. Though Camus feels these concepts, he does not explore them in depth, in the sense that Sartre, for example, links his phenomenological descriptions of shame, fear, and anguish to a complete and rigorous view of man. In our opinion, the value of Camus's processes of thought derives from the very fact that they are lived rather than reasoned. "I am not a philosopher and I know how to speak only of what I have experienced" (*Actuelles II*). This does not mean, of course, that a philosopher must of necessity speak about what he has not experienced. But insofar as he integrates experience within a system, he transforms it. Dialectics gradually take the place of intuition.

Phenomenology is set in motion, truths must fall in and be arranged. In contrast, Camus has no system, no general framework, no philosophy. He grasps firmly only a few discontinuous truths which grip him: "I held on to truth as much as it held me" (*The Stranger*). We may as well get used to it. We can argue for and against, put in balance . . . integrity and entirety, existence and philosophy, and raise all the problems of a philosophy of existence. This is what Jaspers did, and others besides. At any rate — and this is to the point — it is impossible to extract a "morality" from Camus's various intuitions and an "ethic" from his meditations on ethics. Camus's thought has been reproached both for its lack of practical application and for its excessive morality. But we may well question the notion of an ethic devoid of practical applications, an ethic, if ethic there be, defined as an ensemble of rules and precepts. What Camus's monotonous and powerful appeal to "justice" or to "happiness" reveals is in fact, an existentialist tension, rather than any rules for living. Above all, Camus is a poet, or to be more exact he has the sensitivity, the vision of a poet. But can a man innocently be a poet in our century? Insofar as Camus clothes his intuitions with reasoning, he distorts them.

"A man's work is nothing other than the long voyage to rediscover by the detours of art the two or three simple and great images which first gained access to his heart" (*L'Envers et l'endroit*, preface). All Camus's thought resides in a few elementary childhood experiences, in the way they "opened" him to the world. The famous "Mediterranean wisdom" with which he was so often taunted, is not, as was wrongly claimed, a luxury born of a bourgeois culture. As a child, and a child of illiterates, Camus, at the time of his fundamental experiences had not attained the realm of culture. He attempts rather, consciously and sometimes awkwardly, to recapture the *precultural* springs of existence. The fundamental existential experience that haunts Camus and which he tried to express through the lyrical descriptions in his first essays — works to which one must always return because they never ceased to be true for him — through the myths of the "Algerian race" and the "towns without pasts" (is there a writer who does not create his own myths?), in the last chapters of *The Rebel* in brief, is the world lived as heat and light, is the sun.

Sartre, in the analyses at the end of *Being and Nothingness*, has sufficiently emphasized the importance of the tangible in presenting immediate symbols for the interrelation of our consciousness and the world; in his "psychoanalysis" — to use Bachelard's word — of snow, of the viscous, etc. It is not surprising that no theoretical analysis of the solar can be found in Sartre since, after all, the sun seems absent from his personal universe. Or, to state matters more exactly, it plays a negative role: "I shan't do anything worthwhile, except perhaps, at nightfall. That's because of the sun. . ." (*Nausea*). The redeeming virtues of night are defined in relation to the negated sun; it is because they are *anti-solar* that they give Roquentin a temporary respite from nausea. There is, of course, the disappearance of light ("Nausea remained down below, in the *yellow light*"), but what especially counts is the disappearance of heat: "I am happy: the cold is so pure, so pure tonight." Night leads back to cold, cold to purity. We follow the slope, the orientation of Roquentin's existentialist reverie: "Am I not myself a wave of chilled air? To have neither blood, nor lymph, nor flesh . . . To be only a part of the cold." The sun is no longer "Noon the just" of Valéry's "Graveyard by the Sea," "Noon up there, motionless Noon," the plentitude of being against which the revolt of life must be affirmed: it is the *vital* force itself. Camus considers the sun in the same way as does Sartre, but only to oppose Sartre as he opposed Valéry. Camus's sun, unlike Valéry's, is not the manifestation of a spherical form of being, closed in on itself. . . . It is always the sun shining on the ruins of Tipasa, the sand beach of *The Stranger*, or the sea. It is light felt not as a distant purity, but as a fecundating bath. It is the unifying force of the cosmos: "From the earth to the sun a heady alcohol rises over the whole expanse of the earth, making heaven sway" (*Noces*). Gliding over all things, penetrating all things, overwhelming in its presence, the sun is the very symbol of that vital participation through which the realms of nature and of man are united: "Outside the *sun*, *kisses* and wild *perfumes*, all seems futile to us" (*Noces*).

The theme of the "sun," therefore, defines the fundamental category in Camus's ontology: participation. It is perhaps worth recalling here young Camus's vivid interest in Plotinus. His experience is the very opposite of Sartre's nausea. Sartrean "nausea" has its source in the double awareness of subject and object, of the absolute separation of consciousness and nature — in man's impotent negation of being as he tries symbolically to "reject" a world from which he is effectively rejected. With Sarte, we live a godless Cartesianism, whereas in Camus we detect a Bergsonism but without teleology. Though life in Camus's work no longer moves in an ascending and reassuring direction, it still has impetus; though it has lost its finality, it has preserved, so to speak, all its vitality. The body is the place where man and nature meet in a happy "marriage."

In the solar world of Camus, the muscular indolence and eurythmy of bodies reigns without contest. Animality is fully accepted. Camus is far from thinking in terms of self-enjoyment or of a hedonistic retreat within. ("To take pleasure in oneself is impossible." *L'Envers et l'endroit*, preface). The body is the privileged place of joy, because it is the locus of harmony, and union is in fact unison. Physical love places human beings against the background of Being, and participation in the act of love is the symbol of a deeper participation. Meursault feels his love for Marie while swimming: "The water was cold and I felt all the better for it. We swam a long way out, Marie and I, side by side, and it was pleasant to feel how our movements matched, hers and mine, and how we were both in the same mood, enjoying every movement." Nor is it by chance that Meursault's love for his mother, instead of being a latent and permanent sentiment, as required by psychological myths which are only disguised forms of morality, always wells up from sudden perception: "Through the rows of cypress trees . . . that tawny brown and green earth . . . I understood Mother." The spontaneous identification of earth and mother defines Meursault's "cybelian" [Cybele: goddess of the earth] mode of existence, plunging to the telluric sources of his being where in the words of the poet Claude Vigée, all love is "a happy incest."

It is easy to see how an ontology such as this can affect ethics. Vital participation is both act and value. We can mask fact for others and for ourselves, but a value will emerge precisely at the time of the unmasking. In this light it should be noted that at the end of *The Stranger*, Meursault's famous "awakening" and his accession to the ethical life do not arise out of the rejection of his past "animality," or of his physical mode of existence; of his adherence and adhesion to the moment, to the earth, given him in a succession of sensations; of his fidelity to the present and to presence in spite of all the attempts of society to create a continuous time and a logical world. On the contrary, the imminence of death makes explicit those values which heretofore had been implicit only. Meursault's life, suddenly limited and arrested, is not struck retrospectively with absurdity, as happens for Sartre's Pablo, in *The Wall:*

> Death had disenchanted everything. . . . If someone had come to tell me that I could go home peacefully . . . it would have left me cold: a few hours or a few years of waiting, it's all the same, when one has lost the illusion of being eternal. I was anxious about nothing; in a sense, I was calm.

In contrast, Meursault says,

> That meant, of course, I was to die. Also, whether I died now or twenty years hence, this business of dying had to be got through, inevitably. Still, what troubled me in my reasoning was the terrible jump my heart gave at the thought of twenty years of life yet to come.

Threatened with annihilation, life gathers and concentrates its force, becomes conscious of itself and proclaims that it is the only value: "And I, too, felt ready to start life all over again." Far from rendering life absurd, death is the element which gives it its full meaning. Life retrieves and reabsorbs death, and in its very defeat triumphs, since death which denies life succeeds only in reaffirming life. In Cybele, Apollo and Hades were reconciled:

> In a few moments, I shall throw myself down among the absinth plants letting their fragrance invade my body and, all prejudices to the contrary, I shall know that I am fulfilling the truth which is the truth of the sun and will also be that of my death (*Noces*).

This, of course, suppresses neither the reality nor the horror of death. For death is not manifest only at the end of a life, but at its very heart, and then it is called suffering. With Meursault, the problem, in a sense, was posed too simply, too neatly. His beautiful animality is to be destroyed, but it is not impaired. He is going to die a lusty young man, but he will not suffer in the flesh.

With *The Plague*, we move from death suffered in full health to death suffered in illness. Pus mingles freely with the absinth plants of *Noces* (Nuptials), which reappear at the end of *The Stranger*: "The cool night air, veined with smells of earth and salt, fanned my cheeks. The marvelous peace of the sleepbound summer flooded through me like a tide." Flesh does not perish only, it disintegrates. It does not disintegrate after death only, but in life. Life and death are not only opposed one to the other, they inter-penetrate. The problem becomes more painful and more complex, but it remains fundamentally unchanged. This is made clear in the significant episode toward the end of *The Plague*, the end of the long combat with Evil and the long conversation between Rieux and Tarrou, who from all this draws the lesson: "Do you know," he said, "what we ought to do for friendship's sake?" "Whatever you wish," said Rieux. "Take a dip in the sea; even for a future saint, it's a worthwhile pleasure." The friendship between the two men, like the love of Meursault and Marie, regains its essential truth in the contact with water, as the two men swim "in the same cadence": "For some minutes, they advanced with the same cadence and vigor, alone, far from the world, liberated at last from the city and the plague." The narrator had already spoken, at the beginning of the passage, of "the outer world which can always save everything . . ." Rather than the stoic pronouncements he sometimes coined, this is the intuition which lies at the center of Camus's ethic.

If our analysis is accurate, it ought to help us get rid of two misunderstandings which weigh disastrously on the work and the person of Camus. First, the famous "heroism," to which we are told his message can be reduced. This error contains a share of truth, like all errors. The Tarrou side of Camus, in truth the temptation of heroism, is apparent in Camus's tendency to refuse emotion, in the kind of inflexibility with which he comes to grips with fate and which is often reflected in stiffness in his style, in his constant search for the concise phrase. "What interests me," says Tarrou with simplicity, "is to know how one becomes a saint." Evidently, Camus, too, is interested. But in his moments of weakness, when the demands he makes upon himself grow weak, Rieux, who, after all, is the narrator of the book and who survives whereas Tarrou dies, answers his friend, his alter ego: "I have no taste, I believe, for heroism and sainthood. What interests me is to be a man." "Yes, we are seeking the same thing, but I am *less ambitious*." One can easily understand why heroism is a facile solution, a least effort: as the characters of Malraux's

*Man's Fate* show, heroism is essentially a turning in on oneself by a confrontation with death. . . . Camus moves in the opposite direction when at the end of *The Rebel*, he says that "in order to be a man" one must "refuse to be God"; when he breaks away from the ultimate ambition of heroism, it is because he is not thinking in terms of a closed, circular ethic; it is because all his thought tends to define an ethic of "openness" to the world and to others, an ethic of participation.

There is a certain form of participation that is called enjoyment. A propos of Camus, Gide has often been mentioned, and Camus has been taken to task for affinity with the apostle of hedonism, at a time when "commitment" was considered indispensable. Hedonism, too, is one of the temptations Camus faced (who does not have his own?) but it is incompatible with the fundamental direction of his thought, with his "existential project." "Self-enjoyment is impossible; I know it, in spite of the great talents I could have applied to it" (*L'Envers et l'endroit*, preface). Camus finds this hedonism impossible, not in the name of an abstract morality, but because it is the nature of the body, of the "body proper" as the philosophers would say, to turn toward the world and be in harmony with the world. Resemblances with Gide in vocabulary or thought—sensation, present moment, light, sun, landscapes, etc.—are only superficial. . . .

There is no Gidian hedonism in Camus. Camus's faithfulness to ever-repeated fundamental experiences is quite opposed to Gide's variety of experiences. The fundamental paucity and poverty of Camus's imagery of nature contrast sharply with Gide's varied landscapes, with Gide's many sentimental wanderings through reality as flitting "from flower to flower, from one thing to another" (La Fontaine). Camus's imagery is always drawn from the ruins of Tipasa, sun on rock, or the Mediterranean, the sea. When removed from his element, visiting Prague or the Scandinavian countries, Camus becomes lost, bewildered. Whereas Gide experiences everything in the plural, Camus experiences things in the singular. His solar experience is one of destitution and denudation. His is a "proletarian" relationship to the world, the relationship of someone who has nothing and whose contact with objects is not expressed in terms of having. Camus's domain is *being*, and this returns us to our preceding analyses of the vital force. The only possession is a rejoicing which is a participation.

Since heroism and hedonism are rejected, more from an ontological point of view than an ethical one, or to put it otherwise, once the concept of possession in the form of domination of self or of the world is disqualified, there obviously remains a basic problem to be solved in Camus's thought: that of the relationships between being and doing. This is the very heart of the quarrel between Camus and existentialism, a quarrel that caused so much ink to flow over the last ten years. One can easily follow the evolution of Sartre from *Nausea* to *Red Gloves*: all ontological solutions are closed to thought. Where consciousness is the illness of being, where the "for-itself" exists only as a continuous opposition to the "in-itself," and where the aim of the human being underlying all others is to synthesize the two contradictory entities—in other words, where, as Malraux had already stressed in *Man's Fate*, man's dream is to be God, any position which seeks a solution in being is necessarily doomed to failure. "Bad faith," which all Sartre's work is there to uncover and track down in all its machinations, is nothing but man's desperate effort to give the consistency of being to his existence, *to make himself exist* through symbolic possession of the world, through other people's view of him, etc. From then on, man is a "useless passion." The concept of authentic action is opposed to the state of real transcendence of the "absurd." "A priori, life is senseless . . . but it is up to you to give it a meaning" (*Existentialism is a Humanism*). The important word here is *give*. "Bad faith" can introduce itself in our way of "giving a meaning," in such a manner as to have this meaning remain intentional, symbolic. Meaning can be given to one's life through deeds alone, or more precisely through actions, that is to say, a manner of behaving which is not an end in itself (this would be falling into heroism, an attitude denounced in *The Flies*), but which aims at an objective transformation of the world. Since history is the actual medium in which man comes into contact with the world, the existentialist philosophy of action will be a philosophy of historic action, entirely oriented toward *the future*. Sartre: "Existentialism will never take man as an end, for a man is always in a state of formation" (*Existentialism is a Humanism*). De Beauvoir: "It is in the light of the future, which is the meaning and very substance of the act, that a choice will become possible" (*For an Ethic of Ambiguity*). Simone de Beauvoir herself draws the consequences of this attitude in the following statement: "Men of today will be sacrificed to those of tomorrow because the present appears as the 'facticity' that one must transcend toward freedom." In this respect, the whole purpose, the whole effort of Camus's philosophy is directed at shutting this door so dangerously left open on the sacrifice of the living to the men of the future and at reinstating the inalienable value of the present in opposition to the future.

"This argument accepts life as being the only necessary good . . ." (*The Rebel*). The moral philosophies of Sartre and Camus are what one could call "unidimensional philosophies," the one basing itself completely on the idea of liberty, the other on that of life. It is not accidental that throughout this essay we have pursued the parallel, or rather that we have been pursued by this parallel between Sartre and Camus. A perpetual confrontation such as this—which faces us in our every thought and action—does no more than express the absolute need of our time to redefine itself completely. Malraux had already said, "The age of the fundamental is beginning again," and in spite of the complexity of the problems, the fundamental choices are simple. A philosophy of liberty directed exclusively toward action is a philosophy of abandon, of the radical separation of man and world, a philosophy in which the world becomes acceptable only when transformed by man. This explains the value given to the manufactured object in Sartre's work, the detailed analysis of the artifact and of all relations connected with the use of things, whereas, in contrast, Roquentin's "nausea" is triggered by the feel of a pebble on the beach. The dangers of such an existentialist attitude can easily be grasped: by denying itself communion through actual presence, it does away with the present in favor of the world transformed, "acted upon," i.e. the future. By cutting off humanity from being, by enclosing man in the humane and denying being to the human, it tends to upset the balance of existence leaving it in a false equilibrium, so to speak.

Philosophers like Merleau-Ponty have attempted to help man out of this dead end and to re-establish him on his ontological foundations. That is exactly what Camus does in the realm of ethics. To expect salvation to emerge from action is to postpone the justification of the action indefinitely, to perpetually refer to the problematical end of history. In her systematic effort to define an existentialist philosophy, Simone de Beauvoir was aware of the dangerous mirage inherent in the concept of distant goals: "The end justifies the means only if it remains present to us, if it is completely revealed during the enterprise itself" (*For an Ethic of Ambiguity*). However, because of the lack of a point of reference, of a permanent criterion, in short, of an absolute value, or, more exactly, because liberty is the only absolute value he possesses, the existentialist philosopher finds himself placed in a position forever oscillating between the end and the means: "One cannot judge the means without the end which gives it meaning, any more than one can detach the end from the means which define it." But from where then will the definition, the meaning, come? Under its humanized surface the world is absolute chaos. Man, we have been told, cannot be taken as an end since he is perpetually in the making. The refusal to take man himself as an end is all the more understandable since Sartre's theoretical analyses of our relationships to others as well as his literary investigation reveal that "hell is other people" and that for man "his number one enemy is man"; and this without our being able to blame any political system, since Sartre considers that it is an unchangeable ontological situation, a characteristic of man's condition and therefore impervious to any possible modification.

Freedom then remains as the supreme goal. But since freedom is a fact or if one wishes, facticity, as well as transcendency (we cannot not be free, we are *condemned* so to be), and therefore differs from a value that has yet to be, we can conceive of goals *for* freedom but not of freedom as a goal. For we cannot confuse liberty and liberation without being insincere. The chained slave is free as both the theoretician in *Being and Nothingness* and Orestes in *The Flies* know[1]; if he wants to be freed, it is because he wishes to find himself moving once again within the circuit of humanity; it is because he wishes to *live*.

Here we discern another value that liberty can no longer define. It is no longer possible to shut man up inside his own ipseity, to say with Simone de Beauvoir that man's problem consists in "pursuing the expansion of his existence and in recovering this very effort as an absolute." In a different manner, we have come back to the fruitless circularity of heroism. Human activity must open itself to the world, must surrender itself to the world and rediscover its natural source and dwelling, must live the experience of the sun. Simone de Beauvoir herself says this admirably well when she writes:

> To wish man free is to wish for being, it is to wish for the revelation of being in the joy of existence. . . . It is when our movement toward freedom takes on the consistency of pleasure, of happiness, that it assumes its real and palpable form in the world. . . . If we do not love life in our own selves and through our fellow man, it is useless to try to justify life.

This is exactly what Camus says throughout his work. But one can wonder how such an existential outlook is compatible with the existentialist attitude. How can the revelation of being be made through joy if the basic experience of being is expressed through "nausea"? How can one desire being and at the same time set up consciousness as the very negation of being? An orientation toward happiness, an unconditional love of life are indeed the concrete basis of all ethics, but then we need to change ontologies. What happened in fact was that the ethics of ambiguity surreptitiously passed from Sartre to Camus. And if in the last analysis we wish to give a concrete basis to moral philosophy, we must go back to the words of Camus: liberty opens upon life and the philosophy of existence upon the philosophy of being.

We now have before us one of these arresting Camus truths. The "yes" triumphs over the "no." "I came to realize that at the core of my revolt lay a consent. . . . How does one sanctify the union of love with revolt?" (*Noces*). But simultaneously an inverse reaction takes place: revolt exists side by side with consent: both find expression in an equilibrium of opposites. Therefore we have not reached one of those philosophical "principles" that would allow us tragically to "deduce" a philosophy, an axiom from which we could draw laws and precepts as in the good old days of rationalism. Hardly has the "yes" been posited before the "no" rises in opposition. "Man is the only creature that refuses to be what he is" (*The Rebel*). Horror and injustice exist within our own selves, in others, and in the world. Thus in a simultaneous "yes" and "no" Camus defines a dialectic of confrontation, of opposition, of anguish without transcendence. Camus's well-known "concept of limitations" simply means that an affirmation of life must be made which does not end in a complete negation of the world. Camus knew full well that to emphasize the "vital" was not without danger. Nietzsche had encountered the same problem only to fall into the "superman" trap and into the error of biological expansionism; we are well aware of what followed when these ideas were taken up by others. Life can be deadly; the sun kills, as Meursault finds out when he shoots the Arab without reason: "My eyes were blinded by a curtain of salty tears. I felt only the sun beating down relentlessly upon my forehead. . . ." The pure and simple submission to vital forces without the counterweight of moral revolt ends in the destruction of these forces; vitalism escapes nihilism only on the condition that life accept a sacrifice; it must cease to limit itself to the individual; it must transcend itself by moving into the realm of the universal: "Within the limits of the 'absurd' experience, suffering is individual. Starting with the movement of revolt, we are aware of suffering as a collective experience, as everyman's adventure. I revolt, therefore we are" (*The Rebel*). This defines the evolution of Camus's thought from *The Stranger* to *The Plague*.

A moral philosophy of action is thus superimposed upon — one might even say spans — a philosophy of being. This is the sensitive core, the touchstone of any doctrine today. Action in Camus's eyes must remain faithful to its twofold origin, the "no" sitting in judgment, and the "yes" ready to "change life but not the world." Divided at its source, action can only be charged with anguish. Since it no longer attempts to reach the absolute, which is found only on the level of being, it can only be imperfect. "Poverty prevented me from believing that all is well in history and in the world; the sun taught me that history is not everything." Camus has often been criticized for rejecting history because he did not accept it exclusively. The fact that he set it in a broader ontological context does not mean that he substituted the concept of history for something else. But at a time when history, in the case of many, has become the only dimension of the human drama, Camus refers us to something which underlies history and without which history could not exist.

In the course of the debate caused by *The Rebel*, Sartre criticized Camus for placing human values in "the battle of man against heaven" and by so doing forgetting the concrete and historical reasons for action. It is quite true that in a way *The Plague* presents a perfect situation in which all human beings can unite to fight the inhuman. But, after all, the book is also an allegory and must so be understood. It does not negate history, but extracts an ultimate meaning from it. If man habitually can and should (most of all, perhaps) fight man, it is insofar as man becomes a scourge and assumes the role of the plague. The oppressed says to the oppressor: "Get out of my sun." Action as conceived by Camus can never be satisfied with being a praxis; it is never a form of salvation in itself; it is never circular at any time. Though necessary, it is always deceptive, in fact somewhat mystifying if it is not rooted in the world of the present, in life itself. As Simone de Beauvoir so aptly said, "If the satisfaction of an old man drinking a glass of wine has no value, then production, wealth, are only empty myths." Man is not "the future of man"—to use the words of the poet Francis Ponge, so dear to the existentialists—he is man's present.

Immediate practical consequences stem from Camus's moral philosophy which some have described as being so ethereal: "I shall have pleaded my case . . . so that *from this very moment* the agonizing pain of man be lessened" (*Actuelles*). No appeal to the realm of ends, of the future, can justify any attack on the present, on life which is an inalienable value. Camus squarely sets up an ethic of being in opposition to the ethics of action, and at this point he breaks with existentialism and Marxism. Camus never denied that in certain exceptional cases, the use of violence might be a weapon, but he always refused to accept that it might become a policy. A simple nuance perhaps, but for millions of human beings, one which is capital in importance. In this sense certainly, Camus was the conscience of our time, repeating in vain perhaps what Ionesco was to illustrate in his play *The Killer*: that we could not build the "shining city" in defiance of nature without immediately bringing the Killer into existence.

One might object that it is very easy to be a "conscience" and this obviously raises the whole problem of the "clean" and "dirty" hands having an equal chance of bringing some consolation. But, we ask, how does the evolution from *The Stranger* to *The Plague*, from the subjective to the "we are" attitude find its application on the practical level? Camus proposes an ontology; nevertheless a concrete ethic, in other words, a policy, still has to be defined, for it would be pointless to establish an "Algerian" ethic which would not begin by dealing with Algeria, for example. And how will the "yes" and "no" offset each other in this particular instance? "What we need is to define a modest policy, a policy just as free from any trace of Messianism as from the nostalgia of a Garden of Eden" (*Actuelles*). Will Camus's ethic of moderation then end up only in a policy of moderation? When Camus writes, "There is only one thing left for us to try, and that is honesty without illusion, a wise loyalty . . . ," this wisdom may seem limited and disappointing, but we must admit that there exists no ethical or political position that does not have its pitfalls. The pitfalls inherent in the concepts of absolutism in action or history are too obvious these days to require any comment. What Camus called the nihilism of efficiency at any cost has more than shown its inhuman consequences. But the opposite danger of abstention and inactivity is also present. It is a real danger and no formula exists which allows us to evade it. Both the middle of the road and the royal road can be fatal. The first, however, offers our civilization more chances of survival than the second, whose end we know only too well.

We shall not discuss those personal commitments or refusals to be committed which concern Camus alone. We merely note that, when necessary, Camus paid with his own person, and that his reticence very often coincided with a near withdrawal. But he never claimed that he was playing an exemplary role nor did he ever set himself up as a model. Passionately in search of an ethic, he never claimed he was a moralist. As his preface to *L'Envers et l'endroit* (Betwixt and Between) clearly shows, he was aware that he was fallible. The exponents of virtue who dream of being judges are dealt with in *The Fall*. To those who demand coherent, satisfying, and clearly stated policies—to systematic minds, to the organizers and administrators—we can only answer that Camus, like the most beautiful girl in the world, can give only what he possesses.

In contrast to the fundamental experience described in most contemporary philosophies, he had a certain happy experience of being which appeared basic to him: he passed it on to us. Around him and in history he sees the consequences of uprooting: he tells us about them. Camus, who is a thinker though not a philosopher, instinctively perceives certain truths. They had escaped minds dialectically better prepared than his own, but minds that did not know how to extract consequences from these truths or who did not wish to extract them. He recalls these consequence inexorably, monotonously. He rediscovers the values of life and happiness lost in the tumult and terrors of our age. He places happiness, that is to say, the reconciliation of man and nature, above ethics and simultaneously rectifies the indifference inherent in nature, his own nature, through an ethic: solitude exploding in the movement of the heart toward his fellow-man. "Rieux straightened up and said in a firm voice . . . that there was no shame in preferring happiness. — Yes, said Rambert, but there may be shame in being happy all alone" (*The Plague*).

This is the existentialist tension in Camus's thought that no theoretical formulation, no dialectic process can resolve. Camus gives us only two ends of the chain which we must hold at any cost. In its authenticity, Camus's "moderation" is quite the antithesis of comfortable, mediocre moderation. It is a painful and perpetual effort. The true contact with being and with others is not given. It can only be conquered over the commonplace, over habit. The tenacious will to come to grips with the present is not easy to maintain when one knows just how easy it is to count on the future or the past for one's own justification. "Moderation" is the only way through which to live and adhere completely to life. Basically, the discontinuous intuitions powerfully restated by Camus, once elucidated, reveal less what we should do than *what we should not do*. One cannot be a hero, a pleasure seeker, or a judge, and this is the sense of Camus's opposition to Malraux, Gide, or Sartre.

Camus's work does not set up an ethic, but in a way it does propose "prolegomena to any future ethic." As Claude Bourdet said in the conclusion of an article "Camus and the problem of Clean Hands," "If the time should come when in spite of present ups and downs France turns toward socialism . . . then the warnings of Camus against the degradation of revolution may be useful to those who will then be facing certain dangers . . ." If we lose a certain relationship to being, existence founders. These are the "traps" detected, the warning cries, desperate at times, that Camus raises in our time, clarion calls of the poet echoing through a city of philosophers and rhetoricians. Lacking that logical coherence which so often is only superficial and illusory, the warnings, the cries, the call possess an internal cohesion born of an unshakable certainty. If it goes deeply enough, analysis uncovers not a mine of ideas but an outpouring, a vital spring. There we must take our arguments to be refreshed. It seems that for Camus this is what constitutes all ethics. It must be *existential* in the full sense of the word, or it does not exist, or it becomes an anti-philosophy dedicated to man's destruction. No formula, no effort of discursive thought can absolve us from recreating experience ourselves within ourselves. Human beings though interdependent stand alone. Today, this is a truth not easily acceptable. Camus is neither the man in the street nor the "organization man." He is the man in the sun, on the lone naked rock, who knows that once the plague has come he must re-enter the city. It is he who said, "My human passions have never been 'against,' " and who during the struggle and beyond it, never forgot the reasons to love. This sun, this knowledge mean little to empire builders or creators of systems. Nevertheless, should the era neglect them, it will rush to its doom, and man's fate will be sealed the day he forgets how to love — in spite of evil and suffering — this creation without a creator.

### Note

1. "*Jupiter*: If you dare pretend that you are free, then the freedom of the prisoner loaded down with chains in the corner of his cell will have to be vaunted as well as that of the crucified slave. — *Orestes*: Why not?"

# Tribute to Albert Camus                    Jean-Paul Sartre*

Six months ago, even yesterday, people wondered: "What is he going to do?" Temporarily, torn by contradictions that must be respected, he had chosen silence. But he was one of those rare men we can well afford to wait for, because they are slow to choose and remain faithful to their choice. Some day he would speak out. We could not even have dared hazard a guess as to what he might say. But we thought that he had changed with the world as we all do; that was enough for us to be aware of his presence.

*From *Situations IV* (Paris: Gallimard, 1964). © Editions Gallimard, 1964. Reproduced by permission of Gallimard and Hamish Hamilton Ltd.

He and I had quarreled. A quarrel doesn't matter — even if those who quarrel never see each other again — just another way of living together without losing sight of one another in the narrow little world that is allotted us. It didn't keep me from thinking of him, from feeling that his eyes were on the book or newspaper I was reading and wondering: "What does he think of it? What does he think of it *at this moment?*"

His silence, which according to events and my mood I considered sometimes too cautious and sometimes painful, was a quality of every day like heat or light, but it was human. We lived with or against his thought as it was revealed to us in his books — especially *The Fall*, perhaps the finest and least understood — but always in relation to it. It was an exceptional adventure of our culture, a movement of which we tried to guess the phases and the final outcome.

He represented in our time the latest example of that long line of *moralistes* whose works constitute perhaps the most original element in French letters. His obstinate humanism, narrow and pure, austere and sensual, waged an uncertain war against the massive and formless events of the time. But on the other hand through his dogged rejections he reaffirmed, at the heart of our epoch, against the Machiavellians and against the Idol of realism, the existence of the moral issue.

In a way, he *was* that resolute affirmation. Anyone who read or reflected encountered the human values he held in his fist; he questioned the political act. One had to avoid him or fight him — he was indispensable to that tension which makes intellectual life what it is. His very silence, these last few years, had something positive about it: This Descartes of the Absurd refused to leave the safe ground of morality and venture on the uncertain paths of practicality. We sensed this and we also sensed the conflicts he kept hidden, for ethics, taken alone, both requires and condemns revolt.

We were waiting; we had to wait; we had to know. Whatever he did or decided subsequently, Camus would never have ceased to be one of the chief forces of our cultural activity or to represent in his way the history of France and of this century. But we should probably have known and understood his itinerary. He said so himself: *"My work lies ahead."* Now it is over. The particular scandal of his death is the abolition of the human order by the inhuman.

The human order is still but a disorder: it is unjust and precarious; it involves killing, and dying of hunger; but at least it is founded, maintained, or resisted by men. In that order Camus had to live. That man on the move questioned us, was himself a question seeking its reply; he lived *in the middle of a long life*; for us, for him, for the men who maintain order and for those who reject it, it was important for him to break his silence, for him to decide, for him to conclude. Some die in old age while others, forever on reprieve, may die at any minute without the meaning of their life, of life itself, being changed. But for us, uncertain without a compass, our best men *had* to reach the end of the tunnel. Rarely have the nature of a man's work and the conditions of the historical moment so clearly demanded that a writer go on living.

I call the accident that killed Camus a scandal because it suddenly projects into the center of our human world the absurdity of our most fundamental needs. At the age of twenty, Camus, suddenly afflicted with a malady that upset his whole life, discovered the Absurd—the senseless negation of man. He became accustomed to it, he *thought out* his unbearable condition, he came through. And yet one is tempted to think that only his first works tell the truth about his life, since that invalid once cured is annihilated by an unexpected death from the outside.

The Absurd might be that question that no one will ask him now, that he will ask no one, that silence that is not even a silence now, that is absolutely *nothing* now.

I don't think so. The moment it appears, the inhuman becomes a part of the human. Every life that is cut off—even the life of so young a man—is at one and the same time a phonograph record that is broken and a complete life. For all those who loved him, there is an unbearable absurdity in that death. But we shall have to learn to see that mutilated work as a total work. Insofar as Camus's humanism contains a *human* attitude toward the death that was to take him by surprise, insofar as his proud and pure quest for happiness implied and called for the *inhuman* necessity of dying, we shall recognize in that work and in the life that is inseparable from it the pure and victorious attempt of one man to snatch every instant of his existence from his future death.

# SELECTED BIBLIOGRAPHY

Primary Sources

*Révolte dans les Asturies (Revolt in Asturias)*. Algiers: Charlot, 1936.

*L'envers et l'endroit*. Algiers: Charlot, 1937. "The Wrong Side and the Right Side." In *Lyrical and Critical Essays*. Edited by Philip Thody. New York: Knopf, 1968.

*Noces*. Algiers: Charlot, 1939. "Nuptials." In *Lyrical and Critical Essays*. Edited by Philip Thody. New York: Knopf, 1968.

*L'Étranger*. Paris: Bibliothèque de la Pléiade, Editions Gallimard, 1942. *The Stranger*. Translated by Stuart Gilbert. New York: Vintage Books, 1958.

*Le Mythe de Sisyphe*. Paris: Bibliothèque de la Pléiade, Editions Gallimard, 1943. *The Myth of Sisyphus and Other Essays*. Translated by Justin O'Brien. New York: Knopf, 1955.

*Caligula*. Paris: Bibliothèque de la Pléiade, Editions Gallimard, 1944. *Caligula and Three Other Plays*. Translated by Stuart Gilbert. New York: Knopf, 1958.

*Lettres à un ami allemand*. Paris: Bibliothèque de la Pléiade, Editions Gallimard, 1945. "Letters to a German Friend." In *Resistance, Rebellion and Death*. Translated by Justin O'Brien. New York: Knopf, 1961.

*La Peste*. Paris: Bibliothèque de la Pléiade, Editions Gallimard, 1947. *The Plague*. Translated by Stuart Gilbert. New York: Knopf, 1948.

*Les Justes*. Paris: Bibliothèque de la Pléiade, Editions Gallimard, 1950. "The Just Assassins." In *Caligula and Three Other Plays*. Translated by Stuart Gilbert. New York: Knopf, 1958.

*Actuelles*. Paris: Bibliothèque de la Pléiade, Editions Gallimard, 1950, 1953, 1958; New York: Knopf, 1968. Partial English translation in *Resistance, Rebellion and Death*. Translated by Justin O'Brien. New York: Knopf, 1961.

*L'Homme révolté*. Paris: Bibliothèque de la Pléiade, Editions Gallimard, 1951. *The Rebel*. Translated by Anthony Bower. New York: Vintage, 1958.

*L'Été*. Paris: Biobliothèque de la Pléiade, Editions Gallimard, 1954. "Summer." In *Lyrical and Critical Essays*. Edited by Philip Thody. New York: Knopf, 1968.

*La Chute*. Paris: Bibliothèque de la Pléiade, Editions Gallimard, 1956. *The Fall*. Translated by Justin O'Brien. New York: Knopf, 1957.

*L'Exil et le royaume.* Paris: Bibliothèque de la Pléiade, Editions Gallimard, 1957. *Exile and the Kingdom.* Translated by Justin O'Brien. New York: Knopf, 1958.

*Discours de Suède.* Paris: Bibliothèque de la Pléiade, Editions Gallimard, 1958. "Speech of Acceptance upon the Award of the Nobel Prize in Literature," translated by Justin O'Brien, *Atlantic Monthly,* May 1958.

*Carnets, 1935–1942; Carnets, 1942–1951.* Paris: Bibliothèque de la Pléiade, Editions Gallimard, 1962, 1964. *Notebooks.* Translated by Philip Thody. New York: Knopf, 1967, 1970.

*La Mort heureuse.* Paris: Bibliothèque de la Pléiade, Editions Gallimard, 1971. *A Happy Death.* Translated by Richard Howard. New York: Knopf, 1972.

## Secondary Sources (English)

### 1. Bibliographies

Hoy, R. *Camus in English: An Annotated Bibliography of Albert Camus's Contribution to English and American Periodicals and Newspapers.* Wymondham, Melton Mowbray: Brewhouse Press, 1968.

Roeming, Robert F. *Camus: A Bibliography.* Madison: University of Wisconsin Press, 1968.

### 2. Books

Brée, Germaine. *Camus: A Collection of Critical Essays.* Englewood Cliffs, N.J.: Prentice-Hall, 1962.

———. *Albert Camus.* Columbia Essays on Modern Writers, no. 1. New York: Columbia University Press, 1964.

———. *Camus.* New York: Harcourt, Brace, Harbinger Books, 1964.

———. *Camus and Sartre: Crisis and Commitment.* New York: Dell, 1972.

Champigny, Robert A. *A Pagan Hero: An Interpretation of Meursault in Camus's "The Stranger."* Philadelphia: University of Pennsylvania Press, 1969.

Cruickshank, J. *Albert Camus and the Literature of Revolt.* London: Oxford University Press, 1959.

Freeman, E. *The Theatre of Albert Camus: A Critical Study.* London: Methuen, 1971.

Hanna, Thomas. *The Thought and Art of Albert Camus.* Chicago: Henry Regnery Co., 1958.

King, Adèle. *Albert Camus.* New York: Grove Press, Evergreen Books, 1964.

Lebesque, Morvan. *Portrait of Camus.* New York: Herher and Herher, 1971.

O'Brien, Conor Cruise. *Camus.* London: Fontana/Collins, 1970.

Onimus, Jean. *Albert Camus and Christianity.* Tuscaloosa: University of Alabama Press, 1970.

Parker, Emmett. *Albert Camus: The Artist in the Arena.* Madison: University of Wisconsin Press, 1965.

Peterson, Carol. *Albert Camus.* New York: Frederick Ungar, 1969.

Pollman, Leo. *Sartre and Camus: The Literature of Existence.* New York: Frederick Ungar, 1970.

Quilliot, Roger. *The Sea and Prisons: A Commentary on the Life and Thought of Albert Camus.* University: University of Alabama Press, 1970.

Rhein, Philip H. *Albert Camus.* New York: Twayne Publishers, 1969.

Scott, Nathan A. *Albert Camus.* London: Bowes and Bowes, 1962.

Thody, Philip. *Albert Camus: 1913-1960.* London: Hamish Hamilton, 1961.

Willhoite, Fred. *Beyond Nihilism: Albert Camus's Contribution to Political Thought.* Baton Rouge: Louisiana State University Press, 1968.

# INDEX

Abbou, André, 89, 90
absurd, the, 1, 6, 8, 46, 47, 49, 50, 51, 58, 104, 115, 138, 147, 151, 152, 155, 161, 165–66
*Actuelles II*, 12
"Adulterous Woman, The," 11, 55, 82–83, 108, 109–10, 116
aesthetics, male, 145–51
affirmation, 152, 160–61, 165
*agonia*, 7, 135–36
Albert, Henry, 24
*Alger Républicain*, 10, 38, 80, 90, 92, 93, 94
*Alger Soir*, 10, 90
Algeria, 16, 17, 18, 19, 21, 24–25, 56, 73–88
alienation, 1, 19; *see also* estrangement
ambivalence, 146–48
Amola, Alba, 10, 11; "Sun, Sea, and Geraniums: Camus *en voyage*," 10
anguish, 160, 161
animality, 154–56
Arabs. *See* Algeria; exteriority
Archambault, Paul, 28; *Camus's Hellenic Sources*, 28
Aristotle, 27, 135
Arnold, James A., 137; "La poétique du premier *Caligula*," 137–38
"Artist as witness of freedom, The," 34
"Artist at Work, The," 108, 109, 110, 113–14
asceticism, 62–64; *see also* poverty
Attlee, Clement, 41
Auden, W. H., 3
Augustine, 28, 104
Azev, Boris, 130

bad faith, 158
Balzac, Honoré de, 21, 119

Bancquart, Marie-Claire, 146
Barbusse, Henri, 118; *L'Enfer*, 120
Bartfield, Fernande, 122
Barthes, Roland, 52, 78, 79
Batchelard, Gaston, 153
Baudelaire, Charles, 22, 113
beauty, 44–45, 52, 53, 57–59, 92, 108
Beauvoir, Simone de, 16, 89, 146, 158, 159, 160, 161–62
Belcourt, 91
Bergson, Henri, 6
Bernanos, Georges, 16
Bersani, Leo, 32
Bespaloff, Rachel, 7
Bianquis, Geneviève, 24
*Bible*, the, 118
Bishop, Michael, 11; "The Compulsion of the Minimal: The Aesthetics of *La Chute*," 11
Blanchot, Maurice, 11: "The Fall: The Flight," 11; *Friendship*, 11
Bloch-Michel, Jean, 119; "Une Littérature de l'ennui," 119
*bomba-menbois*, 66
Borges, Jorge Luis, 118
Bossuet, 30
Bourdet, Claude, 39; "Camus and the Problem of Clean Hands," 163–64
Breton, André, 44
Braun, Lev, 6
Bréhier, Emile, 28
Brée, Germaine, 4, 7, 10, 18, 20, 25, 101, 102–3; "Climates of the Mind: Albert Camus 1936–1940," 10
Brilliant, Dora, 130
Brody, Jules, 32
Brombert, Victor, 34
Bukharin, Nikolay, 26
Butor, Michel, 16

*Caliban*, 40
*Caligula*, 7, 31, 38–39, 47–49, 128, 137–38
Calvino, Italo, 90
Camus, Albert: and Algeria, 16, 17, 18, 24–25, 73–86, 90–97; as artist, 17, 102–4, 106, 108, 113, 120–21; childhood of, 4; and Christianity, 8, 15, 17, 29–30; as classicist, 7, 115, 119, 142; and criticism, 1–12; death of, 15, 54, 166; genealogy of, 116–26; and Hellenism, 17, 27–29, 81–82, 87n15; influences on, 23–24, 116–26; as introvert, 4, 8; as journalist, 17, 38, 90–99; and Mediterranianism, 7, 21, 38, 45–46, 50, 57–58, 87–88n15, 91–92, 108, 113, 117, 153; as moralist, 12, 151–66; as philosopher, 4, 5, 12, 27–28, 152; as *pied-noir*, 73, 126; and politics, 9, 20–21, 36–42; and Sartre, 20, 25–26, 151–65; and travel, 56–69, 157; and women, 17, 22, 29–32

WORKS: FICTION
"Adulterous Woman, The," 11, 55, 82–83, 108, 109–10, 116
"Artist at Work, The," 108, 109, 110, 113–14
*Caligula* (play), 7, 31, 38–39, 47–49, 128, 137–38
*Cross Purpose*, 46, 51
*Exile and the Kingdom*, 7, 10, 16, 29, 34, 54, 55, 74, 80, 81–82, 90, 92, 107–16
*Fall, The*, 1, 8, 11, 15, 16, 24, 29, 32, 33, 34, 54, 103, 104–5, 107, 119, 125, 140–51, 163, 165
"Growing Stone, The," 109, 110, 114–15, 116
*The Happy Death, The*, 22, 46, 50
"Host, The," 11, 55, 83–85, 108, 109, 110, 112–13, 116
*Just Assassins, The* (play), 128, 131–37
*Misunderstanding, The* (play), 3, 7, 32, 132
*Plague, The*, 1, 2–3, 7, 10, 19, 25, 32, 33, 42, 51–52, 59, 74, 78–80, 100–102, 103, 105, 106, 107, 116, 140, 141, 156, 161
"Renegade, The," 11, 34, 108, 109, 110–11, 115, 116
"Révolt dans les Asturies (play)," 38
"Silent Men, The," 109, 110, 111–12
*State of Siege* (play), 8, 132

*Stranger, The*, 1, 5, 6, 9, 10, 12, 16, 19, 24, 32, 46, 47, 49–51, 74–78, 79, 80, 90, 102, 103, 104, 116, 121, 134, 140, 150, 155, 161

WORKS: NONFICTION
*Actuelles II*, 12
"Artist as witness of freedom, The," 34
"Desert, The," 10, 61, 62–63
*Essais*, 211
*Fragments d'un Combat*, 90
"Helen Exiled," 28–29, 53, 69
"Historical Revolt," 30–31
*Le premier Camus, suivi des Écrits de Jeunesse*, 22
*Letters to a German Friend*, 34
*Métaphysique chretiénne et Néo-Platonisme*, 27
"Minotaur, The," 52
*Myth of Sisyphus*, 1, 5, 6, 10, 16, 27, 31, 46, 47, 51, 152
*Notebooks*, 10, 21, 32, 35, 57, 59, 80–81, 101, 137
*Nuptials*, 7, 10, 43, 48, 50, 53, 57, 60, 69, 107, 144, 156
"On the Subject of Tragedy's Failure," 132
"Poème sur la Méditerranée," 69
*Rebel, The*, 8, 16, 24, 27, 41, 51, 53, 80, 88, 89, 97, 128, 129, 131, 138, 152, 157, 161
*Réflexions sur la guilletine*, 121
"Return to Tipasa," 54, 60
"Revolt and Revolution," 129
"Sea Close By, The," 54, 67–69
*Summer*, 10, 52, 53, 54, 57, 58, 67
*Travel Journals*, 10, 57, 63, 65, 67
"Wind at Djemila, The," 43, 60
*Wrong Side and the Right Side, The*, 10, 45, 50, 57, 59, 91, 101, 105, 106, 117, 163

Camus, Baptiste Jules Claudius, 117
Camus, Claude (great-grandfather), 117
Camus, Francine Faure (second wife), 17
Camus, Simone Hié (first wife), 17
*candomble*, 66
capital punishment, 122–23, 135
*Carnets. See Notebooks*
Casarès, Maria, 24, 30
Caute, David, 97
Caws, Mary Ann, 9
Champigny, Robert, 32, 102

Char, René, 3, 9; "L'Eternité à
   Lourmarin," 9
Chardin, Teilhard de, 30
Charney, Hanna, 10; "Supplementarity in
   Camus," 10
Chateaubriand, François René, 74
Chatrian, Alexandre, 117
Chedid, Andrée, 146
Christianity, 8, 15, 17, 27–30, 34
Churchill, Winston, 40, 41
Cixous, Hélène, 145, 146
classicism, 7, 114, 118–19, 142
Claudel, Paul, 31, 132
claustration, 19
Cocteau, Jean, 119
Cohen, Lionel, 24; "Une lignee humaniste
   au vingtième siècle: Martin du Gard et
   Camus," 33; "Signification du sacré dans
   La Chute," 33
cold war, the, 40, 85
Combat, 37, 39, 40, 51, 152
Combat Organization, 130
Commentary, 34
communism, 1, 17, 20–21, 26–27, 37,
   85–86, 128, 131; see also Marxism
Constant, Benjamin, 21
Corneille, Pierre, 7, 135; Polyeucte, 132
Costes, Alain, 22–23, Camus et la Parole
   manquante, 22–23
criticism. See Camus, Albert; New
   Criticism; normative criticism; thematic
   criticism
Cross Purpose, 46, 51
Cruikshank, John, 18; Albert Camus and
   the Literature of Revolt, 20–21
Curtius, E. R., 19

Daly, Mary, 145
d'Astier de la Vigerie, Emmanuel, 37
Das Kapital (Marx), 37
Daudet, Alphonse, 16
death, 19, 100, 155–56
Deguy, Michel, 150
Delpeche, Jeanine, 24
depersonalization, 80–85
Derrida, Jacques, 10, 99–100, 106: Of
   Grammatology, 10, 99
Desbordes-Valmore, Marceline, 146
Descartes, René, 108, 154
"Desert, The," 10, 61, 62–63
detachment, 44–45, 46
Djemila, 42, 43, 44, 46, 60, 61
Don Juan, 17, 18, 24, 31, 34, 47; see also
   Camus, Albert: and Women

Dos Passos, John, 19
Dostoyevski, Feodor, 7, 15, 17, 24, 34,
   118, 119, 135; Diary of a Writer, 119;
   The Idiot, 135; "Krotkaia," 119; Notes
   from Underground, 24, 33; The
   Possessed, 24, 135
Doubrovsky, Serge, 3–4, 11–12, 19; "The
   Ethics of Albert Camus," 11–12
du Gard, Roger Martin, 4, 16, 17, 23–24,
   31, 57; Jean Barois, 24
Duhamel, Georges, 16, 31
Duras, Marguerite, 150

Eliade, Mircea, 58
Empedocles, 28
Erickson, John, 10; "Albert Camus and
   North Africa: A Discourse of
   Exteriority," 10
Essais, 24
estrangement, 77–78; see also alienation
Etcherelli, Claire, 146
ethics, 151–64; see also morality
Euripides, 135
Europe, 118
evil, problem of, 1, 2, 7, 46, 78, 110–11,
   152, 156
Exile and the Kingdom, 7, 10, 16, 29, 34,
   54, 55, 74, 80, 81–82, 90, 92, 107–16
existentialism, 3, 20, 112, 151–52, 157–62
exteriority, 73–88
Eyck, Jan van: "le panneau des juges
   intègres," 23

facticity, 159
Fall, The, 1, 8, 11, 15, 16, 23, 24, 29, 32,
   33, 34, 54, 103, 104–5, 107, 119, 125,
   140–51, 163, 165
fascism, 27
Faulkner, William, 15, 19, 24
Festa-McCormick, Diana, 10; "Existential
   Exile and a Glimpse of the Kingdom,"
   10–11
Festugière, P., 30
Fitch, Brian, 88–89: Bibliographie d'A.
   Camus, 33; Camus nouvelliste, 33; Le
   Sentiment l'étrangeté chez Malraux,
   Sartre, Camus, 33
Flaubert, Gustave, 74, 107
Florence, 44–45, 46, 52
Fouchet, Max-Pol, 17, 118
Fragments d'un Combat, 90
France-Soir, 133
Franc-Tireur, 41
France, Anatole, 16

freedom, 159
Fréminville, Claude de, 118
Frénaud, André, 150
Freud, Sigmund, 106; *Beyond the Pleasure Principle*, 106; *see also* psychoanalysis

Garfitt, J. S. T., 23; *The Work and Thought of Jean Grenier 1898-1971*, 23
*Galerie privée*, 5
Gassin, Jean, 23; "*La Chute* et le retable de l'agneau mystique; étude de structure," 33; *L'Univers symbolique d'Albert Camus*, 23
Gautier, Théophile, 74
Gay-Crozier, Raymond, 89; *A. Camus*, 33
Gide, André, 17, 22, 31, 118, 119, 122, 157, 163; *Counterfeiters*, 17; *Fruits of the Earth*, 23; *Prétextes*, 119; *The World of the Thibault*, 17, 24
Giono, Jean, 16
Giotto, 44
Girard, Jean Baptiste, 32
Giraudoux, Jean, 29
Gobineau, Arthur de, 124-26; *Les Pléiades*, 124
Grand Duke Sergei, 130
Greece and the Greek ideal. *See* Hellenism; Mediterraneanism
Grenier, Jean, 9, 22, 23, 37, 118; *Essai sur l'Esprit d'Orthodoxie*, 37; *Les Isles*, 23
Grenier, Roger, 37, 39; *Les Monstres*, 122
Groult, Benoîte, 145, 146
"Growing Stone, The," 109, 110, 114-15, 116
"Guest, The." *See* "The Host"

Hagnaret, Roger, 41
*Happy Death, The*, 22, 46, 50
*Hebrew University Studies in Literature*, 33
hedonism, 157
Hegel, G. W. F., 6, 27, 128
Heidegger, Martin, 5, 44, 53
"Helen Exiled," 28-29, 30, 53, 69
Hellenism, 17, 27-29, 30, 53-54, 69-70n8, 81, 87-88n15, 108
Hemingway, Ernest, 19, 20, 24
Heraclitus, 28
heroism, 156-57, 160
"Historical Revolt," 30-31
historicism, 26, 36n14, 132, 158, 161
Hitler, Adolf, 26, 34, 38, 95
Hodent Affair, 38
Hoffmann, Léon-François, 119

Holderlïn, Friedrich, 11, 140
hopelessness, 5
"Host, The," 11, 55, 83-85, 108, 109, 110, 112-13, 116
Hoy, Peter, 89
*hubris*, 53, 151
Hugo, Victor, 31, 121-23; *L'Homme qui rit*, 31; *Le dernier jour d'un condamné*, 121
Husserl, Edmund, 45

imitation, the, 20
Impressionists, 6
intertextuality, 116-26
Inter-Trade-Union Liaison Committee, 41
Ionesco, Eugene, 129; *Fragments of a Journal*, 129; *The Killer*, 152
irony, 141-51

Jacobson, Norman, 89
Jaspers, Karl, 5, 153
*Journaux de voyage*. *See Travel Journals*
*Just Assassins, The*, 128, 131-37

Kabylia, 38, 80, 81, 87n14, 90, 92, 94-97
Kafka, Franz, 15, 24, 118; *The Trial*, 90
Kaliayev, 130-32
Kierkegaard, Sören, 6, 7, 24
Koestler, Arthur, 117

La Bruyère, Jean de, 117
*La Chute*. *See The Fall*
La Fayette, Mme de, 117
*La Gauche*, 41
*La Nouvelle Revue Français*, 118
*La Peste*. *See The Plague*
*La Révolution prolétarienne*, 41
La Rochefoucauld, François, 117, 141, 147
Labriolle, Pierre de, 28
Labyrinth, the, 52
Lacan, Jacques, 123
Lamont, Rosette C., 11; "Two Faces of Terrorism: *Caligula* and *The Just Assassins*," 11
landscape, 76, 81
language, 104, 147-51
Lautréamont (pseud. of Isidore Ducasse), 128
Lazère, Donald, 19-20; *The Unique Creation of Albert Camus*, 19-21
*Le Monde*, 25-26
*Le premier Camus, suivi des Ecrits de Jeunesse*, 22
*Le Soir Républicain*, 92, 93

Leclerc, Annie, 146
Lemarchand, Jacques, 9
*L'Envert et l'endroit*. *See The Wrong Side and the Right Side*
*Les Cahiers du Sud*, 29
*Les Temps modernes*, 21, 24, 26, 33, 119
*L'Été*. *See Summer*
*Letters to a German Friend*, 34
Lévi-Valensi, Jacqueline, 90; "Le Temps et l'espace dans l'oeuvre romanesque de Camus; une mythologie du réel," 33
"L'Exile d'Hélène." *See* "Helen's Exile"
Leynaud, René, 39
*L'Humanité*, 9
light. *See* sunlight
Lorrain, Claude: *D'Acis et Galatée*, 119
Lorrain, Jean: *Monsieur de Bougrelon*, 119
Lottman, Herbert R., 17; *Albert Camus: A Biography*, 17–18, 89

McCarthy, Patrick, 4, 18–19, 123; *Camus*, 18–19
*macumba*, 66
Madariaga, Salvador de, 117
Maeterlinck, Maurice, 30
Mallarmé, Stéphane, 44, 113
Malraux, André, 19, 21, 22, 24, 29, 30, 33, 45, 104, 118, 163; *Days of Wrath*, 24; *The Human Condition*, 129; *Man's Fate*, 24, 48, 151, 156–57, 158
Mansfield, Katherine: *Journal*, 118
Marx and Marxism, 20–21, 26–27, 35, 37–38, 128, 162; *see also* communism
Massignon, Louis, 23
Maupassant, Guy de, 16
Mauriac, François, 151
measure, law of, 54, 138; *see also mésure*, moderation
Mediterraneanism, 7, 21, 38, 45–46, 50, 57–58, 87–88n15, 91–92, 108, 113, 117, 153
Mendès-France, Pierre, 41
Melville, Herman, 24, 118; *Benito Cerrino*, 24; *Billy Budd*, 24; *Moby-Dick*, 24
Memmi, Albert, 86
Merleau-Ponty, Maurice, 21, 26–27, 159; *Adventures of the Dialectic*, 26
*mésure*, 22; *see also* measure; moderation
*Métaphysique chretiénne et Néo-Platonique*, 27
Micha, René: "L'agneau dans le placard," 119
Miller, Rev. Samuel, 30

"Minotaur, The," 52
*Misunderstanding, The*, 3, 7, 32, 132
Mitterand, François, 20
moderation, ethic of, 162–65; *see also* measure; *mesure*
Montaigne, Michel de, 7, 89
Montherlant, Henry de, 31, 118
morality, 12, 102–3, 108–9, 152, 162, 165; *see also* ethics
Morot-Sir, Edouard, 89
Mounier, Emmanuel, 3, 8
Murchland, Bernard, 25
Musset, Alfred de, 119
*Myth of Sisyphus*, 1, 5, 6, 10, 16, 27, 31, 46, 47, 51, 152

Naudin, Marie, 122
nausea, 154, 159, 160
Nazism, 26, 39, 51, 94, 101, 110; *see also* fascism
Nerval, Girard de, 74
New Criticism, 10, 11
New York, 63–64, 67
*Ni Victimes ni Bourreaux*, 40
Nietzsche, Friedrich, 22, 24, 27, 29, 35, 118, 128, 137–38, 161
nihilism, 3, 46, 47, 128, 161
Nobel Prize, 15, 16, 22, 24, 41, 57
*Noces*. *See Nuptials*
Noël, Marie, 146
normative criticism, 2, 6, 7, 8, 9, 10, 11
*Notebooks*, 10, 21, 32, 35, 57, 59, 80–81, 101, 137
*Nuptials*, 7, 10, 43, 48, 50, 53, 57, 60, 69, 107, 144, 156

O'Brien, Conor Cruise, 19, 20, 25–26, 77, 89
O'Brien, Justin, 19
Oedipus, 11, 140, 144
"On the Subject of Tragedy's Future," 69–70n7, 132
Onimus, Jean, 29–30; "Les ecrivains devant Dieu," 29–30
Oran, 52, 57, 58, 59, 68, 78, 79, 87n10, 97, 100, 101, 105

pantheism, 10, 43, 44, 109
paradox, 104
*paratext*, 11
*Paris-Théâtre*, 132
participation, 154–57
Pascal, Blaise, 6, 7, 15, 56–57, 104, 108
Peri, Gabriel, 39

*Permanence de la Grèce*, 29, 30
Peyre, Henri, 7, 9; "Presence of Camus," 9
phenomenology, 153
Pia, Pascal, 17, 39, 90
Picon, Gaëtan, 3, 5
*pied-noir*, 18, 73, 86n2, 126
Piero, 44
*Plague, The*, 1, 2–3, 7, 10, 19, 25, 32, 33, 42, 51–52, 59, 74, 78–80, 100–102, 103, 105, 106, 107, 116, 140, 141, 156, 161
Plato, 27; *Dialogues*, 27
Platt, Bruce, 29; *L'Evangile selon Albert Camus*, 29
Plotinus, 28, 154
Plottel, Jeanine Parisier, 11; "Intertextuality in Albert Camus," 11
"Poème sur la Méditerranée," 69
Ponge, Francis, 39, 145, 148, 161
poverty, 62, 92, 101, 161; *see also* asceticism
*Preuves*, 119
Proust, Marcel, 21, 31
psychoanalysis, 22–23, 106, 123, 153; *see also* Freud, Sigmund

Quilliot, Roger, 2, 9, 53, 89, 119; "Camus's Libertarian Socialism," 9

R. D. R. Party, 41
Racine, Jean, 22, 135; *Iphigenie*, 124
*Rebel, The*, 8, 16, 24, 27, 41, 51, 53, 80, 88, 89, 97, 128, 129, 131, 138, 152, 157, 161
récit, the, 33, 107, 148–51
*Réflexions sur la guillotine*, 121
"Renegade, The," 11, 34, 108, 109, 110–11, 115, 116
Resistance, the French, 39, 56, 63, 137
"Return to Tipasa," 54, 60
Revel, Jean-François, 21
revolt, 8, 19, 21, 37–38, 41, 45, 78, 104, 128–29, 138, 152
"Revolt and Revolution," 129
"Révolt dans les Asturies," 38
*Revue des Lettres Modernes*, 89
*Revue d'Histoire de la France*, 119
Rey, Pierre-Louis, 33
Richaud, André de: *La Douleur*, 118
Rimbaud, Arthur, 22, 128
Robbes-Grillet, Alain, 16, 32
Roblès, Emmanuel, 17
Rolin, Dominique, 9
Rolland, Romain, 121
Romains, Jules, 16, 31

Rousseau, Jean Jacques, 10, 100–101, 108
Rousseaux, André, 9
Roy, Jules, 8
Rozès, M., 38, 95, 96

Sade, Marquis de, 21, 128
Saïd, Edward, 73, 81
Saint-Clair, M., 5
Saint-Evremond, Charles, 7
Saint-Exupéry, Antoine de, 16
Saint Francis of Assisi, 62, 64
Saint-Just, Louis Antoine Léon, 128
Samson, J. P., 41
Sartre, Jean-Paul, 1, 5, 6, 12, 16, 19, 20, 25–26, 27, 29, 51, 103, 107, 119, 131, 157–60, 161, 163; *Being and Nothingness*, 153, 159; *The Flies*, 159; *Nausea*, 157; *Red Gloves*, 157; *Situations 1*, 6; "Tribute to Albert Camus," 12; *The Wall*, 155; *What Is Literature*, 34
Saurraute, Nathalie, 16, 32
Schiller, Friedrich, 26; "Resignation," 26
sea, the, 56–69, 75, 78, 80, 157
"Sea Close By, The," 54, 67–69
Shakespeare, William, 135
Sheik el Okhy, 38
"Silent Men, The," 109, 110, 111–12
Silone, Ignazio, 117
Simon, Pierre-Henri, 2, 8, 53
Sisyphus, 47, 48, 52
Sophocles, 135; *Antigone*, 132; *Oedipus*, 54
source, the, 120
South America, 65–67
Spitzer, Leo, 19
Stalin, Joseph, 26
*State of Siege*, 8, 132
Stendhal (Marie Henri Beyle), 106, 142
*Stranger, The*, 1, 5, 6, 9, 10, 12, 16, 19, 24, 32, 46, 47, 49–51, 74–78, 79, 80, 90, 102, 103, 104, 116, 121, 134, 140, 150, 155, 161
style. *See* language
*Summer*, 10, 52, 53, 54, 57, 58, 67
sunlight, 56–69, 74, 75–76, 77, 80, 153–54, 161, 164
*supplément*, 99–107
Symbolists, 6

Tantalus, 48, 53
*Temoins*, 41
terrorism, 11, 128–38
Tertullian, 28
*Théâtre du Travail*, 4

thematic criticism, 2, 4, 5, 8
Tillion, Germaine, 90
Tipasa, 42, 46, 51, 54, 60, 61
Tison-Braun, Micheline, 9; "Silence and the Desert: The Flickering Vision," 9
Tolstoy, Leo, 17, 118
tragedy, 22, 32, 51, 69–70n7, 132, 135
*Travel Journals*, 10, 57, 63, 65, 67
Treaty of Versailles, 38

Unamuno, Miguel de, 118

Valéry, Paul, 22; "Graveyard by the Sea," 154
Vauvenargues, Marquis de, 5
*Venture*, 27, 33
Viallaneix, Paul, 22
Vigée, Claude, 155
Viggiani, Carl, 32
Voltaire, François Marie Arouet, 6; *Candide*, 6; *Zadig*, 6

Walzer, Michael, 89